Special Educational Needs Review

Education and Alienation Series

Series Editor: Neville Jones, Oxfordshire

Special Educational Needs Review
Volume 3

Edited by

Neville Jones

The Falmer Press

(A member of the Taylor & Francis Group)
London, New York and Philadelphia

UK   The Falmer Press, Rankine Road, Basingstoke, Hampshire,
           RG24 OPR

USA   The Falmer Press, Taylor & Francis Inc., 1900 Frost Road,
           Suite 101, Bristol, PA 19007

First published 1990

British Library Cataloguing in Publication Data
Special educational needs review. – (Education
  and alienation series).
  Vol. 3
  1. Great Britain. Special education
  I. Jones, Neville, *1930–*   II. Series
  371.90941

  ISBN 1-85000-670-9
  ISBN 1-85000-671-7   pbk

**Library of Congress Cataloging-in-Publication Data is available on
request**

Jacket design by Caroline Archer

Typeset in 10/12 Garamond by
Chapterhouse, The Cloisters, Formby L37 3PX

Printed in Great Britain by Burgess Science Press, Basingstoke
on paper which has a specified pH value on final paper
manufacture of not less than 7.5 and is therefore 'acid free'.

Contents

Introduction

Neville Jones

The chapters in this book serve as a reminder that the integration of pupils with special educational needs into mainstream schooling is now a well established feature of education in many schools in Britain. This is not to say that integration is widespread; there are many contradictory practices both between LEAs (local education authorities) and within individual LEA administrations. Where there is integration taking place this can occur in spite of constricting and curtailing practices at all levels: the LEA administration, those working in support services like educational psychology, and by headteachers in some of our schools. Prejudice towards those who are disabled, where this is a term covering all those with learning disabilities in one form or another, is never far from the surface. It finds expression in the way LEAs develop their policies and how decisions are made which in outcome create a climate for individual behaviour and school ethos. It finds expression in the daily contact with others.

Integration practices appear to flourish in school communities when headteachers, well supported by LEA services at the personal as well as the managerial level, together with parents and governors, adopt a truly whole-school philosophy. Both pupils and adults are alert to the clear statements of intent in such schools: in school policy documents; in pronouncements; and in the behaviour of staff, parents and governors. But the matter can be more subtle than this. The touchstone is often those occasions when there is conflict in daily intercourse, in lessons and the playground, which call for a restating of attitudes towards disability and a reaffirmation of policies and practices that bring about new learning and social harmony. Schools that take a positive line about matters of prejudice find little space for marginalization practices. For example, pupils are not further handicapped by being unable to participate in the normal life of a school and prevented from having access to and participation in a normal full-time curriculum.

Schools that adopt such a participative philosophy and approach do so because they are prepared to deal with problems relating to integration as they arise: these 'problems' are not found in the 'statements' drawn up by local authorities on the basis of professional opinions, nor as the outcome of case-conference convened when the disabled pupil is in the unfamiliar learning context of a special institution. As with any other pupils in a school, learning and management problems, whatever their source, are and can be responded to at the time they occur and in the context in which they take place. This is what is meant by being integrated and being treated as a normal human being.

If integration is to do with a preparedness to respond to pupil needs, wherever they emerge, and for this to be done in an individual way, then this action alone provides some evidence that positive steps are being taken to correct and minimize prejudicial attitudes.

It is also necessary, however, because to look at those kinds of development which undermine such ideals as, for example, the introduction of the 'statementing' procedure as set out in the 1981 Education Act. Not only did this legislation sustain the historical dichotomy as between so-called normal and abnormal children as a legal process, but it also raised high expectations on the part of parents. Here was a procedure accepted by all parties, the pupils, teachers, doctors and psychologists, and parents, that this would by the very nature of the process itself bring about a better deal educationally for the child with disabilities and learning problems. But in practice the LEA still determines the resources that will be made available for a particular pupil, and sometimes refuses to provide any in spite of what professionals recommend in their 'statement' reports. It is the LEA, in its bureaucratic role that sustains the marginalized facilities (like separate units and schools), and it is the same arm of local authority bureaucracy that determines whether these institutions should be filled or not. In such circumstances a headteacher finds it very difficult to pursue a whole-school policy as far as pupils with special educational needs are concerned. Those concerned with the preparation of 'statements' also find themselves in a position of difficulty when encouraged to curtail their assessment reports to suit the policy and practices of the LEA that employs them.

There seems to be very little expectation of cooperation between the concerned parties in the statementing processes as set out in the 1981 Education Act. Parents often find themselves caught between the desire to improve the quality of the education of their disabled child and the recognition that a normal life for the child becomes more and more difficult if the child is statemented, and thus categorized legally. Some parents have found the statementing procedure advantageous as far as school provision is concerned and are prepared to forego what advantages there might accrue by not having their child categorized.

There were expectations, following the publication of the Warnock Report, that all classifications of the disabled would be dispensed with. Only in this way would inappropriate educational expectations for the disabled be minimized and it was hoped that it would lead to less discrimination in the wider community. But even the Warnock Report itself did not come out wholeheartedly in favour of across-the-board integration as is now being advocated by the London-based organization Centre for Studies on Integration in Education. The Report applauded the general principle and then went on to list those groups of pupils it thought would still need to be placed in special schools.

Resistance to integration also takes place within ordinary schools and is expressed in a variety of ways or disguises. One argument put forward is that integration has the effect of lowering the educational standards for other pupils who are not disabled. There is not as yet any research data that substantiates this claim. The arguments are soon lost in the wider debates about the merits and otherwise of mixed ability teaching. In the arguments that follow there is seldom an appeal to rights (of the pupil) or obligations (of those responsible for managing schools). The arguments intensify the older the pupils: in primary schools mixed ability education is almost a *sine qua non*. But then the arguments shift to such issues as resourcing, teacher preparation and problems of classroom organization.

It is sometimes difficult, if not impossible, to determine what resources may be required until a pupil is actually in an integrated circumstance. Only then are teachers, who are best placed to determine needs, able to assess needs and requirements for any individual pupil. The 'resource' argument is seldom an objection raised by headteachers who deliberately follow a whole-school policy and, by doing so, systematically build up ways and methods of securing extra support and resourcing. Such resources do not necessarily all come from the LEA budget.

An argument against integration that follows closely on the heels of the resource issue is that of preparing teachers for the time when the disabled pupil will attend their class. A slogan on this matter has emerged — no integration without preparation and training. It is difficult to know how meaningful such preparation can be when every pupil with special needs has very individualized needs, expresses them in very individual ways, and often exhibits a different set of needs according to the context of the school in which the pupil attends. This is a reminder that when we are discussing pupil needs in education they are not necessarily those needs which in the past formed the categorized listing of disabilities favoured by the government and used at that time as a method for allocating pupils to respective special schools or other segregated institutions. Furthermore, a pupil's needs in a special school will differ from the needs that require a response when the pupil attends an ordinary school. It is one reason why it is important that in-service work related to pupils with special needs, if it is to be of maximum benefit, needs to take place in the school where the pupil is integrated. Thus training should be addressed not only to one or two teachers who have direct responsibility for the pupil on a daily basis, but to all members of staff in the school.

In spite of difficulties of the kind outlined above the integration movement has developed in Britain in what might be regarded as three, though not necessarily consecutive, stages. These stages appear to follow a ten-year cycle and may well reflect other changes in the education system which also follow such cyclical patterns.

In the 1960s much pioneer work was being carried out in Scandinavian countries and this under-pinned a strong parents' movement for better conditions for the mentally disabled. This brought about a United Nations Declaration in favour of countries developing better services for the mentally disabled within a framework of policies for integration. Emerging slowly was the Rights issue and this found expression in American legislation based as it is on Rights within the Constitution.

A second stage in the integration process in Britain took place during the 1970s when there was increasing discussion on the merits of integration, both as a practical strategy and a philosophical idea in education. Again, pressure grew from active parent groups, voluntary societies and individuals working in the public sector of education. In practice, change came about because of the initiatives of individuals working in public and private sectors of education, and in teaching institutions. Few, if any, LEAs introduced a unified and comprehensive education system of integration though intentions were, and continue to be, scattered through many LEA policy documents. Special schools remained open and special units became fashionable particularly for pupils with behaviour disorders of a disruptive nature.

A further difficulty arose as ordinary schools began to open their doors to the disabled. Since the beginning of state education a perimeter has been drawn around those who would be allowed to attend ordinary schools. Those with too low a measured intelligence quotient were excluded; those beyond a certain degree of physical impairment or sensory disability were educated elsewhere; those with behaviour problems treated as more sinning than sinned against.

This raised some basic problems of school organization when it became apparent that those with special needs should be part of ordinary school communities: either retained once identified, or returned if already marginalized in some special institution. Headteachers experimented with total integration, with placing pupils in special classes in the ordinary school and with systems of extra support through methods of team teaching. As a consequence of these explorations three kinds of development took place: the idea of a flexible Resource Room as pioneered in America; the integration of remedial teachers to become classroom assistants working together with the class teacher; and the use of non-professional classroom aides. A few special schools began to experiment with schemes of joint working with neighbourhood mainstream schools.

This second stage in the integration process was one of management strategies: how to re-integrate pupils meaningfully, what changes were required in the structure and organization of classroom work where the term 'ordinary' would now have a different meaning, and how to ensure that those integrated back into ordinary schools were not just attached to ordinary schools, participating in a physical sense, but like limpets attached to a ship as far as their social and learning needs were being met.

By the early 1980s ordinary schools were moving towards considering issues like appropriate curriculum and realistic assessment of their disabled pupils. It was a period to look at student-led learning and a recognition that education was not a horse race with a few winners, all competing against each other without reward appropriate to achievement. Schools would be places for collaboration, individual and group learning, and where every pupil's learning needs and capabilities were met and extended with individual appraisal and reward. Schemes of modular curriculum and student profiling began to replace methods which were only geared to those pupils whom it was thought would fail. Such pupils included most of those deemed as having special educational needs.

The early 1980s was a period of high optimism when it was thought that we should begin to see the end of national schemes of testing and examination. Educational psychologists could with reason and purpose be encouraged to put away their norm-related tests and all pupils, whatever their needs, would finalize their compulsory education with positive records of their life, work and achievement. For all this the curriculum in a school was centred to a pupil's success, untouched by political considerations, and where ownership of the teaching and pupil learning was fairly and squarely the responsibility of the teachers. All this continues to be the aims and objectives of most committed educationalists despite the stressful changes brought about by some provisions in the 1988 Education Act — the introduction of the National Curriculum and national schemes of examination and testing.

We still have to discover the impact of this new legislation, coupled as it is with what appears to be a systematic under-valuing of the teacher's role, on the needs and achievements of pupils with special needs and particularly those attending ordinary schools. It seems that the 1990s is appropriately the time when the needs of pupils, particularly those with special needs, has to be considered in terms of their rights, and for this to be a dominant theme for the next decade in education.

Already much work has been carried out on rights by voluntary organizations like the Centre for the Study of Integration in Education (CSIE) with its Integration Charter and the work of the Children's Legal Centre, also in London. The fact that the United Nations has adopted a new Convention on the Rights of the Child, taking effect from November 20th, 1989 should also be noted. It has yet to be seen which political party will take forward the idea that there should be a minister for children with powers to ensure that in local situations the rights of all children are protected.

Although there are still LEAs and schools wary of integrating the disabled, much constructive work has already been carried out into the process required for what is a very sensitive area of school practice. We are now at a stage when research into integration is a major concern of researchers looking at individual schemes, at LEA practices, with national initiatives, and bringing together in comparative studies what is happening as between countries. The work of voluntary organizations has a continuing place in all this. These matters are the subject of the contributions in Part One of this book (Fulcher, Lin, Gow and Chow, Wilson, Williams).

A second area of importance is that of appropriate curriculum and pupils having access to and meaningful participation in a full normal curriculum. These matters are covered in contributions in Part Two (Carpenter and Cobb, Wotton) and Part Three (Field, McPherson, Foster and Holcomb, Hutchinson). An appropriate curriculum embraces both specific subjects together with skills needed to maximize learning (Le Prevost, Wallace and Waller, Baldwin, Tann). These cross-curriculum competencies do, of course, apply equally to all other pupils in a school and not only to those designated as having special educational needs.

Much that has been achieved over the past three decades in the interest of normalizing the education for pupils with special needs now seems to be at risk. [Through the 1990s we shall discover the effects of the 1988 Education Act and whether the provisions of this legislation will, while seeming to offer greater educational opportunities and entitlement to all pupils, place even more pupils in marginalized education. There are fears that the systematic testing of pupils will increase the numbers who are disaffected with their educational experiences. Schools coping well with pupils with special needs are likely to be undermined, if not closed, should parents begin to judge a school on the sole criterion of examination results within the framework of the National Curriculum and annual testing. Already there is some evidence that teachers in mainstream schools are showing reluctance to include pupils with special needs where the lessons are related to the National Curriculum. The 1988 Act has thrown greater responsibility on the shoulders of headteachers and their staff not to give way to pressures which have a basis in the philosophy of the Act, namely those of debilitating competition and economic considerations, and to stand firm for a positive creative education that can be participated in by all pupils irrespective of their educational or other needs.

Part One
Integration Policy and Practice

1
The Politics of Integration Policy: Its Nature and Effects

Gillian Fulcher

Introduction

Before we can understand the outcomes of policy we need to conceptualize and theorize policy adequately: only then can we examine its substance. This chapter argues that policy is made at all levels; it outlines a model of policy which is located in a wider model of social life as struggle about objectives which deploys discourse, thus theory about how to attain these objectives. It contrasts the English and Victorian policies on integration, outlines their counter-effects, and suggests why both policies have 'failed' and puts forward some ways out of these effects.

To assess the effects of any policy we must first understand the nature of policy as a general category of action and intervention in social life: we need to conceptualize policy clearly and then to theorize it adequately; only then can we usefully look at its substance.

Both administrative theorists and sociologists have taken positions on the nature of policy. Administrative theorists and others have tended to talk about policy and implementation, or of policy versus practice; when they are on theoretical jaunts, they have talked about a top-down model of government policy, or, more recently, perhaps faced with the extraordinarily complex effects of various government policies, of a complex chain effect (Barrett and Hill, cited by Welton and Evans, 1986 p. 212) or even of policy as the layers of an onion (Whitmore, cited by Welton and Evans, 1986 p. 213). Despite these different concepts and theoretical endeavours, administrative theorists — those caught up in an administrative approach — have tended to regard policy as special, to see government as making policy. This approach views policy as something separate from other seemingly more mundane actions of citizens.

On the other hand, sociologists, or those whose task it is to have adequate social theories of how social life works, have quite frequently taken the position that policy is unimportant theoretically: what has mattered to this kind of sociologist has been class struggle, or the 'state' reconciling its internal structural problems, or the rule of bureaucracy, or aspects of situational interaction. In these concerns policy as substance and action drops out.

My view is that both these positions on policy, the administrative and the sociological, have got it wrong. Policy is neither 'special' nor unimportant. Both views are analytically mistaken and politically misleading. More recently, a number of those who study policy and its effects have argued that the policy-implementation dichotomy is false: policy is remade at all levels of, say, the educational apparatus: this is now becoming conventional wisdom amongst political scientists and this analysis has included special education legislation and its effects, namely the 1981 Education Act in Britain (for example, Goacher, *et al.*, 1986). But those who work with this insight, and I shall argue that thus far they have got it right, fail to locate this political concept of policy in a wider model of social relations. They thereby remain trapped in the perception that policy is all important and miss further theoretical insights which can derive from seeing policy making as a social practice and thus as having characteristics common to all social practices.

As an aside, I use the notion of educational apparatus rather than, say, education system, deliberately, since apparatus connotes how things get done and this term belongs more appropriately in the sort of model I shall draw on to theorize social policy, since the model's starting point concerns how people achieve objectives: this, however, is to leap, several theoretical links in the model I want to put forward.

Far from being separate from practice, policy *is* a form of practice; it seeks to intervene in social life and this intervention is theoretically based.[1] It derives from some image of how society ought to work and it includes notions of how to achieve this: it therefore involves theorizing, if only implicitly, about how society, or aspects of it work. In the case of special education policy, for instance, it should include some pedagogic theories of how children learn and therefore of how children fail. Policy as intervention, has certain objectives though these may not always be clear. In this respect, policy is no different from all other social practices. Social life may be theorized as a series of practical projects, in each of which we struggle to achieve our objectives. Failing to achieve our objectives may be due to our inadequately understanding the nature of our project, that is, to an inadequate social theory if you like: this inadequacy may include presenting the project in the wrong way to others — presenting the wrong discourse; or our failure may be due to our not being clear about our project. This model derives from Foucault's work and recent interpretations which put the notion of discourse at the centre of theorizing social life (for instance, Ball, 1988). A useful and brief paper from which the implications for theorizing policy can easily be drawn, although they are not spelt out, is Barry Hindess's paper 'Actors and Social Relations' (1986).[2]

Three further aspects of the model which are highly relevant to conceptualizing and theorizing policy are firstly, that policy, as social practice, is made at all levels of the educational apparatus and secondly, that at each level of policy making whether, for instance, at government, school or union level, we may *write*, *talk about* or *enact* policy. These are different forms of policy practices — the written, the stated and the enacted (as Macdonald, 1981, has pointed out) — and they are worth distinguishing analytically: for instance, government *written* policy often appears to conflict with funding allocation or goverment *enacted* policy.

This model sees policy, and all social practice, as political, thus as struggle. Thus where technical aspects are concerned, such as medical knowledge about the learning implications of profound hearing impairment or pedagogical theories of how children learn, or of how we can and should teach, these views, while they have a technical component, are also embedded in political practices: to assert a view is to exercise power of one sort or another.

Thirdly, who makes policy? — or writes, talks about or enacts it? We can draw further insights from Hindess's position. In Hindess's view, only social actors carry out social practices: social actors are those who can make decisions, and are thus the individuals and bodies of individuals who have decision-making powers. In the Victorian educational apparatus, the key actors are the Minister, bureaucrats, committees, teacher unions, professional associations, the regional board of directors, teachers as individuals and as members of committees, school councils, Enrolment Support Groups, the Cabinet (since its members make decisions about funding), and so on. Social actors make decisions on the basis of the discourses available to them. This means, as social actors, we do not make decisions on the basis of full information (much as we might like to think we do), but on the basis of the discourses — modes of thinking and talking — available to us. Where integration is concerned, and given the present focus on disability in integration policy, this means the discourse available to various participants in decision-making processes on the nature of particular disabilities or impairments, and on their general understanding, with all its limits, about the causes, consequences and pedagogical implications of various types of disability.

This view of policy, I shall argue, can be usefully applied to disentangle the nature and effects of policies called integration. The rest of the paper will seek to answer three questions. What is the nature of recent written integration policies in the educational apparatuses in Victoria and Britain? What are the effects of these policies? How shall we understand these effects?

The Nature of Recent Written Integration Policies at Government Level in Britain and Victoria

In Britain,[3] the White Paper *Special Education Needs* (1980), the 1981 Education Act and the regulations and circulars the Department of Education and Science (DES) issues to the 104 local education authorities (LEAs) and other bodies, can be taken as government national level written policy on special education. The Warnock Report *Special Educational Needs* (DES, 1978) is seen as being the key source for developing the 1981 legislation. This written policy is widely interpreted as integrationist, despite (according to Booth, 1983) occasional disclaimers by DES officials and from Mary Warnock (1978), who chaired the Warnock Committee: 'People have said we fudged the issue of integration but we fudged it as a matter of policy'.

In Victoria, there is no legislation or regulations on integration. There is however very widespread understanding that the educational apparatus has an integration policy. The key policy documents are the *Integration in Victorian Education* report (1984), and various memoranda from the then Minister of Education, Robert Fordham, and his successor, Ian Cathie, and various officials in the former Department, now Ministry of Education. These memoranda appear to be as follows:

(a) Minister of Education (Robert Fordham), memorandum to presidents of school councils, principals and staff of all schools, *Integration in Victorian Schools* (no date).

(b) Deputy Director-General (M. K. Collins), memorandum to presidents of school councils, school principals and staff, *Integration in Victorian Schools*, August 31, 1984.

(c) Acting Chief Executive (M. K. Collins), memorandum to executive directors, directors of branches and units, regional directors of education, principals of schools, presidents of school councils, officers in charge of student services centres, teachers in charge of education support centres *Guidelines for schools: Integration Teachers: Role, Rationale and Responsibilities (Primary and Post Primary)* (no date).

(d) Director of Student Services (Alan R. Farmer), memorandum to regional directors of education, OICs, student services (CG and CS) centres, *Special School Placement Procedures* 28th March 1985.

(e) Minister for Education (Ian Cathie), memorandum to presidents of school councils, school principals and staff, regional directors of education, *Integration in Victorian Schools*, May 20, 1985.

(f) Acting Chief Executive (M. K. Collins), memorandum to regional directors of education, principals of schools, presidents of school councils, officers in charge of student services centres, teachers in charge of education support centres, *Enrolment and Support Group Guidelines for Regular Schools*, 13 March 1986.

(g) Director Integration Unit (Bernard Lamb), memorandum to All Members Senior Officers Group Integration Committee, 29th April 1986.

(h) General Manager (M. K. Collins), memorandum to regional directors of education, *Delayed Admission to School of Parent's Choice*, 19th January 1987.

(i) General Manager (Schools Division, M. K. Collins), Executive memorandum No. 144 to regional directors of education, principals of schools, presidents of school councils, officers in charge of student services centres, teachers in charge of education support centres, *Integration Support Group Procedures for Regular Schools (Formerly Enrolment and Support Group Guidelines)*, 17 August 1987.

These memoranda variously interpret the 1984 report and, in the absence of legislation and supporting regulations, they effectively *remake* Victorian government level policy on integration as it has been negotiated following the Report. The memoranda may be seen both as responses to, and attempts to direct, policy practices at other levels: they indicate struggle over integration objectives.

There is extensive negotiation, struggle, between the Ministry and other levels of the Victorian educational apparatus; policy is remade rather than 'implemented'. This is in line with Goacher *et al.*'s (1986) observations on policy practices in the British educational apparatus following the 1981 Education Act.

In Victoria, policy practices on integration have a much more tenuous legal basis than their counterpart in Britain. The State Board of Education, as recommended in the Victorian Report (1987) has recently provided advice to the Minister on developing legislation. The current legislation in Victoria which relates to the education of children with impairments and disability is the *Education Act 1958*, Division Two, Section 64A-K (*Integration in Victorian Education*, p. 123) and Regulation VI 662 regulations promulgated under section 82(q) of the Education Act 1958:

> Section 5–9 and 16 and 17 of Regulation VI relate to education policies of previous decades which emphasized segregated rather than integrated options for children with impairments and disabilities (*Integration in Victorian Education*, p. 133).

Thus, despite an integration policy document, current legislation and regulations appear to emphasize segregated practices. Moreover, a number of the new practices which have emerged in the Victorian educational apparatus (see section below) have administrative and political rather than legal bases; some of these practices appear to be extra-legal.

Both the British and Victorian policies are seen as integration, yet their approach to the issues varies considerably. This is not surprising: positions on integration can be antithetical. Moreover, as is often the case with policy, a written policy can be internally inconsistent: this reveals struggles in the policy-writing process, struggles which occur despite a Report being presented as consensus (this is tactical). These 'inconsistencies' in policy are often articulated in policy analysis as 'tensions' between principles, but in a political concept of policy they are more accurately seen as the outcome of struggles between parties contending to achieve their different objectives; such inconsistency indicates the politics of policy making as well as a 'mix' of discourses. As we shall see, this struggle is apparent in both the British and Victorian government written policies but the winner in each differs.

In Britain, according to the 1981 Education Act, parents are entitled to new rights in decision making: they are to be partners. Yet decisions are also to be a matter for professional judgment (Kirp, 1983). Since professional judgment means professional control, this is hardly consistent with the view that parents have a right to influence decisions. Parent rights are thus token rather than real in British policy. Thus at the heart of British policy lies a paradox: the concerns for social justice for parents and students (Stobart, 1986) are submerged by the view that professionals should control this area of educational practice. Thus Kirp (1983) describes British national policy in special education, though his focus is on Warnock rather than the 1981 Act, as a policy which chooses professionalization as the means for making decisions in that arena. I would argue for a more political concept of policy than Kirp provides but for an analysis which relates closely to his view. In line with

Welton and Evans (1986), my view is that the predominant discourse in British government policy on special education is professionalism (Fulcher, 1986). Professionalism — the view that expertise should prevail — is the key tactic in professionalization, the struggle which occupational groups have historically waged in order to gain control of a particular area of social practices. In the British context, we see professionalism strongly endorsed in the Warnock Report and as dominating the much weaker discourse on parents as partners to whom advice, consideration and assistance is due in their suffering (p. 74). While this language denies the politics of its position, it is precisely political in assigning a position of dependence to parents, in using a particular discourse and in excluding other issues from discussion. This is not the language of the discourse on rights in American legislation and which was attempted in the Victorian Report.

In discourse theorizing, language is seen as significant both theoretically and politically, since how you present an issue suggests which courses of action should follow and, at the same time, excludes other themes and courses of action. Welton and Evans (1986) suggest the Warnock Committee and its agenda for discussion illustrate 'Luke's contention that power operates in such a way as to exclude certain points of view so completely that they are not seen as part of that debate' (p. 214).

Professionalism is thus a discourse available to individuals and groups who wish to use it: in Britain it is available to administrators, regular teachers, special teachers, the DES, educational psychologists and parents who may prefer that experts retain control. But it is false to assume this tactic is adopted by a professional in the educational apparatus before establishing what her tactic is: not all professionals use professionalism. There is evidence that some professionals in this arena in Britain take a democratic position and use democratism (the view that those affected by decisions should take part in them) as tactic in an attempt to achieve parent rights and control. The evidence is, however, that these professionals are in the minority in integration struggles in Britain. Moreover, the institutional bases for professionalism are more strongly established than they are for parent rights. These institutional bases consist of special teacher associations, teacher training institutions, wherever there are courses which focus on disability or special educational needs and wherever these topics are excluded from courses on pedagogic practices in general; paradoxically they exist potentially even in courses such as The Open University's on special educational needs, where nevertheless, there is a substantial critique both of professionalism and of its themes and practices which construct both difference, and subsequently distance, between the 'able' and those tagged different, disabled or special in an abnormal sense.

In sum, British government written policy on integration (Warnock, the 1981 Education Act, and associated regulations and circulars) takes a weak position on integration (see paragraph 1 of this section), and strongly endorses professionalism as a mode of regulating this arena of educational practices; it therefore presents issues as largely technical, a tactic which obscures the politics of this position.

The Victorian Report is framed in a different discourse: it adopts a rights discourse which is overtly political in contrast to the covert politics of professionalism. But the dominance of the rights discourse in the Victorian Report is tenuous despite a serious attempt to address issues of rights. Professionalism surfaces strongly in the Report's recommendations that the membership of Enrolment Support Groups (the key structure and tactic proposed to ensure parent and student rights to participate in decision making) may include specialists who may then outnumber non-specialists and thus potentially, if this is the way a particular ESG works, submerge a parent's claim that their child has a right to a regular education. The Extension Note to the Report, inserted at the last minute by the parent member of the Review, which disputes the proposed membership for ESGs, is evidence of the struggle between democratism and its opponent, professionalism.

The democratism in the Victorian Report consists in its view that all children have a right to a regular education, in the recommendations for participatory decision-making structures at various levels in the educational apparatus (though the membership proposed for these groups is mostly professionals), and in its attempted critique of educational practices via the notion of 'problems in schooling' with its suggestion that school practices may disable, This theme makes only a brief appearance in the Report, it is not followed, as politically and pedagogically it should be, by a discussion of curriculum — that set of learning experiences and pedagogic practices which undoubtedly contribute to some children's failing in school. The Victorian discourse on democratism is thus undermined by professionalism, by not following through the pedagogical implications of a rights position which would have taken it in the direction of a debate about comprehensive education and non-divisive curriculum practices, and by the wider legal context: insofar as the Australian Constitution lacks a Bill of Rights, a discourse on rights for any disadvantaged group is, at one level, fictitious since in this context rights lack legal remedies and thus remain moral imperatives subject, of course, to the politics of all moral positions. While the Victorian discourse on democratism is thus seriously undermined by professionalism and a lack of constitutional underpinning, it nevertheless contrasts strongly with the entrenched version of professionalism which characterizes British national policy, particularly as it is presented in the Warnock Report.

The integration objectives in the British and Victorian Reports differ, as noted earlier. The British concept of integration is weak: Kirp (1983) an American professor of social policy, says 'The concept of integration found its way into British law, but in toothless form' (p. 77). Effectively, the Warnock concept provides no impetus towards moving from the extensive segregation which occur. The Victorian concept is clearly different: it refers to processes of maintaining and increasing the participation of all children in regular schools. Such a process could be monitored: the notion allows for accountability (Gow and Fulcher, 1986) and seeks to promote a shift from the extensive provision of educational facilities segregated from regular schools. The Warnock concept of integration is consistent with past practices of extensive segregation and with the co-existent practice of *some* children with disabilities being present in regular classrooms. But this has always been the case in special education practices. Warnock's comment on integration ('we fudged it as a matter of policy') seems accurate.

9

There are other similarities and contrasts between the British and Victorian policies. Both fail to address seriously the question of why children fail in school, to which the answer cannot accurately be because of factors solely to do with what goes on outside school. Yet the question of why children fail in school ought to proceed any serious review of special education provision. The Victorian Report briefly rescues itself from this failure in its notion mentioned earlier, of problems in schooling: this concept was meant as a potential critique of schooling practices. Warnock does a somewhat better job by including a chapter on curriculum in which it is appropriately critical of aspects of the special school curriculum. But these concerns are submerged by a discourse on disability which characterizes both reports though it is much more deeply entrenched in the British version. There, many of the themes of suffering, burden, guilt, shame, medical advice, discovery (p. 74) belong properly only to a discourse on severe disability. But as we know, Warnock included 20 per cent of school children in the notion of special educational needs, of whom only a very small proportion have severe or profound impairment, and to present a discourse which belongs to severe impairment where the objects of that discourse are 20 per cent of school children, without clarifying the limited relevance of such a discourse, is political in the extreme, and is politics submerged by the professionalism in the report.

The Victorian Report, in its discussion of a conceptual framework in Chapter 2, attempted to point out the limited relevance of traditional concepts and themes in what has largely been a medical discourse in education practices concerning disability. However, the limited success of such an attempt, given the institutional bases such as special education training institutions and resource negotiations where this discourse is well entrenched, is one of the effects considered in the next section of this paper. What then are the effects of these somewhat different integration policies in the Victorian and British educational apparatuses?

What are the Effects of British and Victorian Government Written Integration Policies?

We need to use the notion of 'effects' of government or national written policy carefully. It suggests a top-down model, whereas the model outlined above suggests that policy is made at all levels in the educational apparatus. Thus no level of policy making, whether government or regional or union, has a determinate effect on policy practice at other levels. Some levels, such as government funding or lack of it — what may be seen as government level enacted policy— may have an extensive influence on other levels, particularly if extra resources are seen as a key matter but it does not determine policy practices at other levels. We know this empirically: examples of good integration practice (despite restricted funding) can be found in both British and Victorian schools. But this may occur despite, rather than because of, policy at other levels in the education apparatus. The model's notion that policy is made at all levels thus suggests we should look for effects other than direct programme implications of a government written policy. Offe (1984) has suggested that the role of state social policy is to control the production of wage labour and that the function of state policy is to set up conflictual interaction at other levels in the state apparatus. What evidence is there in both the British and Victorian educational apparatuses for (a) the notion that policy is made at all levels and (b) for Offe's view on the role and function of state policy?

In Britain there is ample evidence of diversity in integration practice (see especially Evans, 1986, and Goacher *et al.*, 1986). This seems to be evidence of policy as practice being made at all levels. Secondly educational policy on disability is clearly a form of social policy which controls the production of wage labour and which institutionalizes the production of non-wage labour via its non-credentialling curriculum and where, in segregated settings, deviant behaviour may be tolerated (Tomlinson, 1982). There is plenty of evidence too, of conflict at various levels of the British educational apparatus following the issuing of national policy: this supports Offe's claim that the function of state policy is to control the production of wage labour and that its role is to initiate conflictual interaction at other levels. Metaphorically then, government written education policy on disability appears as a referee: the bell rings and the fight begins, but when a foul occurs the metaphor fades, since (as we shall see, for example, in the Victorian apparatus) the rules are redefined.

In addition, others provide evidence of new practices following the British government written policy on integration. Tomlinson (1985) argues that special education control in regular schools has increased; Goodwin's (1983) study of the introduction of support services in regular schools showed an increase in referral rates in these schools; Booth (1983) shows there has been no systematic move towards integration. Swann's (1985) analysis of statistics reveals that children with physical disabilities are being increasingly integrated in regular schools but that those tagged under the largest category, that of 'learning difficulties' who were formerly tagged as ESN(M) are being increasingly segregated. There are many reports that the statementing procedures of the 1981 Education Act are used differently in different LEAs, and that they are time-consuming and increase bureaucratic regulation.

In Victoria, there is also clear evidence that policy is made at levels other than government written and enacted levels. Research on school council written policies revealed a discourse of professionalism where ESGs were concerned.[4] The emergence of a debate about resources rather than one on rights to a regular education, and the memoranda confirming this (31 August 1984; 20 May 1985) attest to struggle between central level, unions and schools, and to the remaking of policy at various levels. The written responses of various professional associations adopt professionalism as a topic, (for example the former CG and CS), while union responses have adopted resource arguments, which are broadly part of the approach of specialism and therefore professionalism. This is the negative side of policy remade at various levels.

There is also evidence of good practice in integration in various Victorian schools (see especially Huish, 1986). But these practices have existed for some time; many therefore predate the 1984 report. Unless they follow in time, and follow politically from, the Victorian Report they can hardly be seen as an effect of government policy. We urgently need research in Victoria which reveals whether there are systematically produced good effects which have depended upon and been encouraged directly by Victorian Government written and enacted policy on integration. It is no good merely citing instances of good practice since such instances have been part of school practices for some time: we need, as evidence that the Victorian Report has encouraged integration, research on new and successful practices where links to government written and enacted policy can be empirically demonstrated and which overall show increasing integration in the sense the Report uses it. Such system-level data is not available and the provision of additional, though limited, resources does not provide this (see below).

As the evidence stands, and in the absence of demonstrating these links, there are a number of counter-effects which have undoubtedly followed the issuing of Victorian Government written education policy on disability. These counter-effects consist of the following practices which have emerged in the Victorian educational apparatus since the 1984 report. They include:

1 initiating extensive negotiation on — struggle over — practices concerning disability at all levels in the education apparatus; this has resulted in
2 a resource discourse dominating the issue of rights and curriculum (see especially memoranda 31 August 1984; 20 May 1985; 19 January 1987), and in
3 the introduction of '*delayed admission*' a procedure which applies only to students tagged as disabled (see memorandum 13 March 1986).
4 The attempted use by some schools of the notion of delayed admission in order to effectively suspend students already in schools who were suddenly discovered in regular classrooms to be integration students who required extra resources (see memorandum of 29 April 1986).
5 The marginalization of students already in regular schools who were nominated as an 'integration child' (see Tschiderer, 1986). This marginalization is encapsulated by one teacher's reply to the question: What does it mean when you call someone an integration student? 'WATCH HIM!' she replied.

These effects indicate a *politicization* of educational practices organized around a notion of disability, a politicization which systematically deflects attention from the pedagogical issues central to educational practices. Closely related to these political effects, are

6 the increasing bureaucratic regulation of the procedures for admission: see especially memorandum No. 34 of 13 March 1986 which is ten pages long and includes a diagram of six sets of sequences, some of which have subsets, even sub-subsets.

It is worth noting here, that the social theorist most concerned with the analysis of bureaucracy, the German Max Weber (1964), saw the development of bureaucracy (which he thought would increase as capitalism developed), as a fundamental threat to key values in Western democracy of privacy and (relative) freedom. His view, according to one of his interpreters, is of bureaucracy as an iron cage. Finally, these effects include

7   the reported failure of ESG processes.

The provision of resources in the form of allocation for teacher aides, for instance cannot be taken *prima facie* as evidence that integration is occurring, since integration is more than resource allocation. Marginalization may follow from tagging a student an integration child; resources are short-term funded and thus create a contingent status for these students; teachers state there is a widespread stated need for curriculum development and there is no clear information on the extent to which integration might be occurring. The available data on resource allocation such as that from the Integration Unit (1987), would have to be supplemented by, for example, information on where children were previously at school and if this was already in the regular school, whether they had progressed educationally. Moreover extensive allocation to the segregated sector continues to be made at per capita amounts of approximately four times what it costs for a primary age student to be in a regular school (Fulcher, 1987).

Overall then, and despite instances of successful integration practices in both British and Victorian schools, the evidence suggests that the effects of, or new practices which have emerged since both governments issued written education policy on disability, do not reveal a systematic move either in British or Victorian schools towards integration as a process of increasing the participation of all children in regular schools. On the contrary, many of these new practices have systematically made such a process more difficult. New practices in both apparatuses reveal increasing regulation by bureaucracy and an increasing politicization of the issues. Overall, these practices amount to counter-effects, particularly in the case of Victoria where there was a serious intent to democratize this area of educational practices and to move from the exclusion which children tagged as disabled have historically experienced. How shall we theorize the counter-effects of these new practices?

Theorizing these New Practices

If policy as practice is remade at all levels in the educational apparatus, as the model outlined earlier suggests, why is it remade in a way which, far from redressing inequalities children tagged disabled have hitherto experienced in the British and Victorian education apparatuses (and others), appears to regulate their lives in more unequal ways, in ways which politicize their experiences and make more tentative and contingent their existence as school children effectively without an equal place in regular schools? None of this is to deny that there are instances of successful integration and good practice but this is not what the new practices outlined above encourage. How should we explain this increasing politicization and bureaucratization in both the British and Victorian educational apparatuses?

The easy way out theoretically and politically is to appeal to some notion of the 'state' wielding its power and having its unseen way via the mindless actions of bureaucrats. This theoretical solution may sound ridiculous but it has been the subject of recent extensive debate on the nature of the 'state'. But this form of theorizing avoids the key political problems of everyday life and it occupies a politically pessimistic stance. Other theoretical solutions are more conceptually and politically, that is, strategically, demanding, and the model proposed here to theorize policy falls into this category. Before drawing on this model, both to suggest why this government or national policy has been associated with counter-effective practices and what some solutions might be, I shall turn briefly to some of the theorizing others have offered on the nature of practices in special education.

Sally Tomlinson's (1982) answer to the question: Why have special education practices developed historically, and continue to develop, in the way they have, that is, as an arena professionals control? is that powerful groups are able to shape educational practices in ways which protect and advance their interests rather than those of parents and students (p. 107). Hugh Mehan's (1983) conclusions about the way Eligibility and Placement Committees in Californian schools work (these are the Californian version, more or less, of Victorian Enrolment Support groups) both relate to and contrast with Tomlinson's position. Mehan argues that some professionals use techniques of linguistic persuasion in these settings. This is similar to Tomlinson's (1982) observation that it is much more difficult for working-class parents to negotiate with professionals than middle-class parents (p. 110). (It is this knowledge that makes parent advocacy such an important and political act, but this is to open another can of political worms.) Mehan suggests that a key effect of Federal law PL 94–142 (The Education for All Handicapped Students Act) is that it creates institutional procedures or practices at lower levels in the educational apparatus where decisions made about special education referrals are the outcome of available discourses (information held) on disability and on the services available. These decisions are therefore contingent on a number of constraints beyond the control of the decision-makers and do not conform to the rational model of decision making implied in much legislation and policy writing at government level (Mehan, Meihls, Hertweck and Crowdes, 1981). In Mehan's theorizing personal responsibility for counter-effects dissolves once again into the 'mindless' practices of institutional processes where individuals respond to higher level policy: in California, this higher level of policy-making is the Federal legislation, PL 94–142.

> Our daily observations, interviews, and discussions shows that educators were honest and genuinely concerned for the welfare of students in their charge; they were not trying to discriminate against any children. Nevertheless, special education services were made differentially available to students in the district. Differential educational opportunity seems to be more of an unintended consequence of bureaucratic organization than is a matter of individual or collective intentions. (Mehan *et al.*, 1981, pp. 390–1).

Thus in Mehan's account individuals who make decisions are apparently not to be held fully responsible for the consequences of their actions.

But again, this form of theorizing (special education placements are the outcome of routine procedures) tends to be pessimistic as far as taking courses of action to achieve different outcomes is concerned: if actors are not responsible for the consequences of their decisions with whom shall we negotiate to achieve different effects? Or is it the case that we need to think more carefully about the complexities, not only of educational practices, including writing policy and enacted policy organized around a notion of disability, but also of the undoubtedly complex educational apparatuses in which all this takes place? Do we also need to think more carefully about the wide array of social practices surrounding perceptions of disability in contemporary society, practices which Abberley (1987), for one, theorizes as a form of social oppression?

From the theorizing suggested in this paper the following reasons can be drawn to account for some at least of the counter-effects which have followed 'integration' policies, both written and enacted, at national or governmental level in Britain and Victoria.

First the debate uses the *wrong* discourse. To focus on disability is not only to draw on the prejudice and oppression which characterize a wide array of current practices (Abberley, 1987) but also to enter a political logic whose end result has historically been exclusion from regular classrooms for most of the school children tagged disabled. *Asserting* a different objective, that of integration, yet retaining a discourse on disability is inappropriate. This is partly because, in these educational apparatuses, as in the wider society, there is a view that deficit and difference underlie 'disability' or its many synonyms. These derive from the influence of medical perceptions — 'the social world is steeped in the medical model of disability' (Brisenden, 1986, p. 174). But for most of the 20 per cent of school children deemed to have special educational needs (which is ultimately defined as disability, see the 1981 Education Act) this assumption is clearly inaccurate. The themes of impairment and difference in the discourse on disability are nevertheless sufficiently well conveyed, even via terms such as disruptive and learning difficulty, that the political logic of that discourse is established. It is here that the politics of disability lie, a politics which is especially evident in educational practices.

Disability is primarily a procedural category by which welfare states regulate an increasing proportion of their citizens (Fulcher, 1989; 1990). Thus disability, as inability to work, has no necessary connection with a particular impairment but is relative to regional variations in labour tasks, to the supply of labour and to employers' work practices. Similarly, in educational apparatuses disability, or special educational needs, are relative to schools. This is Warnock's position:

> Whether a disability or significant difficulty constitutes an educational handicap for an individual child, and if so to what extent, will depend upon a variety of factors. Schools differ, often widely, in outlook, expertise, resources, accommodation, organisation and physical and social surroundings, all of which help to determine the degree to which the individual is educationally handicapped . . . We wish to see a more

positive approach, and we have adopted the concept of SPECIAL EDUCATIONAL NEED, seen not in terms of a particular disability which a child may be judged to have, but in relation to . . . indeed all the factors which have a bearing on his educational progress. (1978 p. 37)

The failure of the Warnock attempt to shift educators' thinking from a discourse on disability, and the failure of the Victorian Report's notion of 'problems in schooling' which was intended to achieve the same shift, is evidence of the deeply entrenched discourse on disability and of the institutionalized bases which construct that discourse. Disability is seen as requiring expertise, thus professional control beyond the reasonable commitment of regular teachers. This lack of commitment, however, is systematically produced by the prior experience of these teachers, including their teacher training experiences. Why should we teach these children — we haven't the expertise? is a question and answer which, in part, comes out of training experiences which establish, in their courses and in the separation of special teacher training institutions, from regular teacher training institutions, a discourse that disability is the issue. Thus professionalism for disability is a discourse institutionalized in teacher training institutions.

Much of the responsibility for institutionalizing a discourse on disability, which politically generally leads to exclusion, must lie with those who presume to teach teachers and intending teachers how ro teach. One solution therefore is to address the issue of specialism which presently characterizes teacher training institutions. This, of course, is much easier said than done, as the politics of a recent Accreditation Process for a Postgraduate Diploma in Integration at a Melbourne teachers college shows.[5] The resistance to this endeavour shows how powerful the mobilization of interests that wish to retain separatism can be.

If disability is the wrong discourse for an objective of real integration, what is the right one? Clearly this has to do with curriculum, that is, with pedagogy, rather than with perceptions of difference which are informed by a powerful medical discourse about impairment. The curriculum issues have to do not only with what might be taught to students, some of whom clearly have different capacities from students of similar age, but with pedagogic practices such as those discussed by Biklen (1985) in the US, Quicke (1986) in the UK, and Baird and Mitchell in Victoria (1986). But this takes us back to what is taught in teacher training institutions. Curriculum surfaces every now and again in the debate on integration (for instance, Varley and Howard, 1985) but it is submerged by the more powerful discourses on resources, professionalism and disability.

A second reason why the policies under consideration may have counter-effects can also be drawn from the theorizing I've proposed. If policy, as intervention, is informed by social theories of, for instance, how integration might be achieved, then one possible reason for the failure of this policy is that its social theories are inadequate. This subsumes the claim just made that a discourse on disability or special educational needs is the wrong discourse for an objective of integration. But there are a number of other instances of possibly faulty theorizing which may work against an objective of integration as increasing participation. In Victoria, for instance, if the extent of resistance to the policy proposed in *Integration in Victorian Education* had been properly anticipated, as it could have been since there is plenty of evidence that those tagged disabled do not participate equally in Australian society (for example, Human Rights Commission, 1986a and 1986b; Bodna 1987), then a potential strategy would have been to make better use of the political process. As it was, the report was dumped on schools, moral panics ensued which could have been headed off by more astute negotiation, and bureaucratic regulation and thus the politics of bureaucracy were in fact encouraged by the Report: this contravened the objective in Ministerial Paper no. 1 for a more responsive bureaucracy (1983). There is overseas evidence, from countries such as Norway where, admittedly, some key factors affecting educational practices differ from those in Victoria, that integration policy and other educational policies can be introduced with less resistance, lower conflict and fewer counter-effects, through a more astute use of the political process (Vislie, Kierulf and Pukstad, 1987). This strategy assumes the political process is well understood and there is evidence that key figures in policy formulation in Victoria do not have this. An instance of misunderstanding the political process is the notion that demonstrating a real need for extra resources will gain them: extensive research of schools in one of the non-government sectors is currently (1987) being undertaken in Victoria based on this premise. In an economic situation where education has fallen on the political agenda, and this is what has happened in Australia and Victoria, and as against Harris's view (1986), strategies other than resource demand need to be explored. What might those be?

One possible course of action, might be based on the premise that people in education believe in the main belief which underpins educational practices, namely that people can learn about the world in ways which open their minds to new courses of action. A clear strategy would be to mount a course for teachers, and intending teachers, which shows:

(a) that tagging children as disabled, while a means of personal survival for a teacher, is a practice which repeated many times in many places constructs a discriminatory system not only of schooling but, contributes too, to a discriminatory market place and social life;

(b) that there are curriculum strategies to deal with the issues which presently are tagged as to do with disability;

(c) that democratism and equality may not be such a bad thing after all; and

(d) to demand of their past or present teaching institutions the very best in pedagogic practice, including learning about a non-divisive curriculum and non-divisive pedagogic practices.

A second course of action would be to carry out research on good practice, research whose social theory can expose the factors which constitute such practices as opposed to merely describing such instances: since description may encourage others but does not easily lend itself to changing practices elsewhere. This research would be fundamentally different from the research on alleged prevalence or incidence, a medical discourse which currently informs research and information for policy development in the area. It would have to be well funded and if it were to be government funded there is a political task here, since there is persuasive evidence that educational apparatuses in Australia as against Swedish practice for instance tend, with some notable exceptions, to use research poorly, to mis-understand the nature of research (perhaps intentionally) and to fund it expediently (Burns, 1979).

A third course of action is raised by what has happened in Enrolment Support Groups (now renamed Integration Support Groups: ISGs). While there are undoubtedly instances where parents have achieved a place for their child in a regular school through an ISG, there are many reports that the process is undemocratic. We must ask then, whether ISG practices help to reduce the inequalities children tagged disabled have experienced in the Victorian educational apparatus? Do such instances illustrate once more a failure to understand the political process (Mehan's research shows what the political processes in such Groups might be) both among those involved in the policy-writing process and among some members in these Groups. Are Integration Support Groups (as they are now known) part of what some call the swamps of participatory decision making? Have they merely bureaucratized integration processes? This democratic socialist strategy has been found wanting in Victoria and this invites us to think of better courses of action.

Notes

(This chapter was originally presented at the Australian Association for Special Education's 12th Annual Conference, Melbourne, October 1987).

1   My thanks to Robin Burns, Centre for Comparative Study and International Studies in Education, La Trobe University, for pointing this out.
2   See his more recent book (1987).
3   More accurately, in England and Wales, Scotland has a separate educational apparatus and separate legislation.
4   This was conducted by third year students in sociology at Monash University in 1985. A random sample of sixty primary School Councils in the metropolitan area of Melbourne were contacted, of whom forty provided School Council policy documents on integration.
5   The writer was a member of the Accreditation Committee for a graduate diploma in special education.

References

ABBERLEY, P. (1987) 'The concept of oppression and the development of a social theory of disability', *Disability, Handicap and Society*, 2, 1, pp. 5–20.

APPLE, M. W. (1982) *Education and Power*, Boston, Routledge and Kegan Paul.

BALL, S. (1988) 'Comprehensive schooling, effectiveness and control: An analysis of educational discourses', in SLEE, R. (Ed.) *Discipline and Schools: A Curriculum Approach*, Australia, Macmillan.

BARTON, L. (1987) 'Keeping schools in line', in BOOTH, T. and COULBY, D. (Eds) *Producing and Reducing Disaffection*, Milton Keynes, Open University Press, pp. 242–7.

BAIRD, J. and MITCHELL, I. (Eds) (1986) *Improving the Quality of Teaching and Learning: An Australian Case Study — the Peel Project*, Melbourne, Monash University Printing.

BODNA, B. (1987) *Finding the Way: The Criminal Justice System and the Person with Intellectual Disability*, Office of the Public Advocate, Melbourne, Government Printer, April.

BOOTH, T. (1981) 'Demystifying integration', in SWANN, W. (Ed.) *The Practice of Special Education*, Basil Blackwell for the Open University, pp. 288–313.

BOOTH, T. (1983) 'Policies towards the integration of mentally handicapped children in education', *Oxford Review of Education*, 9, 3, pp. 255–68.

BIKLEN, D. (1985) *Achieving the Complete School: Strategies for Effective Mainstreaming*, Teachers College, Columbia University.

BRISENDEN, S. (1986) 'Independent living and the medical model of disability', *Disability, Handicap and Society*, 1, 1, pp. 173–8.

BURNS, R. (1979) *The Formation and Legitimation of Development Education*, with particular reference to Australia and Sweden, PhD thesis, La Trobe University.

DEPARTMENT OF EDUCATION AND SCIENCE, SCOTTISH EDUCATION DEPARTMENT, WELSH OFFICE (1978) *Meeting Special Educational Needs: A Report of the Committee of Enquiry into Education of Handicapped Children and Young People*, London, HMSO.

DEPARTMENT OF EDUCATION AND SCIENCE (1978) *Special Educational Needs*, Report of the Committee of Enquiry into the Education of Handicapped Children and Young People (The Warnock Report), London, HMSO.

DEPARTMENT OF EDUCATION AND SCIENCE (1980) *Special Needs in Education*, White Paper Cmnd 7996. London, HMSO.

DEPARTMENT OF EDUCATION AND SCIENCE (1981) Circular no. 8/81, Education Act 1981, 7 December, 1981. London, HMSO.

DEPARTMENT OF EDUCATION AND SCIENCE (1983) Circular 1/83, *Assessment and Statements of Special Educational Needs*, London, HMSO.

EVANS, R. (1986) 'Children with learning difficulties: Contexts and consequences', paper presented at the Australian Association of Special Education 11th National Conference, September.

FINKELSTEIN, V. (1980) *Attitudes and Disabled People — Some Issues for Discussion*, New York, World Rehabilitation Fund.

FISH, J. (1985) *Special Education: The Way Ahead*, Milton Keynes, Open University Press.

FULCHER, G. (1986) 'Australian policies on special education: Towards a sociological account', *Disability, Handicap and Society*, 1, 1, pp. 19–52.

FULCHER, G. (1987) 'Bureaucracy takes round seven: Round eight to commonsense?' *The Age*, 14 April.

FULCHER, G. (1989) 'Disability: A social construction', in NAJMAN, J. and LUPTON, G. (Eds) *Health and Australian Society*, Macmillan, Australia.

FULCHER, G. (1990) *Disabling Policies? A Comparative Approach to Education Policy and Disability*, Lewes, Falmer Press.

GOACHER, B., EVANS, J., WELTON, J. WEDELL, K. and GLASER, D. (1986) *The 1981 Education Act: Policy and Provision for Special Educational Needs* a Report to the Department of Education and Science, University of London Institute of Education, October.

GOW, L. and FULCHER, G. (1986) Part 2 *Towards a Policy Direction on Integration*, discussion paper prepared for the Commonwealth Schools Commission, June 26.

HARRIS, R. (1986) 'Recognition of special education needs: Co-operation at the political level', *The Australian Journal of Special Education*, 10, 1, May, pp. 6–12.

HINDESS, B. (1986) 'Actors and social relations', in WARDELL, M. L. and TURNER, S. P. (Eds) *Sociological Theory in Transition*, Boston, Allen and Unwin, pp. 113–26.

HINDESS, B. (1987) *Freedom, Equality and the Market: Arguments on Social Policy*, London, Tavistock Publications.

HUISH, R. (Ed.) (1986) *Integration — A Place for Everyone*, Melbourne Participation and Equity Program.

HUMAN RIGHTS COMMISSION (1986a) *The Treatment of Disabled Persons in Social Security and Taxation Law*, Occasional Paper No. 11, Canberra, Australian Government Publishing Service.

HUMAN RIGHTS COMMISSION (1986b) *Ethical and Legal Issues in the Guardianship Option for Intellectually Disadvantaged People*, Human Rights Commission Monograph Series No. 2, Canberra, Australian Government Publishing Service.

Integration in Victorian Education (1984) Report of the Ministerial Review of Educational Services for the Disabled, Melbourne, Government Printer (chair M. K. Collins).

KIRP, D. L. (1983) 'Professionalization as a policy choice: British special education in comparative perspective', in CHAMBERS, J. G. and HARMAN, W. I. (Eds) *Special Education Policies*, Philadelphia. Temple Press, pp. 74–112.

MACDONALD, I. (1981) 'Assessment: A social dimension', in BARTON, L. and TOMLINSON, S. (Eds) *Special Education: Policy, Practices and Social Issues*, London, Harper and Row, pp. 90–108.

MEHAN, H. (1983) *The Role of Language and the Language of Role in Institutional Decision Making*, Cambridge, Cambridge University Press.

MEHAN, H. (1984) 'Institutional decision-making', in ROGOFF, B. and LAVE, J. (Eds) *Everyday Cognition: Its development in Social Context*, Cambridge, Massachusetts, Harvard University Press.

MEHAN, H., MEIHLS, J. L., HERTWECK, A. and CROWDES, M. S. (1981) 'Identifying handicapped students', in BACHARACH, S. B. (Ed.) *Organizational Behaviour in Schools and School Districts*, Praeger, pp. 381–422.

MINISTERIAL PAPER NUMBER 1, *Decision Making in Victorian Education*, Melbourne, March 1983.

OFFE, C. (1984) 'Social policy and the state,' in KEANE, J. (Ed.) *Contradictions of the Welfare State*, London, Hutchinson, pp. 88–118.

QUICKE, J. (1986) 'Pupil culture, peer tutoring and special educational needs', *Disability, Handicap and Society*, 1, 2, pp. 147–71.

STOBART, G. (1986) 'Is integrating the handicapped psychologically defensible?' *Bulletin of the British Psychological Society*, 39, pp. 1–3.

SWANN, W. (1985) 'Is the integration of children with special needs happening? An analysis of recent statistics of pupils in special schools', *Oxford Review of Education*, 11, 1, pp. 3–18.

THE STATE BOARD OF EDUCATION (1987) *Legislative Changes to Implement the Integration of Students with Impairments, Disabilities or Problems in Schooling*, Advice to the Minister for Education, Melbourne, February.

TOMLINSON, S. (1982) *A Sociology of Special Education*, London, Routledge and Kegan Paul.

TOMLINSON, S. (1985) 'The expansion of special education', *Oxford Review of Education*, 11, 2, pp. 157–65.

TSCHIDERER, N. P. (1986) 'A study to identify the nature of integration at the Wonthaggi primary school in 1986', research paper presented to the Faculty of Special Education, Melbourne College of Advanced Education, October, unpublished.

VARLEY, J. and HOWARD, S. (1985) 'Integration — what it's all about', *VSTA News*, 6, 5, March 20.

VICTORIA, EDUCATION DEPARTMENT, STUDENT SERVICES (CG and CS) (n.d. 1984) 'Response to the Report of the Ministerial Review of Educational Services for the Disabled', *Integration in Victorian Education*.

VICTORIA, MINISTER OF EDUCATION (The Hon I. Cathie) (1985) memorandum on 'Integration in Victorian Schools', 20 May.

VICTORIA, MINISTRY OF EDUCATION (1986) *Curriculum Guidelines for the Education of Students with Impairments, Disabilities or Problems in Schooling*, Curriculum Branch, Curriculum Committee, May.

VICTORIA, MINISTRY OF EDUCATION (1986) Executive Memorandum No. 34 from the Acting Chief Executive (M. K. Collins) 'Enrolment Support Group Guidelines for Regular Schools', 13 March.

VICTORIA, MINISTRY OF EDUCATION (1986) memorandum to all members Senior Officers Group Integration Committee from the Director, Integration Unit (B. W. Lamb) 29 April.

VICTORIA, MINISTRY OF EDUCATION (no date) memorandum to presidents of school Councils, Principals and staff of all schools, *Integration in Victorian Schools*.

VICTORIA, MINISTRY OF EDUCATION(1984) memorandum to presidents of school councils, principals and staff, 31 August.

VICTORIA, MINISTRY OF EDUCATION (no date) memorandum to executive directors, directors of branches and units, regional directors of education, principals of schools, presidents of school councils, officers in charge of student services centres, teachers in charge of education support centres *Guidelines for schools: Integration Teachers: Role Rationale and Responsibilities (Primary and Post Primary)*.

VICTORIA, MINISTRY OF EDUCATION (1985) memorandum to regional directors of education, OICs, student services (CG and CS) centres, *Special School Placement Procedures*, 28th March.

VICTORIA, MINISTRY OF EDUCATION (1987) memorandum to regional directors of education, *Delayed Admission to School of Parent's Choice*, 19 January.

VICTORIA, MINISTRY OF EDUCATION, (1987) Integration Unit, 'Resource Briefing Paper for Ministerial Reference Group', February.

VICTORIA, MINISTRY OF EDUCATION executive memorandum no. 144 (1987) to regional directors of education, principles of schools, presidents of school councils, officers in charge of student services centres, teachers in charge of education support centres, *Integration Support Group Procedures for Regular Schools (Formerly Enrolment and Support Group Guidelines)*, 17 August 1987.

VISLIE, L. in collaboration with KIERULF, C. and PUKSTAD, P. (1987) *Review of the Current Status of Special Education in Norway*, made for UNESCO by the Institute of Educational Research of Oslo, typescript, June.

WARNOCK, M. (1978) *Times Educational Supplement*, 25 May.

WEBER, M. (1964) *The Theory of Social and Economic Organization*, New York: The Free Press.

WELTON, J. and EVANS, R. (1986) 'The development and implementation of special education policy: Where did the 1981 Act fit in?', *Public Administration*, 64, pp. 209–27.

Acts

England
Education Act 1981, HMSO.

Victoria
Education Act 1958.

US
Public Law 94–142, The Education for All Handicapped Students Act, 1975.

2
Evaluating Integration Processes in Brazil

Wen T. C. Lin

Introduction

This chapter addresses the issue of how schools can, using their own human and other resources, ensure that a continuous effort is made to achieve the aims of integration once a process of integration is initiated. It presents a methodology for evaluating and improving integration processes (MEIIP), a methodology developed in the Brazilian context, as an alternative by which schools can monitor system-atically the integration process of individual pupils. The focus is placed on how one can evaluate and improve, systemactically, the integration process of children trans-ferred from special classes into ordinary classes within the context of Brazilian schools. It is specially concerned with pupils who were previously from the so called special classes for the Educable Mentally Deficient (EMD) in Brazil.[1]

The Integration of Children Categorized as Educable Mentally Deficient (EMD) in Brazil

In Brazil, the first educational provision for the mentally retarded appeared in 1874. However, it was only in the 1960s, when the *democratization* of education became a central government policy, that accompanying the growth of popular education, special education gradually increased the size of its services and became more institutionalized. Since this time, the dominant type of provision for the EMD has been special classes within regular schools.

According to the 1981 national statistics, within the first level regular school system, the EMD category accounts for 81.1 per cent of the total number of children receiving some kind of special educational provision. This overwhelming predominance of the EMD category is confirmed by the more recent data, obtained from a questionnaire survey carried out by the author in the first semester of 1988.[2] According to this survey, an average of 70.5 per cent of children with special educational needs were catered for under the EMD category. The highest percentage was found in the São Paulo State, with 84 per cent; and the lowest was in the Goiás State, with 59 per cent. Regarding the prevalence of the special class type provision, the survey also showed that, over 85 per cent of the EMD (within the state school system) were provided for in special classes within regular schools rather than in special schools. In fact, in five states (Bahia, Espírito Santo, São Paulo, Rio Grande do Sul and Santa Catarina) the percentage of EMD provided for in special classes within regular schools was as high as 100 per cent.

The majority of EMD classes are located in schools of poorer urban areas and, not infrequently, children in these special classes come from the lowest income families. Most of them would have failed the first year of primary education once or more. Officially, these special classes are aimed at providing education for children diagnosed as EMD. EMD, in the official definition, are children with IQ between 69–50 (Wechsler), i.e. 'children who, although they possess an intellectual level below average, can be initiated in literacy, can follow the curricular program adapted to their personal conditions, can achieve social and occupational adjustment, and, in adulthood, partial or total independence'. (BRAZIL-MEC-CENESP, 1984, p. 11). However, in practice, failure in first year primary education with additional behavioural maladjustment often become the main criteria for transfer to special class. Thus, it is possible to find in EMD special classes children whose EMD label could be challenged. Moreover, schools often denominate their special classes as classes for children with learning difficulties, abandoning or camouflaging the EMD categorization. When attributing causes to the failure of these children, the predominant view is that the problem dwells with the child and the poverty of the family. The notion of *special need* as a resulting state from the interaction between personal characteristics, environmental (including school) factors and the cultural definition of normality is rarely present.

Once entered into the special class, for how long do these children stay there and how many of them are re-integrated into the regular class? Most schools have only one, and at most two, special class, for which the official upper limit of annual in-take is twelve pupils. Having this in view, it appears reasonable to expect that every year a number of these pupils should be returned to regular classes, or further segregated into special schools, in order to allow other pupils to be admitted. One feature that constantly arises from personal contacts with practitioners is the lack of a clear definition of what an EMD special class is supposed to achieve by the end of the academic year. Could or should re-integration into regular classes be a goal to strive for?

The word *integration* has been used in different ways within the field of special education. It is often used to describe a type or location of special educational provision, in terms of its proximity to *normal* children. However, another usage of this word brings a more dynamic meaning: a process of increasing the participation of the handicapped children in school, community and society, which ultimately involves the *democratization* of schools (Booth, 1983).

In 1986, the Centro Nacional de Educação Especial — CENESP[3] (later renamed Secretaria de Educação Especial — SESPE) released a document where five principles for special education were established: participation, integration, normalization, interiorization and simplification. In this document, integration is defined as a dynamic and organic process, involving efforts from different social segments, to establish conditions that enable the persons with deficiencies, behavioural problems, and gifted, to become an integral part of society as a whole (BRAZIL-MEC-CENESP, 1986)

It is possible to find in this definition two components: (a) the integration of different social segments including service providing agencies, aiming at (b) the integration of the persons with deficiencies or the gifted in society, i.e., becoming part of. In addition, this definition seems to acknowledge the importance of society structuring itself, in order to make it possible for the handicapped to become participants of this society. This reflects the current thinking within the field of *integration with necessary support*.

According to the survey carried out by the author, there is a multiplicity of ways in which integration is defined by individual states, despite the existence of a national guideline by CENESP. Only two states followed closely the CENESP's definition, by acknowledging the two components mentioned above. The concept that appeared most frequently in the definitions gathered was that of *participation*, the second component of CENESP's definition. To be integrated was to participate in society, or to become an active part of society. Another concept was that of *equal opportunity*. To be integrated was to have access to the educational or social opportunities available to those classified as normal.

If one is to analyze the education of the EMD in Brazil in terms of its physical and curricular proximity to the normal, it may be considered as one that promotes integration, because of the predominance of the special class type provision. However, if the concept of *a process of increasing participation* is brought into the analysis, it becomes less simple to arrive at a conclusion.

Although transfer back into ordinary classes has been happening, as revealed by the survey, there is a noticeable lack of systematic monitoring as to whether integration is happening. Once the child re-enters the regular classroom further effort is rarely spent on verifying whether the participation of the child is being increased and extended in all aspects of his school life, nor is effort spent on continuously offering the provision to meet his learning needs. It seems that there is a lack of a continuous integrated action from different segments of the education system in furthering the process of integration of the EMD to its full extent.

Does the state of regular education in Brazil propitiate the re-integration of children from EMD classes into regular classes? The education system in Brazil has traditionally been organized on the basis of collectivity and uniformity. Despite the discourse of *democratization* of public instruction and equal opportunity to education, the curriculum organization, the lock-step promotion system, and the deficient human and financial resource ensure the continuation of collectivity, uniformity and selectivity.

Within this context, for a child to be considered ready to return to the regular class, he has to have achieved a level of academic ability which no longer requires a special curriculum programme or intensive individual help from the class teacher. The survey revealed that the prerequisite for transfer back to a regular class is that the pupil must have learnt the basic skills of reading and writing, he must also have acquired some social competence in order to relate to his peers and the teacher in the regular class. Because of the large size of regular classes and the very little, or non-existing, individualization of instruction, he must be able to follow the pace of the class and work independently, with very limited individual attention from the class teacher. Only then, he can be transferred back to regular class, profit from the instruction and education provided, interact with the class and the teacher, and thus have his participation in the regular class increased. The concept of the individualized programme, much emphasized in other countries, does not form part of the integration programme referred to here.

The academic goals of integration effort can, therefore, be described as:

(a) to provide the child with an educational opportunity equal to other children in the regular class — equal in terms of curriculum content, instruction and classroom culture; so that

(b) the child might through achieving a similar level of ability to others, attain promotion by the end of the academic year; and thereafter

(c) proceed in normal schooling.

The social goals can be described as:

(a) to destigmatize the child from the effects of being a member of special class;

(b) to desegregate the child;

(c) to increase the child's participation and interaction with other children within the ordinary class; and thus

(d) to *normalize* the schooling experience of the child.

The educational process that a child in an integration programme experiences would at least include these aspects, adapting to:

(a) a faster working pace and more compact curriculum content;

(b) working more independently with substantially less individual attention from the class teacher; and

(c) working alongside a far larger number of peers.

Brazil, because of its tradition of special class provision, might be in a more favourable position in permitting the integration of pupils categorized as EMD into ordinary schools. However, without the necessary reforms in the regular education system, integration of children into regular classes loses its dimension of respect for the individuality, and also the qualitative dimension of the equality of opportunity. The possibility of adequately integrating EMD class pupils into regular classroom appears to be very limited. Only those who have acquired the ability to cope and to make progress within the existing situation can be successfully reintegrated.

Having in view the existing deficiencies within the current regular education system, and also considering the continuing transfer of children back into this system, it becomes vital to carry out careful monitoring and continuous evaluation of integration processes. While reforms in the education system and more fundamental social changes are yet to be realized, efforts need to be made in order to ensure that integration does happen when a child returns to the regular classroom.

A Naturalistic Evaluation Approach for Evaluating and Improving Integration Process

The study of methodologies for evaluating integration is a field largely unexplored, and it is even more so when evaluation of the integration of individual pupils is concerned. There is a need for an evaluation methodology which has a main purpose of producing a direct and immediate effect on the educational conditions of pupils whose integration process is being evaluated; a methodology which will evaluate the integration process of each pupil individually, detect problematic areas in the actual situation of integration and guide the process of improving the situation. In short, there seems to be a need for an essentially interventionist approach. In addition, integration is a concept susceptible to differing definitions and interpretations from different participants involved in the process of integration, i.e., interested parties. Because of this, the criteria for making value judgments about a particular situation of integration and the definition of what is problematic may vary among these participants, depending on their individual understanding of those concepts and their perception of that situation. Thus, it would be of extreme importance that this methodology should recognize, and incorporate into its evaluation process, this multiplicity of views. Furthermore, this methodology should be devised as a working tool, for the staff of schools, so that they themselves can carry out systematic evaluation and improvement of integration processes.

Considering the purpose of evaluation defined above, and what integration means within our particular context, it seems that the approach required has to present the following three features:

(a) its enquiry paradigm has to be based on phenomenology;
(b) it has to involve active participation of people closely involved in the integration process (i.e., the pupil, the parents, the teacher, the counsellor and the supervisor)[4]; and
(c) it has to lead to an in-depth and holistic examination of individual cases.

The need for a phenomenological enquiry paradigm is intrinsic to the nature of the integration programme. The primary goals of integration are based on the concepts of equality, destigmatization, desegregation and normalization. These concepts are social constructs, and the meanings that people attribute to each of these words might differ from individual to individual, and from one context to another. The phenomena that are considered to represent these concepts depend on two factors: (a) the frame of reference used by each participant to interpret these concepts, and (b) how each participant perceives events, situations and processes within the programme. Therefore, to evaluate an integration process is to deal with the multiple meanings and perceptions that exist in the minds of each participant, and this can only be done through an enquiry process based on phenomenology.

Concerning the need to involve the participants of an integration process in an evaluation study, it can be explained from two dimensions: conceptual and practical. The explanation from the conceptual dimension follows from the previous analysis of the enquiry paradigm. To evaluate integration process is to deal with the multiple ways that each participant perceives and attributes meaning to the process of integration. Hence, if a more accurate and complete picture is to be obtained, the participation of the people involved is essential. It is important that the perspective of each one is made known to the others. Regarding specifically the participation of the child and the parents, if the main concern of integration is to provide equality of educational opportunity and equality of social treatment, it seems obvious that they should also be given equal opportunity to participate in the evaluation process. They should be allowed and encouraged to express their views.

The explanation from the practical dimension is related to the purpose of evaluation, which is improvement. This improvement orientation entails that evaluation must produce relevant and useful results which can help the programme staff in finding out adequate improvement strategies. And, in order to achieve this, a number of authors have proposed active involvement of programme staff in the evaluation study. This is seen as having the strengths of (a) increasing the relevance and usefulness of evaluation findings, (b) increasing the usage of evaluation findings through staff's appropriation of the evaluation knowledge, and (c) allowing a faster information flow among the programme participants (Deshler, 1984; Dawson and D'Amico, 1986). Nevertheless, participation of the child and the parents should not be overlooked, because as far as increasing the relevance of findings is concerned their involvement is essential. Without their perspective the understanding of the integration process becomes incomplete, and hence attempts of improvement might be rendered ineffective.

The need for an in-depth and holistic examination of individual cases is due to the special conditions of integration programmes. There is the complexity of the child's own characteristics, of his past experiences, of the singularity with which each child experiences the integration process, and the complexity of the context of the integration process. Evaluation needs to examine the integration process from different dimensions, e.g., academic, psychological and organizational. It has to evaluate the adequacy of the programme as well as how the programme is working. It has to draw evaluative information from multiple sources. It has to accommodate and capitalize on the multiplicity and diversity of perspectives held by the participants.

These three main features served as the basis for the conceptual framework of the approach developed by the author: MEIIP, a methodology for evaluating and improving integration processes. MEIIP is proposed as an alternative by which school educational counsellors and/or pedagogic supervisors can evaluate and improve, systematically, the integration process of individual pupils. The first part of the conceptual framework deals with the assumptions which underlie MEIIP.

The second part deals with the functional and methodological characteristics of MEIIP.

MEIIP — The Conceptual Framework

Underlying Assumptions

The nature of society

The position taken in MEIIP is that society is formed by groups of people with different and sometimes conflicting interests. One group might have stronger power to influence another than vice-versa, and given this uneven power relationship, consensus will take either the form of *imposed-upon consensus* or of *negotiated consensus*. Therefore, the result of an evaluation effort will be either an 'imposed-upon' decision or a 'negotiated' decision.

An ideal society

It is assumed that an ideal society is one which promotes an equality of participation and diminishment of power difference. The implication of this assumption is that the judgment made about an integration process must be made (a) by the participants of the situation and (b) through a process of negotiation. Each parties' different views, however conflicting they might be, must be more equally represented. The weaker parties' perspectives, normally the pupil's and the parent's, must be given proper consideration, so that the decisions are not imposed-upon them, but rather negotiated with them.

The nature of social reality

Social reality is multiple, divergent and intangible. It is how people perceive and interpret actions, events, situations and processes that make up the social reality.

The nature of evaluator-evaluand relationship

It is assumed that the relationship between evaluator and evaluand is interdependent. The evaluand is the process of integration. This process not only involves physical and organizational arrangements; it involves people. Thus, interaction is observed between the evaluator and the evaluand.

The nature of truth statements

Evaluation conclusions are context-determined and context-bound. Judgments made about a particular integration process can only be understood within the context of that particular pupil. And, the knowledge generated from that evaluation study can only be best applied in effecting changes or improvements in that particular integration process.

Causal relationship

It is assumed that because of the complex nature of social reality, situations and processes can only be interpreted as resulting from multiple interacting factors which shape them and are part of them. Therefore, in evaluating an integration process, one can only interpret and explain the process by looking at the programme holistically.

The role of values in an evaluation study

The evaluation process is value bound. The explicit statement of the ideological and epistemological assumptions is in itself a recognition of this value-boundness. The role of values is especially important in the evaluation of integration process, because the concept of integration itself is based on a set of social values. So, how an integration process is evaluated reflects how the participants handle the related set of social values.

Functional and Methodological Characteristics

The definition of evaluation

Evaluation is defined as a study designed and conducted to assist the participants of an integration programme in judging and improving the integration process. The verb *to assist* is significant here. The concept it brings is that of evaluator as a facilitator, whose role is to create a situation where the participants can arrive at a *negotiated* judgment about the process and about strategies for effecting improvement. (The concept of evaluator as facilitator can be found in Steinmetz, 1983; Kemmis, 1986.) This definition of roles is made to reflect the assumption about ideal society established earlier.

The main function

The major function is that of *improvement* — a formative rather than summative function. In addition to this, it is also expected that the process of evaluating will help to increase awareness and understanding of the participants in regard to other people's perspectives, and hence to produce attitude and behavioural change. It has a psychological, socio-political and educational function (Cronbach *et al.*, 1980).

Who conducts evaluation?

An evaluation study can have either an internal or external, professional or amateur evaluator. The literature on evaluation has largely concentrated on approaches conducted by external-professional evaluators. MEIIP is, however, an approach where evaluation is conducted by an internal-amateur-evaluator: the educational counsellor (EC) and the pedagogic supervisor (PS).

It was stated earlier that active participation of programme staff in evaluation is important to increase the relevance and the usage of evaluation findings. However, MEIIP takes a step further, it is thought that the fact of having the counsellor and the supervisor as the evaluators can present a number of advantages. Firstly, the counsellor and the supervisor, in contrast to an external evaluator, already have an in-depth knowledge of the programme and the school context; thus, they do not need extra time spent on understanding the context of evaluation, and establishing rapport with the programme participants. Secondly, being full-time school personnel, they have a wider opportunity for informal and/or formal contact with the participants; there can be faster information flow and more frequent exchange of ideas, hence the evaluation process can be carried out at a faster pace. Thirdly, counsellor and supervisor can incorporate this evaluation approach into their normal working practice; thus, evaluation and improvement can be carried out periodically and systematically, as part of the integration programme. Fourthly, the fact of having a familiar person as the evaluator might help to avoid feelings of uneasiness or threat that might emerge if the evaluator were from an outside agency. Finally, evaluation carried out internally can dispense with the extra financial expenditure that it otherwise might incur. Although the counsellor and the supervisor are by no means professional evaluators, their professional training does provide them with basic knowledge and skills for conducting evaluation and case studies.

The main cues that guide the study

The main cues that guide the study are the concerns and issues raised by the people involved in that particular integration process. It is the perceptions of the participants regarding the integration process that will determine at a more detailed level how the study should be conducted.

The basic questions to be addressed

The questions that the evaluation addresses are basically (1) how the process of integration is judged by those who are involved in it, and (2) how they think it could be improved.

On which already existing evaluation model or approach MEIIP is based

MEIIP is built from the approach by Guba and Lincoln (1981), i.e., from the responsive evaluation model based on the naturalistic enquiry paradigm. The reasons for this choice are (1) its better paradigmatic fit; and (2) a central focus placed on the perceptions and concerns of programme participants. However, it needs to be emphasized that MEIIP has its special feature as to who should conduct the study, the role of evaluator, the emphasis on negotiation and the improvement orientation.

The basic enquiry methods or techniques

The methods of enquiry will be predominantly qualitative. Interview plus negotiation will be the main methods employed. Other methods such as participant observation and analysis of documents, will often be used in the collection of further information. However, quantitative methods might be included when concerns or issues raised by the participants require them.

The main components of evaluation process

The *detailed* design of the evaluation study is emergent, i.e., it will only take form as the study progresses. Nevertheless, it is expected that the evaluation process should begin by finding out how each participant perceives and evaluates the integration process and what suggestions each one has for the improvement of the integration process. In addition the process should contain an exchange of views so that people are made aware of different perspectives; the process should allow for a negotiation of the final evaluative judgment and strategies for improvement. Moreover, an improvement stage should be added on to the evaluation stage, because it is a process of evaluation aimed at and followed by an intervention. Finally, the intervention stage should be followed or accompanied by a second round of evaluation, in such a way that it becomes a cyclic process, where evaluation and improvement are carried out systematically and periodically. Figure 1 outlines the basic activities of an evaluation-improvement process.

Activities

1 The evaluation conductor starts by interviewing each of the participants to find out how each one perceives the situation, how they evaluate the integration process and what suggestions each one has as to how the integration process can be improved.
2 Each interview data are analyzed in terms of its internal consistency, and are cross examined in terms of differences and similarities.
3 If there is a need for additional information, the conductor selects the sources of information and the method of data collection.

Figure 1   The evaluation-improvement process: its basic activities.

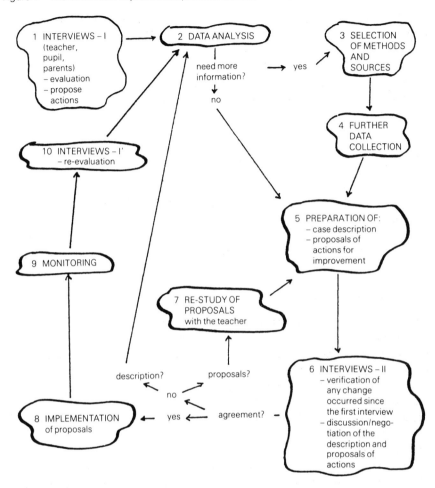

4 The conductor proceeds with collection of additional information.

5 If there is no need for additional information, the conductor proceeds to write up the case description, which should contain: the child's past history; how his integration process is evaluated by each participants, including the counsellor and the supervisor; the improvement proposals.

6 Having prepared the case description, the conductor carries out a second round of interviews with each participant. He will check: whether there has been any change since the last interview; discuss the different perspectives offered by the participants; and discuss the improvement strategies. It is mainly at this stage that the negotiation occurs and each one gets to know other peoples' perspectives.

7 If there is disagreement about the improvement proposal, the conductor re-studies the proposals.

    If there is disagreement about the evaluation of the integration process, the conductor returns to 2, data analysis.

8 If there is agreement, the conductor proceeds to the implementation stage with

9 systematic monitoring.

10 After a period of implementation, the conductor initiates the second cycle of evaluation, by repeating the interviews. In this way, evaluation and improvement are carried out systematically and periodically.

The operational process outlined here should be seen as a guideline for organizing the MEIIP studies. Its sequential order need not be followed rigidly. The experience in practice has revealed that the operational process of MEIIP does not usually follow a single-line sequential order, nor is it a uni-directional sequential process. Often more than one activity is carried out during a same period of time, and frequently the execution of activities makes forward-backward movements along the evaluation-improvement process.

On the Implementation of MEIIP in Schools

Similarly to any other methodology, MEIIP is based on a set of epistemological and ideological assumptions. Those assumptions are reflected in the emphasis on perception, participation and negotiation that the approach advocates. As an implication, the adoption of MEIIP in a school entails democratizing the school, opening up the decision-making process to participation, specially of parents and pupils. Because of this, it is believed that MEIIP cannot and should not be imposed upon schools by the education authority. Rather, it has to be introduced to schools (especially, to the education counsellors and/or pedagogic supervisors) as an alternative working strategy, and the schools should have the final decision on whether to adopt it or not. Before any decision is made, they should have a full knowledge of the methodology and its practical and political implications (opening up the decision-making process to participation is a political act). MEIIP studies would be best developed when the philosophical and ideological bases of the methodology are understood and the commitment to implementing it is made voluntarily and consciously.

    Concerning who should conduct the MEIIP studies, it is recommended that:

(a) whenever possible, the the educational counsellor (EC) and the pedagogic supervisor (PS) should work together as a team;

(b) the working pattern and the task division should take into consideration the nature of their usual functions and working styles; so that

(c) the EC and the PS can complement each other and make the best of their similarities and differences.

Working in a team will provide an opportunity to exchange ideas with a partner (who has a full knowledge of MEIIP, of the case under study, of the context of that evaluation study and of the school culture) about the interpretation of interview data and manner of conducting the evaluation-improvement study.

Before starting a MEIIP study, the first step to be taken is to establish a provisional time schedule, by estimating a length of time for each activity of the operational process of MEIIP. The function of the provisional time schedule is to help the EC and the PS to coordinate more efficiently the MEIIP study within the framework of their overall working programme. This provisional time schedule should be constantly reviewed and modified in accordance to the natural evolvement of each study and to the contextual changes. It serves to guide, rather than to bind, the evaluation-improvement process. Its temporary status does not diminish its importance. Instead, the fact of having to constantly review it leads the EC and the PS to reflect constantly about their work.

During the process of study, it is important to keep individual record files for each case study. The aims of record keeping are: (a) to avoid the loss of data over time; (b) to avoid mixing data from one case study with another; and (c) to maintain the continuity of a study, especially when change of personnel (e.g., EC or PS) occurs. The individual files should contain the interview notes, the record of additional information collected, the record of all activities carried out (e.g., data, what activity and related relevant information), the case description (including the summary of each participant's perspective and improvement proposal), or the brief evaluation conclusion. Record keeping helps the EC and the PS in organizing each case study and in maintaining constantly a clear view of the evolvement of each case. This is important because MEIIP studies constitute only a small part in the overall working programme of these professionals within the school, and the absence of an organized working system might be detrimental to the continuity of MEIIP studies. This problem can become specially serious when these professionals are faced with extra work pressure or great time constraint.

Within the operational process of MEIIP, interviews occupy a position of vital importance. Interviews–I have the objective of drawing from each participant (a) his evaluation of the integration process under study and (b) suggestions on what and how improvement should be made. Interviews–II have the objective of providing an opportunity to each participant to (a) learn about the other participants perspective, (b) negotiate the conclusion of the evaluation, and (c) negotiate the improvement strategies. Interviews–I' have the objective of obtaining from each participant (a) a re-evaluation of the situation, (b) an evaluation of the effects of the improvement strategies implemented, and (c) further improvement suggestions.

These interviews are central to the methodology, because it is the result obtained from these interviews that is going to guide and direct the other activities of the evaluation-improvement process. Furthermore, it is during the interviews that the philosophy of MEIIP is translated into practice, giving value to: (a) the perception of each participant; (b) their participation in the evaluation process; and (c) the negotiation, or the participation of the participants in the decision-making process. Therefore, it is important that the interviews are carefully prepared and executed. The experience in practice has shown that a time of preparation prior to the interviews can be helpful in focusing the conversation on relevant topics and finding the best ways of approaching a same set of questions with different participants. Nevertheless, it also seems important that this preparation should not result in highly structured interviews, where the participants would not feel free to express themselves and to talk spontaneously and openly about their concerns.

Concerning the execution of the interviews, they are to be carried out on a one-to-one basis in order to enable pupils and parents to express their views more freely and to make the maximum use of the opportunity for negotiation. It is believed that in a group situation (involving pupil, parent, teacher, PS and EC), because of the unbalanced power relationship among the participants, the weaker parties (usually the pupil and the parent) might feel overwhelmed by others or might not obtain an equal opportunity to express their view. Thus, they might not be able to negotiate over the evaluation conclusion and improvement proposals. Therefore, the interviews need to be prepared, organized, and executed in a way as to provide propitious conditions for each participant to (learn to) exercise the right to participate and negotiate, a right that MEIIP attributes to them

Conclusion

This chapter briefly presented a methodology developed within the Brazilian context, with the purpose of helping the schools to evaluate and improve systematically the integration process of children transferred from EMD special classes to regular classes. This methodology, MEIIP, has in short four basic inter-related characteristics. Firstly, its enquiry paradigm is based on phenomenology. Perception is central to this methodology. It emphasizes how the process of integration is perceived by people. Secondly, it involves an active participation of the people most closely involved in the integration process (i.e., the pupil, the teacher, the parents, the educational counsellor, and the pedagogic supervisor). These participants are brought to express their evaluation of the process of integration, and to give suggestions regarding how this process can be improved. Their participation is extended to the decision-making process, through the negotiation of evaluation conclusions and improvement strategies. Thirdly, it makes an in-depth and holistic examination of individual cases. Each case of integration is examined individually, from multiple dimensions — e.g., academic, psychological, social — and considered within the pupil's own developmental and schooling history and within the school context. Finally, MEIIP capitalizes on, and also systematizes, what people naturally do when evaluating and improving a situation. Its operational process is made up of two major activities: evaluation and improvement. It is designed to be a cyclic process which only ends when the participants decide, in a negotiated consensus, to do so.

MEIIP was implemented in three state run primary schools of Belo Horizonte, the capital of Minas Gerais State, by their respective educational counsellor (EC) and pedagogic supervisor (PS). In these schools it was found to be a useful, feasible and practical methodology. It demonstrated a great potential in:

(a) making explicit similarities and differences in the perspectives of different participants of an integration process;

(b) helping the EC and the PS to detect problematic areas for improvement;

(c) raising improvement strategies;

(d) providing opportunities for the participants to learn about other people's perspectives;

(e) promoting a negotiation of evaluation conclusions and improvement strategies; and

(f) effecting improvements in an integration process, through the participative evaluation process and through the implementation of improvement strategies.

MEIIP, apart from presenting some specific methodological and functional feature, carries a set of assumptions. The assumptions concerning the nature of society and an ideal society, specifically, establish the sociological and ideological stance taken by MEIIP. The assumption that society is constituted of interest parties, where the relationship between parties is characterized by a differing degree of power influence, and the assumption that an ideal society is the one which promotes equality of power influence are the bases of MEIIP's emphasis on participation and negotiation. MEIIP advocates a more balanced distribution of power, or at least a reduction of the difference of power. It implies a democratiz- ation of the decision-making process in schools. Therefore, to adopt the MEIIP in a school is not a mere act of adopting a working strategy; it implies in assuming an ideological and political stance that it has ideological and political implications. Therefore, MEIIP should not be imposed upon the schools by any education authority. Instead, it should be made known to the schools, and these should have the opportunity of making a conscious decision for or against the use of MEIIP in their establishment. Without this, it would be doubtful whether MEIIP would be appropriately translated into practice and its intended effects obtained.

A question might be raised as to what extent schools would want to open the decision-making process to participation, and questioning, specially of pupils and parents? No optimistic view is held in this respect. Nevertheless, perhaps the political process the country is going through might be propitious to the acceptance of MEIIP. The increasing politicization of the population with the economic crisis, the general elections and the direct presidential election, the growing union movement, the recent initiative from the Federal Government to negotiate with different sectors of society over a range of issues, the newly instituted direct election of school directors in the municipal education system of Belo Horizonte, all these seem to indicate an increasing awareness towards the importance of opening up the decision-making processes to participation of a wider number of people — of interest parties. While the traditionally weaker parties are learning to fight for a right to participate and to make use of this right, the stronger parties are learning to negotiate. Thus, in the middle of this, it seems that MEIIP in some way echoes an ideological trend that is increasingly gaining force. It is expected that MEIIP will make a contribution to the democratization process that Brazilian society is going through.

Notes

1 EMD will be used, hereafter, to mean children categorized as educable mentally retarded.
2 A questionnaire survey was sent to twenty-six Brazilian states, and twelve responses were obtained. The data presented here are based on the data offered by these twelve states.
3 CENESP was created by the Brazilian Federal Government in 1973. Its function is to coordinate, in conjunction with individual states' Special Education Services, the planning and implementation of the development of special education throughout the country.
4 The educational counsellor (EC) and the pedagogic supervisor (PS) are the school staff responsible for promoting and facilitating the transfer of children from special class to regular class, as part of their daily task of assisting and supervising classroom teachers, liaising with parents and counselling pupils. While the EC deals mainly with the affective, emotional, developmental and social dimensions, the PS deals with the pedagogic-learning dimension.

References

BOOTH, T. (1983) 'Integrating special education', in BOOTH, T. and POTTS, P. *Integrating Special Education*, Oxford, Blackwell.
BRAZIL-MEC-CENESP (1984) Subsídios para Organização e Funcionamento de Serviço de Educação Especial: Área da Deficiência Mental, Brasília, MEC/CENESP.
BRAZIL-MEC-CENESP (1986) Portaria No. 69 de 28 de Agosto de Brasília, MEC/CENESP.
CRONBACH, L. J. and Associates (1980) *Towards Reform of Program Evaluation*, San Francisco, Jossey-Bass.
DAWSON, J. A. and D'AMICO, J. J. (1986) 'Involving program staff in evaluation studies: Strategy for increasing information use and enriching the data base', *Evaluation Review*, 9, 2, pp. 173–88.
DES (1978) Special Educational Needs: Report of the Committee of Enquiry into the Education of Handicapped Children and Young People (The Warnock Report), London, HMSO.
DESHLER, D (Ed.) (1984) *Evaluation for Program Improvement. New Directions for Continuing Education*, No. 24. San Francisco, Jossey-Bass.
GUBA, E. G. and LINCOLN, Y. S. (1981) *Effective Evaluation: Improving the Usefulness of Evaluation Results Through Responsive and Naturalistic Approaches*, San Francisco, Jossey-Bass.
KEMMIS, S. (1986) 'Seven principles for programme evaluation', in HOUSE, E. R. (Ed.) *New Directions in Educational Evaluation*, Lewes, Falmer Press.
STEINMETZ, A. (1983) 'The discrepancy evaluation model', in MADAUS, G. F., SCRIVEN, M. S. and STUFFLEBEAM, D. L. (Eds) *Evaluation Models: View Points on Educational and Human Services Evaluation*, Boston, Kluwer-Nijhoff Publishing.

3
Values into Action:
The Work of the Campaign for the Mentally
Handicapped and CMHERA

Paul Williams

Introduction

During the 1960s there was growing concern about two issues affecting people with severe mental handicaps[1] — the exclusion of such children from education within the school system, and the isolation and poor quality of life of the 50,000 people living in mental handicap institutions. Many of the latter were housed in large wards in old uncomfortable buildings and had very few contacts with the outside world (Morris, 1969). Moreover, the origins of the structure both of education (or non-education) of severely mentally handicapped children and of residential services for adults, lay in outdated, negative value systems, particularly the 'eugenics era' at the beginning of the twentieth century (Wolfensberger, 1975; Gabbay, 1983; Kelves, 1985)

The concern felt about these two issues in the 1960s culminated in the inclusion of severely mentally handicapped children within the education system from April 1971, and the publication by the government of an important blueprint for the development of residential services and day services for adults — the White Paper *Better Services for the Mentally Handicapped* (DHSS and Welsh Office, 1971). Although these represented quite radical changes from what had gone before, there were naturally some people who felt they did not go nearly far enough. Special education was still structured around exclusion of some children from ordinary schools, and 'Better Services' still involved large numbers of people living in segregated settings dominated by the 'medical model'.

The Founding of CMH

Three people particularly concerned about this, and wanting much more radical change, were Ann Shearer, a journalist who had written some graphic accounts of the deprivation and poor quality of life of mentally handicapped people in institutions, Sandra Francklin, an architect specializing in the design of housing for handicapped people, and Anita Hunt, a researcher with The Spastics Society. Early in 1971 at a conference of professionals concerned with mental handicap they circulated a manifesto describing their ideas, and received considerable support. With the initial assistance of The Spastics Society, they founded an organization to press for more radical change, through meetings, publications, letter-writing, comment on planning documents and mutual support of like-minded people. They called themselves 'Campaign for the Mentally Handicapped' (CMH).

Their response to the White Paper *Better Services* was entitled *Even Better Services* and argued for a complete dismantling of the institutional system of residential care and its replacement by small units of accommodation which would enable people to stay close to their families and communities.

A group of around forty friends formed around the original founders and met regularly to discuss action. Two local groups were formed, in Bristol and Cardiff, which brought together students, parents and professionals interested in improving the quality of life for people with severe handicaps. These local groups produced guides to local services and commented on local plans for service development, as well as providing a forum for discussion and mutual support. The central group also provided this forum for those involved. Individual members wrote various publications and eventually a regular newsletter was started.

'Our Life'

One of the early ideas of the group was for a conference of people with severe mental handicaps. There had been some conferences of this kind in Sweden in the late 1960s, but the idea was very new and even members of the CMH group were sceptical. However, the first British conference was organized and held at The Spastics Society's staff training centre, Castle Priory College, in Oxfordshire in 1972. Thirty-seven people came from all over the country, twenty-two of them with the label 'mentally handicapped' and the rest non-handicapped friends or helpers. The conference was called 'Our Life' and was structured around small discussion groups on topics to do with daily life, interspersed with activities such as a boat trip, a barbecue and a performance by a classical music group. The event was enormously successful. The proceedings had been tape-recorded and were written-up by Ann Shearer in a report called 'Our Life' (Shearer, 1972).

The event and the report were an important and pioneer part of an embryo movement in several parts of the world to give people with mental handicaps a voice: other key events had been the Swedish conferences (Nirje, 1972) and the publication in Britain of a book written by a man with Down's Syndrome (Hunt, 1967) which was featured in a television documentary.

The 'Our Life' conference was a stimulus to similar ventures in Canada and the USA which led to the development of the 'self-advocacy' movement — the existence now of groups all over the world of people with mental handicaps themselves meeting regularly to discuss their needs and to pursue common interests (Williams and Shoultz, 1982). CMH itself ran a sequence of conferences during the

1970s, reports of several of which were published (Shearer, 1973; Williams, 1973; Williams and Gauntlett, 1974; Tyne and Williams, 1975).

Participation

The second conference and report were entitled 'Listen!' and this reflected the beginning of a change in how the events were perceived. 'Our Life' had had the clear aim of being a conference for people with mental handicaps themselves, with the focus on affording them expression and recording their views. The title of 'Listen!' for the next conference showed awareness that the opportunity for people with handicaps to speak must be accompanied by an effort on the part of others to listen to what is said.

Those of us who organized and attended the conferences observed great effort and learning going into this process of listening amongst the non-handicapped people present, including ourselves. Eventually, we came to believe that the learning and benefits to the non-handicapped participants were as great as those to the people labelled 'handicapped'. Many of the discussions and activities at the conferences forced people to interact with a degree of equality and sharing that many of us were unused to. Professionals and relatives were in a new role which clearly changed their perceptions of their service user or family member. The experience of equal sharing with people with mental handicaps seemed to be of great benefit as an important learning opportunity for non-handicapped people.

So the idea of the 'conference' for people with mental handicaps, with non-handicapped people present to assist, changed to the idea of the 'participation event', deliberately planned and structured to foster equal sharing and learning between handicapped and non-handicapped people. Activities were now chosen in which everyone could take part on an equal basis; simple art and craft activities, country dancing, yoga, walking, watching a film, visiting a museum, all lent themselves well to this. Between activities, discussions were held in small mixed groups with a simple rule which a group leader was briefed to apply: no-one can ask a question without answering it as it applies to them. For example, if you wanted to ask a handicapped person how much he or she earns, you would have to say how much you earn; if you wanted to ask someone if they have a girlfriend or boyfriend, you would have to say if you do; if you asked someone where they lived, you would have to describe where you lived, and so on. Useful topics have been: discussions of possessions of particular importance to us; our childhood; holidays; work; what we do in our leisure time; important people in our lives; where we live; what we spend our money on. Often, the non-handicapped participants found these things quite difficult to talk about in the mixed group, and at the participation events a great deal of learning took place about the major inequalities and the more subtle ones that handicapped people have to live with, and how remedying that situation requires action and effort by all of us.

Growth and development of CMH

From 1971 to 1975, CMH operated as an informal group of like-minded friends. People joined and left, but a consistent direction was maintained. Writing of publications or letters or organizing conferences was done on a purely voluntary basis, roughly coordinated by a small central group. Meetings were held in members' homes or at The Spastics Society. The latter also assisted with printing and storage of publications. Over the years, a succession of small rooms in various corners of The Spastics Society's headquarters in London were utilized as the central office; they are now at Oxford House, Derbyshire Street, London E2.

In 1975, CMH received grant funding to employ a paid Director, and Alan Tyne, a teacher and researcher with a sociology background and extensive knowledge of mental handicap, was appointed. This appointment of a full-time Director facilitated a number of developments: the information base of the organization was greatly strengthened, and could now include sophisticated research and data collection to give CMH's arguments greater validity and credibility; a proper membership structure was established and several new local groups were started. Since then, under the successive direction of Alan Tyne, Alison Wertheimer and Steve Dowson, CMH has become a respected resource of information, based on a clear set of values concerned with achieving a high quality of life and a dignified and rightful place in society for people with severe handicaps.

CMH publications and its newsletter, now approaching its sixtieth issue, have charted the progress of radical thinking on mental handicap and the influence of consistent values on relevant political and service developments over almost two decades. Current publications include papers or books on: normalization (see below), community care, reports from the USA and lessons from American experience, integration in schools, family support, imagery in advertising and media presentation of handicapped people, planning of local services, mental handicap hospital closures, community relationships, innovative models of good service practice, staffing and support in residential services, leisure, the life-style of people with mental handicaps, ethical issues at the time of birth of handicapped babies, employment, self-advocacy, the views of handicapped people, housing, neighbourhood networks, encouraging choice, voting, independent living, common myths about mental handicap, and a brief explanatory leaflet on mental handicap.

As already described, CMH was influential at the very beginning of the movement towards 'self-advocacy' by people with mental handicaps. This interest has been maintained and CMH currently publishes a pack of materials for use by people with mental handicaps themselves, to explain the ideas, skills and practice of self-advocacy (Crawley, Mills, Wertheimer, Whittaker, Williams and Billis, 1988), and a comprehensive survey of the extent of self-advocacy in day and residential services for mentally handicapped adults (Crawley, 1988). CMH is increasingly working in partnership with People First, the London-based self-advocacy group which takes a central role in the coordination and stimulation of self-advocacy in Britain at present (People First — London and Thames Region, 126 Albert Street, London NW1 7NF).

Over the years, CMH has struggled with its name. In the late 1970s it was accepted that 'Campaign for the Mentally Handicapped' was inappropriate, and this was changed to 'Campaign for Mentally Handicapped People'. In the early 1980s this was again changed to 'Campaign for People with Mental Handicaps', to reflect the notion of 'people first'. By 1988 the organization was retaining the initials 'CMH' but using the sub-caption 'Campaigning for Valued Futures with People who have Learning Difficulties'. In 1989 a decision was taken to change both the name and the initials to 'VIA — Values Into Action', reflecting the essential notion of seeking the valuing of people with severe handicaps in society, as an expression of the values held by the organization's members.

Influences on CMH

CMH had always had, initially through Ann Shearer and later many others, strong contacts with developments in America and their pioneers. The latter included Professor Gunnar Dybwad and his wife and colleague Rosemary Dybwad of Brandeis University, Massachusetts, and Professor Wolf Wolfensberger of Syracuse University, New York. The Dybwads have been pioneers for over thirty years of the kind of ideas that CMH stands for. They have worked internationally through forums such as voluntary organizations of families of people with severe handicaps, to spread philosophy and practical knowledge on such issues as integration in schools, self-advocacy by people with mental handicaps and legal protection of the rights of handicapped people (see, for example, Dybwad, 1964).

Professor Wolfensberger has been the world's foremost writer and authority on the set of ideas known as 'normalization'. It is of interest that his views took root during a period he spent in Britain in the early 1960s working with Jack Tizard on a study of adult training centres in what was then the administrative county of Middlesex (see Tizard, 1964). At that time, these centres were oriented towards industrial contract work, usually simple assembly and packaging but also often including more sophisticated work involving high degrees of skill, precision or cooperation within a group. Britain, partly as a result of the earlier pioneer work of Jack Tizard, Neil O'Connor, Alan and Ann Clarke and others, led the world at that time in demonstrating the work capacity of people with severe handicaps (see for example Williams, 1967).[2]

Wolfensberger had seen people with severe handicaps working, albeit in segregated special settings. They could be seen by others as contributors having competence and skills, and could feel themselves to be taking part in similar activities to their parents or brothers and sisters — activities that society as a whole values and expects of its adult citizens. Later, as a response to his analysis of the historical and still prevalent 'social devaluation' of handicapped people (Wolfensberger, 1975), he married these observations on helping handicapped people to have a 'valued social role' to the principle developed in Scandinavia of 'helping handicapped people to attain a lifestyle as close to normal as possible' (Nirje, 1969). The resulting set of principles of 'normalization', later given the term 'social role valorization' (Wolfensberger, 1983), was described in an influential book (Wolfensberger, 1972) and in two instruments designed for evaluating the quality of services from a normalization or 'social role valorization' perspective: PASS — Programme Analysis of Service Systems (Wolfensberger and Glenn, 1975) and PASSING — Programme Analysis of Service Systems' Implementation of Normalization Goals (Wolfensberger and Thomas, 1983).

The most effective way of learning about normalization or social role valorization and their detailed application to services is to attend a course on PASS or PASSING, for which a structure of workshop was evolved by Wolfensberger. This includes a practice evaluation of an actual service by students organized in small teams with an experienced leader. Normalization is sometimes seen on first acquaintance as a highly prescriptive set of principles — even involving coercive imposition on handicapped people (Brechin and Swain, 1988). In practice, however, PASS and PASSING provide a framework for wide-ranging debate about personal and social values in relation to helping handicapped people. Using PASS or PASSING does not involve applying a checklist or imposing a blueprint, but considering at length the nature of the social devaluation of handicapped people, the role of services in that process, and the complex values, principles and practical dilemmas in trying to change that. No-one attending a PASS or PASSING workshop comes away thinking that normalization, or social role valorization, supplies easy answers!

The Founding of CMHERA

In 1978, the Director of CMH, Alan Tyne, attended a PASS workshop in the USA. On his return he suggested the setting up of a sister organization to CMH to develop systematic training in Britain on the principles of normalization as developed by Wolfensberger, which would lead also to a capacity to evaluate services and to assist service organizations wishing to apply the ideas. The new organization was named 'CMHERA — The Community and Mental Handicap Educational and Research Association'. Alan Tyne became its first Director and it became a registered charity and later a limited company.

A colleague of Wolfensberger, Joe Osburn, was invited over from the USA to run the very first comprehensive workshop in Britain on Wolfensberger's framework of normalization, in 1979. Two highly experienced and innovative teachers of PASS — John O'Brien and Connie Lyle — were invited to Britain to introduce the style and process of workshop that had been successfully developed in the USA. Between 1980 and 1982 they supervised about ten such workshops on PASS, through which Alan Tyne and a number of others learned how to present the material and undertake leadership roles in the workshops.

Since 1982, CMHERA has itself run some fifty workshops on PASS or PASSING, attended by around 2,500 people. Others have also developed a capacity to run these workshops and a national programme of between ten and twelve workshops a year is organized by various individuals and agencies. Workshops with an orientation towards mental health rather than mental handicap have been developed by Don Braisby and Peter Wakeford under the auspices of MIND. Other individuals running PASS or PASSING workshops include Graham Harper of Clwyd Social Services Department, David Race of The Children's Society, Alan Tyne who now works freelance under the title 'Constructive Options', and Kristjana Kristiensen — a Norwegian now domiciled in Britain who gained extensive experience of PASS in the USA. CMHERA still has a strong involvement in this teaching, under its current Director, Paul Williams.

CMHERA's Work

On each PASS or PASSING workshop, five or six teams of participants, most of whom have extensive experience of service provision, carry out a practice evaluation of a real service, under experienced leadership. The results, though obviously requiring caution in interpretation, nevertheless are likely to represent data on service quality which is unique in its range, extent and comprehensiveness. Over 300 services have been evaluated, ranging through all types and sizes of residential, day and support services, managed by a wide range of statutory, voluntary and private agencies, for a number of different client groups — children and adults with moderate, severe and profound mental handicaps, children with emotional or behavioural difficulties, adults with mental health problems, homeless people, elderly people, people with drug or alcohol problems, children and adults with physical and sensory disabilities of all kinds. Resources for full analysis of these data have not yet become available, but some preliminary analyses have been carried out (Williams, 1987a, 1987b and 1988a). These tend to suggest that almost all forms of conventional service provision, including much that goes under the name 'community care', severely affect the social valuing of their clients in negative ways. Only a very few models of service provision that encourage 'life-sharing' between handicapped and non-handicapped people seem to offer a basis for extensive re-valuing of people, or 'social role valorization'.

CMHERA has always been concerned to help services to improve their practice, as most of those involved in services wish to do. We have tried to do this through evaluation, advisory project work and teaching (Tyne, 1987a and 1987b; Williams and Tyne, 1988). The development of PASS and PASSING training and related advisory work was greatly helped by a grant from the Joseph Rowntree Memorial Trust between 1983 and 1986.

A number of services have commissioned full PASS or PASSING evaluations, carried out by experienced teams with fuller preparation and over a longer time than is possible on introductory workshops. Such evaluations lead to a written report, and several agencies have given permission for these to be published by CMHERA. The reports illustrate how the results of an evaluation are translated into constructive suggestions for service improvement, usually through a process of dialogue and mutual learning with the service providers during and after the evaluation. Reports are available on evaluations of: two family support services, one run by a statutory authority (Tyne, 1987c), the other by a voluntary organization (Williams, 1987c); a residential service for children before and after a move from a large single building into dispersed ordinary housing (Williams, 1988b); a study of the process of moves out of a large mental handicap hospital in relation to one of the health districts involved (Tyne and Williams, 1987); a plan for a new kind of day service for mentally handicapped adults (Tyne, 1987d); and two residential services for mentally handicapped adults run by voluntary organizations (Tyne, 1987e; Williams, 1988c).

Long-term advisory work on the application of normalization has been carried out with a number of groups and agencies, one of the most extensive being with The Children's Society; a report on the latter has been published (Williams and Race, 1988).

John O'Brien and Connie Lyle of Responsive Systems Associates in Georgia, USA, have worked on a framework for teaching that is more flexible and more conducive to generating ideas for personal action than PASS and PASSING tend to be. They have explored the notion of 'accomplishments' to be pursued through a mobilization of the strengths and interests of communities, services and individuals. In particular, five major accomplishments can be identified: choice, respect, competence, community presence, and relationships. O'Brien and Lyle's 'Framework for Accomplishment' is mainly taught in Britain by Alan Tyne of Constructive Options (17 Belle Vue Road, Wivenhoe, Colchester, Essex). Early work on its application in Britain was carried out when Alan was with CMHERA.

Images of Possibility

One of the important elements in CMHERA's teaching, and in CMH's work too, has been the notion of 'images of possibility' (Wertheimer, 1986). In the 1970s a number of members or associates of CMH visited the USA and came back with accounts, materials and photographs of innovative developments there. These proved invaluable in stimulating thinking about new ways of serving handicapped people in Britain. Particularly influential was a service in the area of Nebraska around the city of Omaha — the Eastern Nebraska Community Office of Retardation (ENCOR). Planned jointly by professionals and parents in the late 1960s, this service sought to bring back to their home communities all those people who were housed in the state institution 150 miles away, as well as to provide a comprehensive community-based service with elements of housing, education, family support, medical care, work, etc. CMH published an account of ENCOR by three visitors from Britain (Thomas, Firth and Kendall, 1978) and Alan Tyne began a series of presentations, of which he gave over a hundred in the years between 1978 and 1983, using slides of the ENCOR service. We believe that the sheer power of seeing pictures of severely handicapped people living in ordinary houses stimulated 'images of possibility' in the minds of many service planners and providers and led to much greater acceptance of this idea amongst professionals, parents and politicians.

Such propagation of 'images of possibility' has also been important in CMHERA's normalization teaching, for which a set of 250 illustrative slides of British services was assembled and made available, and in CMH's promotion of integration, self-advocacy and other issues. It has also been important in the work of other people — for example, in supporting the King's Fund Centres series of 'Ordinary Life' papers (King's Fund Centre, 1982, 1984 and 1988). It is illustrated in particular by Ann Shearer's book 'Building Community' (Shearer, 1986), published jointly by CMH and the King's Fund. A recent video of successful integration of severely handicapped children and young people in education (called 'Regular Lives') is currently being marketed by CMH.

Summary

This brief overview of the work of the two sister organizations — CMH and CMHERA, the former now renamed 'VIA — Values Into Action' — illustrates the major influence that committed and values-led people can have with fairly minimal organization and certainly very few resources. The central office is still little more than a cupboard!

Particularly through greater collaboration with people with learning difficulties themselves, we hope to continue to pioneer work until all handicapped people have a better quality of life and experience the welcome and appreciation in society that should be theirs by right.

Notes

1   I confess failure in the search for acceptable terminology in referring to the people who are the subject of this paper and the work it describes. Most self-advocacy groups in Britain seem to prefer the term 'people with learning difficulties' and to dislike greatly both the terms 'mental' and 'handicap'. I personally think 'learning difficulties' puts too much emphasis on educational needs, which seem to me to be only part of the situation of the people concerned; it is also already a term used more specifically in the field of education. I also dislike the phrase 'people with . . . ' as it conveys that the person has some condition or disease. My lack of resolution of this issue is reflected in the use of several terms and phrases interchangably in this paper, primarily 'mentally handicapped people', 'people with mental handicaps' and 'people with learning difficulties'. The important thing to remember is that all people are first and foremost fellow human beings: 'people first' as the self-advocacy movement would say.

2   Regretfully, a lot of this was lost in the 1970s. Inefficient management of work flow and work processes in centres, some exploitation by firms of the labour involved, lack of proper payment for the handicapped people doing the work, failure to achieve progression of people to ordinary jobs in outside industry, and growing interest in the potential of much more broadly-based further education for people with mental

handicaps, all culminated in 'Pamphlet No. 5 — Day Services for Mentally Handicapped Adults' published by the National Development Group for People with Mental Handicap in 1977. Although this did not dismiss the role of work and work-oriented activities in centres, it did suggest a much wider curriculum with division of centres into sections, most of which would have an educational emphasis. Virtually overnight, a lot of work-based activities in centres stopped and Britain ceased to be a pioneer in this area. (For later developments see Bellamy, Horner and Inman, 1979; Porterfield and Gathercole, 1985; Shearer, 1986; McLoughlin, Bradley-Gardner and Callahan, 1987.)

References

BELLAMY, T., HORNER, R. and INMAN, D. (1979) *Vocational Habilitation of Severely Retarded Adults*, Baltimore, University Park Press.

BRECHIN, A. and SWAIN, J. (1988) 'Professional/client relationships: Creating a 'working alliance' with people with learning difficulties', *Disability, Handicap and Society*, 3, pp. 213–26.

CRAWLEY, B. (1988) *The Growing Voice — A Survey of Self-Advocacy Groups*, London, CMH.

CRAWLEY, B., MILLS, J., WERTHEIMER, A., WHITTAKER, A., WILLIAMS, P. and BILLIS, J. (1988) *Learning About Self-Advocacy*, London, CMH.

DEPARTMENT OF HEALTH AND SOCIAL SECURITY AND THE WELSH OFFICE (1971) *Better Services for the Mentally Handicapped*, Cmnd. 4683, London, HMSO.

DYBWAD, G. (1964) *Challenges in Mental Retardation*, New York, Columbia University Press.

GABBAY, J. (Ed.) (1983) 'Mental handicap and education', Special issue of *Oxford Review of Education*, 9, 3.

HUNT, N. (1967) *The World of Nigel Hunt*, Beaconsfield, Darwen Finlayson.

KELVES, D. (1985) *In the Name of Eugenics*, London, Penguin Books.

KING'S FUND CENTRE (1982) *An Ordinary Life: Comprehensive Locally-Based Residential Services for Mentally Handicapped People*, (2nd edition) London, King's Fund.

KING'S FUND CENTRE (1984) *An Ordinary Working Life: Vocational Services for People with Mental Handicap*, London, King's Fund.

KING'S FUND CENTRE (1988) *Ties and Connections: An Ordinary Community Life for People with Learning Difficulties*, London, King's Fund.

McLOUGHLIN, C., BRADLEY-GARNER, J. and CALLAHAN, M. (1987) *Getting Employed, Staying Employed: Job Development and Training for Persons with Severe Handicaps*, Baltimore, Paul Brookes.

MORRIS, P. (1969) *Put Away: A Sociological Study of Institutions for the Mentally Retarded*, London, Routledge and Kegan Paul.

NIRJE, B. (1969) 'The normalisation principle and its human management implications', in KUGEL, R. and WOLFENSBERGER, W. (Eds) *Changing Patterns in Residential Services for the Mentally Retarded*, Washington, DC, President's Committee on Mental Retardation.

NIRJE, B. (1972) 'The right to self-determination', in WOLFENSBERGER, W. (Ed.) *The Principle of Normalisation in Human Services*, Toronto, National Institute on Mental Retardation.

PORTERFIELD, J. and GATHERCOLE, C. (1985) *The Employment of People with Mental Handicap: Progress Towards an Ordinary Working Life*, London, King's Fund.

SHEARER, A. (1972) *Our Life: Conference Report*, London, CMH.

SHEARER, A. (1973) *Listen! Conference Report*, London, CMH.

SHEARER, A. (1986) *Building Community with People with Mental Handicaps, Their Families and Friends*, London, CMH and King's Fund.

THOMAS, D., FIRTH, H. and KENDALL, A. (1978) *ENCOR — A Way Ahead*, London, CMH.

TIZARD, J. (1964) *Community Services for the Mentally Handicapped*, Oxford, Oxford University Press.

TYNE, A. (1987a) 'Shaping community services — the impact of an idea', in MALIN, N. (Ed.) *Reassessing Community Care*, London, Croom Helm.

TYNE, A. (1987b) 'Some practical dilemmas and strategies in values-led approaches to change', in WARD, L. (Ed.) *Getting Better All the Time? Issues and Strategies for Ensuring Quality in Community Services for People with Mental Handicaps*, London, King's Fund.

TYNE, A. (1987c) *Home from Home: Thinking about Improving Home and Family Support Services for People with Mental Handicaps in Clwyd*, London, CMHERA.

TYNE, A. (1987d) *Report of the Evaluation of a Plan: Day Services for Adults in Central Manchester*, London, CMHERA.

TYNE, A. (1987e) *An Evaluation of an Adult Residential Service*, London, CMHERA.

TYNE, A. and WILLIAMS, P. (1975) *Working Out: Conference Report*, London, CMH.

TYNE, A. and WILLIAMS, P. (1987) *The Relocation of People from Calderstones into Ordinary Housing in Burnley District: Report of the PASS Evaluation*, London, CMHERA.

WERTHEIMER, A. (1986) *Images of Possibility: Rethinking Services for People with Mental Handicaps in the Light of American Experiences*, London, CMH.

WILLIAMS, P. (1967) 'Industrial training and remunerative employment of the profoundly retarded', *British Journal of Mental Subnormality*, 13, pp. 14–23.

WILLIAMS, P. (1973) *A Workshop on Participation*, London, CMH.

WILLIAMS, P. (1987a) 'Evaluating services from the consumer's point of view', in BESWICK, J., ZADIK, T. and FELCE, D. (Eds) *Evaluating Quality of Care*, Kidderminster, British Institute of Mental Handicap.

WILLIAMS, P. (1987b) 'Value-based training and service change', in *Our Lives, Your Jobs — Report of the 13th Annual Congress of the Association of Professions for Mentally Handicapped People*, Ross-on-Wye, APMH.

WILLIAMS, P. (1987c) *The Western Corner Project: Support for Families and Young People — A Report to The Children's Society*, London, CMHERA.

WILLIAMS, P. (1988a) *A Preliminary Examination of Some Questions that Could be Addressed by Analysis of Scores from PASS Evaluations*, London, CMHERA.

WILLIAMS, P. (1988b) *The Move from Barford House: An Account of a Residential Service Before and After a Move to Ordinary Housing*, London, CMHERA.

WILLIAMS, P. (1988c) *Report of the PASS Evaluation of the North Wilts Community Living Project*, London, CMHERA.

WILLIAMS, P. and GAUNTLETT, T. (1974) *Participation with Mentally Handicapped People*, London, CMH.

WILLIAMS, P. and RACE, D. (1988) *Normalisation and The Children's Society*, London, CMHERA.

WILLIAMS, P. and SHOULTZ, B. (1982) *We Can Speak For Ourselves: Self-Advocacy by Mentally Handicapped People*, London, Souvenir Press.

WILLIAMS, P. and TYNE, A. (1988) 'Exploring values as the basis for service development', in TOWELL, D. (Ed.) *An Ordinary Life in Practice*, London, King's Fund.

WOLFENSBERGER, W. (Ed.) (1972) *The Principle of Normalisation in Human Services*, Toronto, National Institute on Mental Retardation.

WOLFENSBERGER, W. (1975) *The Origin and Nature of Our Institutional Models*, Syracuse, New York, Human Policy Press.

WOLFENSBERGER, W. (1983) 'Social role valorisation: A proposed new term for the principle of normalisation', *Mental Retardation*, 21, pp. 234–9.

WOLFENSBERGER, W. and GLENN, L. (1975) *PASS — Programme Analysis of Service Systems* (3rd edition) Toronto, National Institute on Mental Retardation.

WOLFENSBERGER, W. and THOMAS, S. (1983) *PASSING — Programme Analysis of Service Systems' Implementation of Normalisation Goals*, Toronto, National Institute on Mental Retardation.

4
Integration: Is it a New Fad or Just a Remake of an Old Unsuccessful Plot?

Lyn Gow and Rosalia Chow

Introduction

The most significant and controversial debate concerning the education of students with special needs is related to integration. Integration is intended to provide disabled students with the same educational and social environments as their peers who are not disabled and thus allows a normalization of experience which is not attainable in the segregated system that has evolved with special education. It has resulted in a return to greater involvement of students with special needs in regular schools, and is impacting on both the special and regular school systems.

For teachers, the main issues relate to anxiety over their lack of training in the required techniques, irritation at having to assume additional responsibilities, often without adequate preparation and support, and concern over the academic progress of their students, with and without special needs. For administrators, major concerns may relate to expediency and financial matters, especially in a time of cutbacks in education budgets. All of those involved in integration acknowledge, however, that many children with special needs are not being given an opportunity to be effectively integrated into the regular school community. The need to overcome the barriers to integration has become more urgent following the formulation of policies of integration in most education systems throughout the world and the growing controversy surrounding their implementation.

What is rarely acknowledged in the debate of integration is that it is not a new phenomenon. Many of the contemporary concerns were discussed over a century-and-a-half ago when the first recorded experiment took place. This trial of integration failed. The debate, however, did not die but rather has continued in an ebb and tide flow since this first attempt, and has grown in momentum over the past twenty-five years.

The purpose of this chapter is to analyze these developments in order to pave the way for smooth progress towards integration. The path of integration is followed from the earliest attempts through to present day practices from the perspective of a model of educational reform. Brief reference is made to historical developments in the United Kingdom, the United States and Australia as a backdrop to current trends and a few significant studies and review papers are cited. Practical implications of the implementation of integration policies and future directions are viewed from the context of the resource issue and in light of the needs of individual students. The warnings of many against the ingredients of failure are noted: the recurrence of the resource issue and the flexibility required to meet individual needs are underscored. Most importantly, placement decisions must be made on the basis of the best interests of the individual student whose future rests on those decisions. The conclusion is that in satisfying the unique needs of the individual student it is essential to confront and seek to overcome the serious obstacles that stand in the way of educational integration (Mittler and Farrell, 1987)

The old plot

Most people with some knowledge of integration would claim that integration on a large scale is a relatively recent innovation. Nix (1981) (and doubtless many other special education historians), however, contend that watching the current emphasis and implementation of integration is comparable to viewing a cinematic remake of an old plot which unfortunately was unsuccessful. Nix has conducted extensive reviews of the history of special education and lamented that the remake of the old plot is in some respects a poorer version of the earlier drama. The account provided by Nix (1981) is so fascinating that it is worthy of extensive reference.

Nix claimed that Dr Johann Graeser made the first and most thorough and ambitious attempt to integrate disabled students into the regular educational environment in 1821 in Beyreuth, Germany. Dr Graeser placed a class of deaf students in an elementary school for boys where the deaf children associated with the non-handicapped children as much as possible but continued to receive special instruction from a teacher of the deaf. It was expected that the deaf students would enter the regular classes in the elementary school at the end of two years. Nix reported that Graeser and the proponents of integration met with little serious opposition and that the acceptance of integration spread rapidly. Gordon in 1885 recounted:

> it seemed plausible enough that parents, brothers, sisters, pastors and public school teachers might give deaf children a sufficient education through their combined efforts, provided special instruction, adapted to the needs of the deaf, could be given by the school-teacher. The instruction of the deaf was thus made a part of the public school system. Special inducements were held out to teachers to receive deaf pupils, and systematic and persistent efforts were made to qualify teachers for the work. (in Nix, 1981, p. 4)

Nix stated that teacher education was responsive to this shift in pedagogy and one year programmes for the special preparation of teachers to work with the deaf in integrated settings were initiated. To provide practical experiences for teachers, 'lab.' schools were established in conjunction with the teacher education centres in Saxony, Westphalia, Posen, Prussia and Pomerania.

As a reflection of the German Government support for this move, the Federal Government, through the Ministry at Berlin (14 May, 1828), issued an edict which provided a six-year Federal grant for the preparation of ordinary public school teachers to work at the schools for the deaf in Berlin, Koenigsberg and Munster. The province of Brandenberg elected to send public school teachers to Berlin for six weeks of in-service training rather than develop a full-year course of study.

Nix noted that, as might be expected, the professional literature of the time reflected the thrust towards integration with such works as Wilhelm Daniel's three volume work entitled: *The General Education of Deaf-Mutes and the Blind especially in Families and Public Schools*. Daniel's volumes, published in 1825, advocated service options which utilized placements including both special school and regular class settings, Daniel discussed the merits of placement in 'the least restrictive environment' appropriate to the child's needs and he clearly favoured educational placement in the public school setting. He realized, however, that not all families and/or communities were equipped to meet the needs of deaf children and recognized the utility of segregated residential placements for providing an appropriate education for some (Gordon, in Nix, 1981).

Unfortunately, the potential cost-saving effect of integrating hearing impaired students was soon recognized by the German Government. The interest then shifted from the educational to the economic advantage of integration. The provincial governments were 'financially hard pressed' after the Napoleonic Wars and the idea of integrating disabled children into regular public schools apeared to be a cost-effective strategy for the education of deaf children who were not served by the residential schools.

> The Ministry in Berlin had great confidence in the efficiency of the scheme, and said that, 'in the course of ten years it will be easily brought about that in all provinces of the Kingdom provision will be made for the education of all the unfortunate deaf and dumb'. (Gordon, in Nix, 1981, p. 6)

As a result of funding cutbacks, the necessary support services such as special teachers of the hearing impaired and trained regular teachers would no longer be provided. As a result, in spite of the wave of enthusiasm by educators, the Federal Government, the provincial governments and the teacher education centres, the effort to integrate children with hearing impairments failed. Saegert, the official Inspector of Deaf-Mute instruction reported in 1854, twenty-six years after the ministerial order.

> Of a classroom instruction of the deaf and hearing in the same classes no one speaks. (Gordon, in Nix, 1981, p. 8)

He reported that in Brandenburg, at that time, only sixty-eight deaf children were integrated out of a total of 301 elementary school-age deaf children. It was noted that sixty-three of the 301 children were not receiving any instruction at all (Gordon, in Nix, 1981, p. 1–3).

As a direct function of resource constraints, the promise of integration was not realized for the majority of these children. The experiment was running a smooth course until the government capitalized on what it perceived as the potential cost-saving effect of integration. When funds were reduced, the necessary support services were no longer available. The commitment of all concerned atrified and integration was rejected as unworkable. This was obviously an embarrassment for the German Government which may explain why this example of integration is not well known.

Analysis of this Integration Experiment from within a Model of Educational Reform

This historical account of integration can provide the beginning of a reference source for the future implementation of integration. Integration is an educational reform. It is useful, therefore, to examine this experiment from within the context of a model of educational reform. This kind of analysis can help pave the way for the effective implementation of integrated education. One such model has been provided recently by Guthrie (1988). Analyzing this first recorded integration experiment within Guthrie's model, some of the lessons to be learned are:

1 Government support for integration can lead to community support. If the community is not supportive of an educational reform, it is not likely to be implemented;

2 Whilst most educational reform is prompted by economic factors, it can fail from the same springboard. Financial resources are necessary to fund teacher training and support services, without which integration is doomed to failure. The more anxious people are about the economic future, the less likely educational reform will be on the agenda. Unfortunately, integration can be conveniently viewed by government as a cost-saving exercise;

3 Integration may not be effective for all children; segregated placement may be appropriate for some. The flowering of the individual should not be overlooked; the engine driving the machine can be insensitive to the needs of the individual. Care is needed so that we are not enacting policies to placate rather than to enhance educational outcomes for the individual student;

4 People must be made aware of the reform: the more democratically argued, the more likely the reform will occur in the spirit and letter of the reform.

The Debate Continues

Developments in integration have followed the waxing and waning pattern typical of educational philosophy and practice. The debate relating to the merits and demerits of integrated versus segregated settings was not heard again until the end of the last century when it was renewed, complete with advocates and debunkers. One of the advocates was Howe, who in 1886 warned against the possible 'damage' resulting from segregation (in Tay, 1986).

At the turn of the century, in most countries the debunkers grew in force with the introduction of compulsory education when many teachers could not cope with the demands of catering for individual differences with large class sizes (Temby, 1975). This waning period lasted until the 1950s when interest in integration grew. The peak was around the mid-1960s when the 'Principle of Normalization' was popularized (Bank-Mikkelsen, 1969). In the next section of the chapter, these trends in three parts of the world (United Kingdom, United States of America and Australia) are reviewed briefly. The account is by no means exhaustive: its main purpose is to provide a flavour of the developments rather than a total picture. Examination of these current integration trends reveals a hauntingly similar pattern to the earlier, unsuccessful experiment (Gow, Snow, Balla and Hall, 1987a).

UK Developments

In the UK, developments have been facilitated by reports and legislation supporting integrated education. For instance, in Scotland in 1955, the desirability of placing special education within the mainstream of primary and secondary education was recognized in the reports of the Advisory Council, entitled 'The Education of Handicapped Pupils' (in Warnock, 1978). These reports, whilst recognizing the continuing need for separate provision in special schools for some children, supported the integration of disabled students by saying:

> as medical knowledge increases and as general school conditions improve it should be possible for an increasing proportion of pupils who require special educational treatment to be educated along with their contemporaries in ordinary schools. Special educational treatment should indeed be regarded simply as a well defined arrangement within the ordinary educational system to provide for the handicapped child the individual attention that he particularly needs. (Scottish Education Department Circular 300, in Warnock, 1978, p. 25)

The Chronically Sick and Disabled Act (Scotland, 1970) promoted integration further by requiring local authorities to provide, as far as possible, education for deaf, blind, autistic and acutely dyslexic children in maintained and assisted schools. Although this included special schools, the intention was that provision would be made in ordinary schools where possible. The Education of Handicapped Children Act (Scotland, 1970) and the Education of Mentally Handicapped

Children Act (Scotland, 1974), required that all children, however serious their disability, should be educated. The 1976 Education Act (Scotland) shifted the emphasis more firmly towards greater integration and improved provision in the ordinary schools.

Warnock (1978), following an extensive survey of service delivery for people with disabilities in Europe, strongly supported the move towards integration. The Warnock Report suggested that special education provision should no longer be decided in respect of categories of disability, but rather should be organized in relation to a classification system based on the special needs of the individual. This definition of special needs placed the services required within the normal schools in many cases and in so doing recognized those services as additional or supplementary to regular education to enable the teacher to meet the needs of the individual child. In this way, special education would not be separate or alternate but would become integrated into the normal school system (see Chatwin, 1983).

As a result of the Warnock Report (1978), the 1981 Education Act was passed which served to maintain the interest in integration. However, throughout the UK financial constraints have sparked and sustained the resource debate.

There have been a few significant case studies and review papers in the UK on this subject. For instance, 'The Centre for Studies on Integration in Education' conducted a government sponsored three-year study of seventeen integration schemes in fourteen local education authorities. The researchers, Hegarty, Pocklington and Lucas published the studies in two volumes: *Educating pupils with special needs in the ordinary school* (1981) and *Integration in action: Case studies in the integration of pupils with special needs* (1982). During a conference conducted by the UK Spastics Society in 1982, called 'Working Towards Integration', Hegarty and his colleagues presented their conclusions. Their major finding was that much more successful integration should be taking place in regular schools than had been the case. They also reported that:

1 integration is of benefit to the whole school because it enhances educational provisions for all students, particularly in the areas of social and emotional development;
2 students with special needs prefer to stay in regular schools rather than return to segregated settings;
3 from integration, students with special needs can develop self-confidence and independence;
4 students and teachers in regular schools typically develop a realistic approach to the disabling condition of individual children when they are integrated; and
5 once integration has taken place, parents of non-disabled children change from having anxieties about their children interacting with others with disabilities to being the staunchest advocates of the change.

In a more recent paper on integration in the UK, Mittler and Farrell (1987) provided a model for effective integration of more severely disabled children. Again, they called attention to the necessity of providing further resources in order to bring about successful integration. Moreover, they cautioned that the unique needs of the individual child should not be sacrificed on the altar of ideology. Mittler (1987) underscored this need and argued that the major challenge of Special Education today is one of meeting both the ordinary needs of all children as well as any special needs resulting from an individual disability.

US Developments

In the US, a National Department of Education was established in 1896 and a Department of Special Education in 1897. This reflected an awareness of the need to cater for individual differences in education. By 1918, compulsory education was effective in all states. The Children's Bureau was set up in 1912 and special classes and programmes for students with disabilities became established. Professional organizations such as the Council for Exceptional Children were founded in the 1920s and training programmes for special educators were introduced in colleges and universities. In the period to 1950, the foundations were laid for the expansion of the field of Special Education which occurred in the 1960s and 1970s. In the aftermath of the Second World War and with the impetus stemming from Russian advances in science and technology (particularly the launching of Sputnik), special education focused on the gifted. The social programmes of the Kennedy era also had great effects on special education with the result that Federal laws were passed providing training and other services, and funds were provided for research projects on a range of issues associated with integration.

From the turn of the century there was long debate about the merits and demerits of integration, but little action. The overwhelming forces of inertia took over until the 1968 seminal article of Dunn which brought the integration debate into sharp focus. In this frequently cited article, the case against segregated schooling for students with disabilities was eloquently argued. This article sparked off a plethora of studies of integration and a great deal of debate, which provided support for a resurgence of interest in integration (e.g., Kaufman, Gottlieb, Agard and Kukic, 1975; Kauffman and Hallahan, 1981). The debate focused on the following issues.

1   every human has the right to lead a normal life in the community;
2   every child can learn and should be educated;
3   integration is a reflection of the democratic philosophy that equal access to education is the right of all individuals, however different from the majority they may be;
4   through interaction with their non-disabled peers, disabled children can develop social/emotional skills and the skills for living in the community;
5   every child is entitled to a wide range of options so that he or she can make meaningful choices regarding future career and functioning in the community;
6   segregation is often based on questionable diagnostic procedures;

7 these diagnostic procedures have resulted in the assigning of labels with associated stigma often causing irreparable damage;
8 segregation is not economically viable when transport costs, etc. are considered.

Dunn (1968) outlined the following principles for facilitating integration:

1 children with special needs should not be categorized or grouped according to a descriptive label;
2 improvements must be made in the regular class in which the child is mainstreamed, including:
   i. organizational changes such as team teaching and flexible groupings within the school;
   ii. development of resource materials in conjunction with in-service training to demonstrate effective use of new materials; and
   iii. provision of more support staff such as guidance officers, psychologists, remedial teachers, itinerant teachers, physical education teachers, technicians, aides, volunteers, etc.;
3 there must be collaboration of educators with others closely involved with the child such as parents and personnel from other agencies; and
4 the education system must consider personality and attitude development, social interaction training and vocational training.

A great deal of pressure was put to bear on the US Government by parent groups which resulted in 1975 in the passing of PL 94–142, 'The Education of all Handicapped Children Act'. This law was the driving force behind integration in the US and influenced development in other countries as well. It called for individualized education programmes in the least restrictive environment and provided the stimulus for integration of children with disabilities into the normal educational settings. Grants were made to the states to provide the means for initiation of new programmes and expansion/upgrading of existing programmes for the education of disabled children. It was intended that the new provisions would establish educational services which would be the 'right' of students thus avoiding the stigma of social concessions to these students.

In 1977, the 94th Congress of the US began implementing this Law and since this time, there has been constant debate as to whether it has brought about real change or only an illusion of change. In 1985, a report to the US Congress (US Department of Education, 1985) showed that nationally, a staggering 68 per cent of all the children identified as 'disabled' during 1982–83 attended classes with their non-disabled peers at least part of the time.

Evaluation of the effects of integration is provided by a recent review conducted by Gartner and Lipsky (1987) which examined the first ten years of implementation of PL 94–142. They concluded that:

While there was considerable concern about the feasibility of implementating of PL 94:142, and some difficulty in doing so at the compliance level, by and large it has been accomplished. (p. 371)

Gartner and Lipsky (1987) reported that over 650,000 more students are being served now than when the law was enacted and that generally educators believe that few, if any, students needing services have not been identified. They also found that there has been a substantial increase in the funds devoted to special education, from $100 million in 1976 to $1.64 billion in 1985. They noted an improvement in the quality and accessibility of education for students with disabilities, and that there is now wide acceptance of the view that all children must and can be educated. To achieve these developments, state laws have been passed to support the Federal Law and there has been a national resolve that schools will be restructured. The major area of deficiency noted by Gartner and Lipsky (1987) is in programme effectiveness, although some improvement was detected. In addition, administrative requirements have been found to be cumbersome and onerous as teachers are reported to feel overwhelmed.

There are further criticisms of the implementation of PL 94–142 from Wang (1987). Wang reported that many students continue to be segregated in disjointed programmes, and in support of Hobbs and many others (e.g., Hobbs, 1980; Morsink, Thomas and Smith-Davis, 1988), she argued that an inconsistent and scientifically questionable system for classifying and placing students in special education programmes was still in use. According to Wang, as well as to many of her contemporaries (e.g., Heller, Holzman and Messick, 1982, see review in Wang, Reynolds and Walberg, 1988), the full promise and the intent of the dual mandate, an appropriate education (state of the art) in the least restrictive environment (integration), of PL 94–142 is yet to be achieved.

Wang (1987) commented on the barriers to integration caused by the proliferation of the resource model of delivery of services to students with disabilities because it has promoted the acceptability of part-time integration. The resource model entails providing special education outside the regular programme on a part-time basis, while allowing special education students (typically those classified as mildly intellectually disabled, learning disabled, mildly behaviour disordered) to be integrated in the mainstream for part of their school day (Gow, 1982; Gow and Lyon, 1982a). Wang argued that this part-time 'pull-out' approach to providing special education services has been the predominant practice for meeting the integration mandate of PL 94–142. As a result, many variants of this model have evolved. Wang (1987) maintained that these resource models have formulated the basis for, as well as the barrier to, the full delivery of the integration mandate of PL 94–142. One of the major effects has been on funding so that, in practice, schools receive more rather than less funding for placing students in more restrictive placements. Wang (1987) summarized:

> Thus, while the rhetoric in programming may embrace the goal of 94–142, separateness prevails in the reality of current practice. (p. 11)

Singer and Butler (1987) reported the findings of a study of implementation of PL 94–142 in five diverse school districts across the US conducted during the fifth and the eighth years of the Act's existence. While they found both significant transformation of attitudes towards integration and social reforms, they also detected inequities whose roots in the social fabric make them difficult for the schools alone to overcome. They stated:

> ...outcomes that have been measureable suggest that some children have been winners and others losers in the actual degree of entitlement the law confers. (p. 126)

They acknowledged methodological problems in their reviews, caused by individualized learning goals which made it intrinsically difficult to evaluate the impact of integration on individual students, and they also recognized the biases they brought to the review process. Nevertheless, they concluded that PL 94–142:

> ...remains one of the most far-reaching pieces of social legislation ever to benefit children. Since its enactment, it has successfully weathered a decade characterised by declining tax revenues, increasing school costs, and escalating doubts about the value and quality of public education. (p. 152)

Several reviews of integration in the US have been carried out to investigate the effects of integration on the children served (e.g., Armfield, 1985; Guralnick, 1986; Madden and Slavin, 1983; Wang, Reynolds and Walberg, 1988). Madden and Slavin (1983) reviewed 154 individual reports relating to integration of mildly disabled students and concluded that, for these children, the best placement was in the regular class, either with individualized instruction or supplemented with well-designed resource support. They stressed, however, that if such support was not provided, the gains may be no more significant than if the student were placed in a full-time special education setting. They also added that, while regular classes may be more effective for mildly disabled students, special classes may be more effective for moderately to severely mentally handicapped students.

Several other major reviews by study groups and commissions in the US (cf. Heller *et al.*, 1982; Mayor's Commission on Special Education, New York City, 1985; US Department of Education, 1986; Wang *et al.*, 1988) have noted the existence of quality integration programmes. These reviews identified the trend towards more inclusiveness of all marginal groups (e.g., disabled, migrant, bilingual) in regular classes. The major findings of all these reviews is that what actually happens in the classroom is more important than the environment itself (i.e., regular educational setting, resource room or special educational setting) (Biklen, 1985). Successful integration is related to small class sizes, regular monitoring, rapid pacing, formal class environment and positive child self-concept. The consensus of these reviews is that what is needed to advance integration is restructuring of schools and modification of instructional design.

In summary, US reviews of integration have demonstrated that the legal mandate and financial support provided by the Education for All Handicapped Children Act (PL 94–142) have greatly aided the growth of effective practice and innovative programmes for students with all types of disabilities (Polloway, 1984). Once again, this demonstrates the importance of government support, both legal and financial, in promoting integration. The reviews further show that the individual's needs have to be considered in planning for integration.

The impact of PL 94–142 has not only been felt in the US, other countries have watched the North American developments with some interest and used these developments to lobby governments to support integration. One of these countries has been Australia.

Australian Developments

Apart from developments in the US, there have been many other influences on the Australian education system to effect the steady movement towards integration. Among these influences are: pressure groups, consisting of parents and organizations representing people with special needs; Scandinavian efforts to implement the principle of normalization over the past two decades (Nirje, 1985; Perrin and Nirje, 1985); the Warnock Report (1978) and the British 1981 Education Act which was one of the results of the Warnock Report; Equal Employment Opportunity and the International Year of Disabled Persons; and the investment of Labour governments which have given a voice to parental concerns (Ashby and Taylor, 1984). It is not possible to rank these influences in terms of their relative effect, but their timing has been significant, serving to maintain the propulsion towards integration.

In Australia, there is no specific legislation relating to integration comparable to the US PL 94–142 or the 1981 Education Act in the UK (Ashby, Taylor and Robinson, 1987; Gow, Snow and Ward, 1987b). State Education Acts have developed idiosyncratically and in isolated cases (such as Queensland) have been used to support a policy of integration but overall there is only general legislation relating to special education. For instance, the Disabled Persons Accommodation Act was introduced in 1963, and the Sheltered Employment Assistance Act, in 1967. These Acts dealt with specific areas of concern but did not encompass education *per se*. The Handicapped Children's Assistance Act of 1970 and the Handicapped Persons' Assistance Act, 1974, were more comprehensive. However, whilst recognizing the needs of the disabled person, there was still no overall policy concerning the best way to meet those needs.

Historically, in Australia, as indeed in many other parts of the world, the debate concerning the relative efficacy of segregated versus integrated placement of children with special needs commenced at the end of the nineteenth century when schooling became compulsory (Temby, 1975). Children with low incidence disabilities were integrated, but segregation became the predominant mode of delivery of services until the 1970s, particularly for children with intellectual disabilities and behavioural disorders (Drummond, 1978). With segregation being perceived by society as the accepted mode of delivery of service for disabled people, secondary and primary divisions of education could not be convinced that integration was either worthwhile or feasible. As a result, there was little movement of children with special needs in the regular education system until the early 1970s (Gow *et al.*, 1987a). At this time, with the weight of evidence regarding the feasibility and desirability of integration coming from overseas to support them, parents formed lobby groups and demanded that their children be integrated. The range of services began to widen and a growing movement towards integration was witnessed (Elkins, 1981 and 1985).

To this stage, reservations continue to exist in the minds of teachers, administrators and parents who support the philosophical base of integration but question the ease with which it can be implemented without essential backup resources (Gow, Balla, Konza, Hall and Snow, 1986; Pickering and Gow, 1987). Integrated education necessitates the provision of support services for the regular class teacher (Doherty, 1987; Gow and Lyon, 1982b), and this raises the problems of funding levels (Gow, 1987; Gow and Ward, 1988). In addition, teachers in regular schools often question their capacity to cope with the different demands imposed by the inclusion of disabled children in their classrooms (Gow, 1986a and b). In spite of this constant cry for resources, Australia has for many years been committed to the education of children with special needs with their non-disabled peers in regular classrooms, as long as there is some evidence that they can benefit from the experience (Gow *et al.*, 1987a). This has applied in particular with children with a learning disability, or hearing or visual impairment. However, it is children with an intellectual disability, and children with behaviour problems who have been the most difficult to integrate (Gow *et al.*, 1986). The reasons for this are unclear, although one answer may be that for these children who traditionally have been more difficult to integrate, integration represents a radical departure from the trend prior to the seventies in the eyes of teachers and parents alike.

As noted in a survey of Special Education in Australia (Andrews, Elkins, Berry and Burge, 1979), and later confirmed in the review of integration in Australia conducted by Gow *et al.* (1987a) as well as the evaluation of integration in the Catholic school system of Victoria (Pickering, Szaday and Duerdoth, 1988), successful integration of a student with disabilities in Australia depends on a range of factors, some of which are:

1 a positive attitude by both parents and school staff;
2 an appreciation by the school staff of the student's educational and personal needs;
3 the adoption of clear educational goals for the student by teachers and support staff;
4 the organization of the school;
5 the capacity of teachers to cope with new demands on their time and attention;
6 the effects of periodic absence of the student resulting from the requirements for medical attention; and
7 the vulnerability to stress of some students as a result of the social and academic demands of the regular school.

Summary

In the three countries examined, there is widespread acceptance of the desirability of providing of education in an integrated setting, but problems of logistics of implementation are evident. In fact, it can be said with some certainty that the contemporary integration debate no longer focuses on whether or not the ideology of integration is acceptable, for it has been powerfully argued and substantiated by reference to UN Declarations and related laws and reports, and won in most parts of the Western world on philosophical, ethical, moral, social, educational, psychological and economic grounds (Butterfield and Gow, 1987). The area of current contention has more to do with the implementation of integration and relates to determining the most appropriate, beneficial and efficient means of providing integrated education for students with special needs. The main questions of concern are: 'Which students with special needs can be integrated appropriately?', and 'What particular educational provision is required for integration to be successful?'. Unfortunately, with some notable exceptions (e.g., Mittler and Farrell, 1987; Wang *et al.*, 1988), these implementation issues and questions of concern have received insufficient attention from researchers, bureaucrats and practitioners (Jenkinson, 1983 and 1987; Jenkinson and Gow, in press).

Integration has been and will continue to be influenced to a large extent by political and social factors (Gow *et al.*, 1987b). As has been demonstrated in the case of the three countries discussed, government support, in the form of legislation, policy and funding, is often needed to promote integrated education. The central issue is that if resources are not made available, all efforts will fail (Konza, Gow, Hall and Balla, 1987). This has been shown in recent data (e.g., Center and Ward, 1987; Hall and Gow, 1986) indicating the importance of resource availability if positive attitudes regarding integration are to be developed. Therefore, parents and the voluntary organizations formed by them and by other caring members of the community have to persevere with their pressure tactics designed to persuade governments that the responsibility for the provision of education for disabled children is theirs, and that such education should be provided in settings most conducive to social and educational equity.

Furthermore, a policy of integration has to take into consideration the needs of the students concerned (Gow, 1988). The main criterion for a decision on the desirability of an integrated placement for an individual student is that it is clearly beneficial (Hall, Gow and Konza, 1987). Research findings to date have been interpreted in a way that suggests that although regular classes may be more effective for mildly disabled students, more severely disabled students may be catered for best in self-contained special classes. It can, however, be claimed from this review of literature that there is sufficient evidence that some children, presently segregated, can be effectively integrated if resources appropriate to their needs are made available (Gow and Heath, 1988; Thompson, 1983). A further strong recommendation is that support services should be made available for all children in the regular system experiencing difficulties, not just those children transferring from special to regular settings (Gow and Fulcher, 1986). It is this resource issue which has left many questions unanswered (e.g., Thorley and Mills, 1986); the major one relating to the amount and form of resources necessary for maintaining individuals in the regular school situation. However, the point made many times over in the literature is that this question needs to be considered on an individual basis (Gow *et al*,. 1986).

There is little support for the wholesale transfer of all children with disabilities from the special to the regular school, but rather, consistent with PL 94-142, placement within an environment which is considered to be least restrictive for the individual child is preferred. The most important consideration is for the child to be 'accepted'. If within an 'integrated' environment, disabled students are not 'accepted', then they are as isolated as if they were segregated in a separate system. Integration is not merely placement in regular schools, nor is segregation placement in special schools. Integration and segregation are not mutually exclusive because there can be elements of both in any school situation. A child placed in an integrated unit within a regular school can experience isolation or segregation, depending on the process of instruction and active encouragement of social interaction. Unfortunately, however, the movement towards integration has focused on *location* or placement issues. As a result, integration is generally seen as a matter of where a student is enrolled, rather than how or what she or he is learning. What is needed is attention to more qualitative factors such as improved teaching methods and curriculum modifications (Conway and Gow, 1988; Gow and Heath, 1988; Larrivee, 1981; Larrivee and Cook, 1979; OECD, 1988).

In conclusion, it seems clear that the ideology of integration is generally accepted, but the practicalities of implementation have not been thoroughly investigated by researchers, administrators or the teaching profession. Research regarding the effective implementation of integration is in its infancy; a great deal of investigation of implementation of integration programmes is needed (Thompson, Ward and Gow, 1988). Analyses of ongoing programmes, their outcomes and the associated problems are imperative in order to provide guidelines for the future direction of integrated education. In the meantime, many changes must occur, in community attitudes and the teaching profession, as well as in the provision of resources and at the administrative level. While changes are occurring, and attitudes are constantly being modified, unless we can unite and overcome the barriers to effective integration, the impetus for integration will falter and the new plot will end up a simple remake of the original, but unsuccessful, experiment.

Author's Note

The review of integration in Australia reported in this chapter was supported by funds provided by the Australian Commonwealth Schools Commission. The contributions of John Balla, Leonie Miller, Judy Hall and Dianne Snow to this review are gratefully acknowledged. We are also indebted to Jane Cook for her contributions to sections on the history of special education.

References

ANDREWS, R. J., ELKINS, J., BERRY, P. B. and BURGE, J. A. (1979) *A survey of Special Education in Australia. Provisions, needs and priorities in the education of children with handicaps and learning difficulties*, Brisbane, Fred and Eleanor Schonell Research Centre, Department of Education, University of Queensland.

ARMFIELD, A. (1985) 'Special education in the United States', in CRAFT, M., BICKNELL, J. and HOLLINS, S. (Eds) *Mental handicap: A Multidisciplinary Approach*, London, Bailliere Tindall.

ASHBY, G. and TAYLOR, J. (1984) *Responses to Policies, Review of Commonwealth Schools Commission Special Education Program*, Canberra, Commonwealth Schools Commission.

ASHBY, G., TAYLOR, J. and ROBINSON, M. (1987) *Special Education Services Study: Interim Report*, Canberra, Commonwealth Department of Employment, Education and Training.

BANK-MIKKELSEN, N. E. (1969) *Normalisation: Letting the Mentally Retarded Obtain an Existence as Close to the Normal as Possible*, Washington, DC, President's Committee on Mental Retardation.

BIKLEN, D. (1985) *Achieving the Complete School: Strategies for Effective Mainstreaming*, New York, Teachers College Press.

BUTTERFIELD, E. C. and GOW, L. (1987) 'Civil rights and social science answers to the question of how evil are normalisation, deinstitutionalisation and mainstreaming?' in BARTNIK, E. A., LEWIS, G. M. and O'CONNOR, P. A. (Eds) *Technology, Resources and Consumer Outcomes for People with Intellectual Disabilities*, (pp. 141–54) Perth, P.E. Publications.

CENTER, Y. and WARD, J. (1987) 'Teachers' attitudes towards the integration of disabled children into regular classes', *Exceptional Child*, 34, 1, pp. 1–16.

CHATWIN, D. (1983) 'The Warnock Report: Recommendations and reactions', *Australian Journal of Remedial Education*, 15, 1, pp. 13–17.

CONWAY, R. and GOW, L. (1988) 'Mainstreaming special class mildly handicapped students through group instruction', *Remedial and Special Education*, 9, 5, pp. 34–41.

DOHERTY, P. J. (1987) *Integration: A New South Wales Perspective*, Sydney, N.S.W. Department of Education.

DRUMMOND, N. W. (1978) *Special Education in Australia*, Sydney, Torron Press.

DUNN, L. M. (1968) 'Special education for the mildly retarded: Is much of it justifiable?' *Exceptional Children*, 35, pp. 5–22.

ELKINS, J. (1981) 'The changing nature of special education provision', in CONRAD, L. M. and ANDREWS, R. J. (Eds) *Special Education Facilities in Australia*, Brisbane, Schonell Education Research Centre.

ELKINS, J. (1985) 'Disability and disadvantage: Special education in Australia: Past, present and future', *Melbourne Studies in Education*, pp. 163–84.

GARTNER, A. and LIPSKY, D. (1987) 'Beyond special education: Toward a quality system for all students', *Harvard Educational Review*, 57, 4, pp. 367–95.

GOW, L. (1982) 'Organisation and implementation of a service system for pupils with learning difficulties within a school', *A.S.E.T.*, 15, pp. 11–18.

GOW, L. (1986a) 'Overview of a report prepared for the Commonwealth Schools Commission on Integration in Australia', *Bulletin of the N.S.W. Institute for Educational Research*, April, pp. 23–38.

GOW, L. (1986b) Policies and practices on integration in Australia. Paper presented at *OECD Dissemination Conference*, Coolangatta, May.

Gow, L. (1987) Integration or maindumping? *Proceedings of the 12th Asian Conference on Mental Retardation*, Singapore, November.

Gow, L. (1988) 'Integration in Australia', *The European Journal of Special Education*, 3, 1, pp. 1–2.

Gow, L., Balla, J., Konza, D., Hall, J. and Snow, D. (1986) 'Towards effective integration in Australia', *Australasian Journal of Special Education, Gold Edition*, 10, 2, pp. 14–21.

Gow, L. and Fulcher, G. (1986) *Towards a Policy Direction on Integration: A Discussion Paper*, University of Woollongong, Unit for Special Education.

Gow, L. and Heath, S. (1988) 'Teaching techniques for facilitating integration', *The Special Education Journal*, 1, pp. 16–19.

Gow, L. and Lyon, J. (1982a) *Survey of the Resource/Remedial Model in Schools in N.S.W. and Canberra. Volumes I and II*. Canberra, ERDC Monograph.

Gow, L. and Lyon, J. (1982b) 'Training needs of resource/remedial teachers in N.S.W. schools', *A.S.E.T.*, 15, pp. 36–41.

Gow, L., Snow, D., Balla, J. and Hall, J. (1987a) *Report to the Commonwealth Schools Commission on Integration in Australia*, (5 Vols) Canberra, Commonwealth Schools Commission.

Gow, L., Snow, D. and Ward, J. (1987b) 'Contextual influences on integration in Australia: Overview of a report to the Commonwealth Schools Commission: Part 1', *The Exceptional Child*, 34, 3, pp. 1–14.

Gow, L. and Ward, J. (1988) 'Integration in Australia', *The Australian Journal of Remedial Education*, 20, 2, pp. 20–3.

Gow, L., Ward, J., Balla, J. and Snow, D. (1988) 'Directions for integration in Australia: Overview of a report to the CSC: Part II', *The Exceptional Child*, 35, 1, pp. 5–22.

Guralnick, M. (1986) 'The peer relationships of young handicapped and non-handicapped children', in Strain, P. S., Guralnick, M. J. and Hill, M. W. (Eds) *Children's Social Behaviour: Development, Assessment and Modification*, New York, Academic Press.

Guthrie, J. W. (1988) The international dynamics of educational reform. Paper presented at a public lecture organized by *the Hong Kong Educational Research Association*, University of Hong Kong, 17 October, 1988.

Hall, J. and Gow, L. (1986) 'A study of attitudes of regular teachers to the role of the special education resource teacher', *The N.S.W. Journal of Special Education*, 6, pp. 17–26.

Hall, J., Gow, L. and Konza, D. (1987) 'Are we integrating or maindumping students with special needs?' *The N.S.W. Journal of Special Education*, 7, pp. 4–12.

Hegarty, S. and Pocklington, K. (1982) *Integration in Action: Case Studies in the Integration of Pupils with Special Needs*, Windsor, NFER/Nelson.

Hegarty, S., Pocklington, K. and Lucas, D. (1981) *Educating Pupils with Special Needs in Ordinary Schools*, Windsor, NFER/Nelson.

Heller, K., Holzman, W. and Messick, S. (Eds) (1982) *Placing Children in Special Education: A Strategy for Equity*, Washington DC, National Academy of Sciences Press.

Hobbs, N. (1980) 'An ecologically oriented service-based system for the classification of handicapped children', in Salzinger, E., Antrobus, J. and Glick, J. (Eds) *The Ecosystem of the 'Risk' child*, New York, Academic Press.

Jenkinson, J. C. (1983) *The Integration Issue in Special Education: A Review of the Literature*, Faculty of Special Education and Paramedical Studies, Victoria College, Melbourne.

JENKINSON, J. C. (1987) 'School and disability: Research and practice in integration', *Australian Education Review,* 26, Melbourne, ACER.

JENKINSON, J. C. and GOW, L. (in press) 'Integration in Australia: A research perspective', *Australian Journal of Education*.

KAUFMAN, M. J., GOTTLIEB, J., AGARD, J. A. and KUKIC, M. B. (1975) 'Mainstreaming: Toward an explication of the construct', *Focus on Exceptional Children*, 7, 3, pp. 14–25.

KAUFFMAN, J. and HALLAHAN, D. (Eds) (1981) *Handbook of Special Education*, Englewood Cliffs, Prentice Hall.

KONZA, D., GOW, L., HALL, J. and BALLA, J. (1987) 'A functional support network for integration: Why and how?' *The Australian Journal of Remedial Education*, 19, 3, pp. 15–21.

LARRIVEE, B. (1981) 'Effect of inservice training intensity on teachers' attitudes toward mainstreaming', *Exceptional Children*, 48, 1, pp. 34–9.

LARRIVEE, B. and COOK, L. (1979) 'Mainstreaming: A study of the variables affecting teacher attitude', *Journal of Special Education*, 13, 3, pp. 315–24.

MADDEN, N. A. and SLAVIN, R. E. (1983) 'Mainstreaming students with mild handicaps: Academic and social outcomes', *Review of Educational Research*, 53, 4, pp. 519–69.

MAYOR'S COMMISSION ON SPECIAL EDUCATION (1985) *Special Education: A Call for Quality*, New York: Author.

MITTLER, P. (1987) Towards integrated education. Paper presented in a plenary session at the *Conference of Asian Federation for Persons with Mental Handicap*, Singapore, 16 November.

MITTLER, P. and FARRELL, P. (1987) 'Can children with severe learning difficulties be educated in ordinary schools?' *European Journal of Special Needs Education*, 2, 4, pp. 221–36.

MORSINK, C. V., THOMAS, C. C. and SMITH-DAVIS, J. (1988) 'Noncategorical special education programs: Process and outcomes', in WANG, M. C., REYNOLDS, M. C. and WALBERG, H. J. (Eds) *Handbook of Special Education: Research and Practice*, Oxford, England, Pergamon.

NIRJE, B. (1985) 'The basis and logic of the Normalization Principle', *Australian and New Zealand Journal of Developmental Disabilities*, 11, 2, pp. 65–8.

NIX, G. W. (1981) Mainstreaming: A bend in the river. Paper Presented at the *Association of Canadian Educators of the Hearing Impaired National Convention*, Vancouver, British Columbia, August.

OECD (1988) *Report of the working party on the condition of teaching: Integration of the handicapped in schools and its implication for teachers: lessons from research.*

PERRIN, B. and NIRJE, B. (1985) 'Setting the record straight: A critique of some frequent misconceptions of the Normalization Principle', *Australian and New Zealand Journal of Developmental Disabilities*, II, 2, pp. 69–74.

PICKERING, D., SZADAY, C. and DUERDOTH, P. (1988) *One in Eleven: Special Educational Needs of Catholic Schools in Victoria*, Melbourne, Victoria College.

PICKERING, D. and GOW, L. (1987) 'Together we can make it work', *Interaction*, 1, 3, pp. 31–4.

POLLOWAY, E. A. (1984) 'The integration of mildly retarded students in the schools: A historical review', *RASE*, 5, 4, pp. 18–28.

PUBLIC LAW 94: 142 (1975) *Education for All Handicapped Children Act*, 94th Congress of the United States of America.

SINGER, J. D. and BUTLER, J. A. (1987) 'The education for all handicapped children act: Schools as agents of social reform', *Harvard Educational Review*, 57, 2, pp. 125–52.

TAY, A. (1986) *Human Rights for Australia*, Human Rights Commission Monograph Series No 1, A.G.P.S., Canberra.

TEMBY, E. (1975) 'Integration', *ASET*, 3, pp. 37–8.

THOMPSON, D. (1983) 'Inservice training materials for teachers of students with special needs', *The Pointer*, 28, 1, pp. 41–4.

THOMPSON, G., WARD, J. and GOW, L. (1988) 'The education of children with special needs: A cross-cultural perspective', *European Journal of Special Needs Education*, 3, 3, pp. 125–37.

THORLEY, B. and MILLS, L. (1986) 'Special education: A problem of costs and benefits', *N.S.W. Journal of Special Education*, 6, pp. 5–10.

US DEPARTMENT OF EDUCATION (1985) *Seventh Annual Report to Congress on the Implementation of Public Law 94:142: The Education for All Handicapped Act*, Washington DC, Author.

US DEPARTMENT OF EDUCATION (1986) *What Works: Research about Teaching and Learning*, Washington, DC, Author.

WANG, M. C. (1987) Implementing the integration mandate of the Education for all Handicapped Children Act of 1975. Paper prepared for the *Bush Colloquium on Policy Implementation*, the University of North Carolina at Chapel Hill, 14 April.

WANG, M. C., REYNOLDS, M. C. and WALBERG, H. J. (Eds) (1988) *Handbook of Special Education: Research and Practice*, Oxford, England, Pergamon.

WARNOCK, M. (Chair) (1978) *Special Educational Needs. Report of the Committee of Enquiry into the Education of Handicapped Children and Young People*, London, HMSO.

5
Teacher Assumptions and Beliefs about Exceptionality

Anne J. Jordan and Harry Silverman

Introduction

In special education, one is frequently reminded of the extremes of opinions and beliefs of various professionals regarding the solution to children's learning difficulties. The language of special education has evolved from a medical or restorative base, while other disciplines within education have been influenced by child development, sociology and traditions in the behavioural sciences. In some respects, differing viewpoints based on historical antecedents have contributed to making special education programmes and services perhaps the most controversial area in education.

The purpose of the study reported here was to explore the assumptions and beliefs of educators about exceptional children, and about the programmes and services which are appropriate for them. The beliefs of principals and teachers were inferred from their responses to interviews. They were interviewed about their understanding of their roles and responsibilities in delivering special education programmes and services in their school, and about their actions in working with exceptional or potentially exceptional pupils.

This chapter will describe the variety in the belief systems and in the interpretation of school-board level and school-level policy for delivering special education in Canadian schools. We found that teachers and principals hold coherent and consistent belief systems which permeate all aspects of the delivery process; from the identification of a pupil as exceptional and the annual review of the pupil to their beliefs about their own ability to deal with the pupil. Their views about their involvement with other staff, school-board level resource people and parents are also generally predictable within a given belief framework. We will characterize the belief systems of individual educators as locatable on a single dimension. At the opposite ends of this dimension are the 'restorative' and 'preventive' belief frameworks. The restorative framework has the characteristics of a traditional, medical approach to special education. The medical approach is criticized by Hobbs (1980), Ysseldyke and Thurlow (1984) and Gartner and Lipsky (1987) as describing children's needs in the context of mental and physical disabilities and within the framework of medical management. This approach is heavily dependent on identifying the category of exceptionality and on dispatching pupils for specialized interventions, usually in a segregated or withdrawal setting. The purpose of assessment is to confirm the categorical designation at the outset of a child's admission to a special placement and thereafter annually. For this purpose, norm-based, and in particular, psychological tests of ability are central to the assessment process (Ysseldyke and Thurlow 1984).

The preventive framework, at the opposite extreme, places a part of the onus for learning problems on the teaching staff. Special education programmes are seen as not differing from regular education curriculum, except that modifications and adjustments to their manner and rate of delivery are frequently required. Children's learning problems may stem from a variety of sources, some of which are environmental. Problems may be short-term or temporary, provided that they are appropriately handled. Consequently, assessment may involve a variety of professionals, the child's teachers and his or her parents. The purpose of assessment is primarily to design an instructional intervention.

The preventive view of exceptional children and of the services to be provided, emphasizes a more mainstreamed or integrated placement although the choice of a setting may vary, according to the learning needs of the child. If categories are used to label children, these are viewed as the result of administrative necessity and not causal in the delivery process. Table 1 contains a summary of the main points of difference in the two perspectives about the delivery of programmes and services to exceptional children.

The research to be reported here is a part of a larger, longitudinal study (Silverman, Wilson and Seller, 1987). Educators were asked to describe their understanding about how special education worked in their school, their role in the process and their rationale for the actions which they take. The semi-structured interviews addressed each of four topics in the delivery process. These were:

1   Identification of a pupil, from the point that a regular classroom teacher had a concern about the pupil's learning or behaviour to the referral for formal assessment preceding the identification of the pupil by a committee;

2   programming, including (a) the nature and extent of programme modifications and interventions *prior to* formal referral, and (b) the extent of collaborative programme planning for integrated pupils *following* referral, and the selection and monitoring of programmes for pupils designated as exceptional;

3   review and evaluation of the pupil as (a) ongoing evaluation and continuous assessment of the pupil's progress and the frequency and nature of records kept, and (b) the purpose and type of information presented at the formal review meeting which by law is to be conducted at least annually;

4   communication with (a) staff — the perceived purpose of collaboration and consultation among staff both within the school and with the board-level resource staff, the type and frequency of consultation with other

Table 1:   *Major differences in the assumptions and beliefs about restorative and preventive delivery systems*

	Restorative	Preventive
Roles	Special education teachers are specialized to deal with learning difficulties. Curriculum for exceptional pupils is specialized and different from regular curriculum.	Teachers all contribute to collaborative solution. Curriculum is standard, regular, modified in level, rate and method of delivery for exceptional pupil.
	At-risk pupils should be referred as soon as possible for special education.	Referral is the last step after regular classroom resources have been unable to meet the at-risk pupil's need
	The criterion for referral is e.g., two grade-levels behind age peers on standardized tests of achievement	The criterion for referral is that efforts to resolve difficulties with local resources is unsuccessful.
Assessment	Deficits exist exclusively within the pupil.	Difficulties include environmental factors including previous learning opportunities.
	Norm-based criteria confirm exceptionality.	Curriculum-based assessment assists in identifying programming alternatives.
	Categorical labels designate child, and give rise to delivery of services.	Programme and service needs are central to designation
Review	Confirms categorical designation at intervals	Monitors effect of programme and services in enhancing opportunity for pupils to learn.
	Usually annually.	At intervals as instructional goals dictate.
Placement	By categorical label.	By availability of resources identified as needed for instruction.
	Press to segregation: specialized help given to pupil in small group setting.	Press to integration: resources and help given to regular class teachers to maintain progress of pupil.

professionals and with the principal, and (b) parents — the frequency and nature of contact with parents, the methods used for securing parental consents for assessment and placement, and perceived responsibilities of self and others for involving parents.

The selection of the topics was made on several criteria. Primary was the passage in 1980 of special education legislation which amended the Education Act of Ontario. The legislation included a set of detailed procedures for the identification, placement and review of exceptional pupils through a committee, and a detailed provision for parents to appeal the identification of their child as exceptional and the placement of the child. It also contained a definition of a special education programme as 'a programme that is based on and modified by the results of continuous assessment and evaluation, that includes a plan containing specific objectives and an outline of the services that meet the needs of the exceptional pupil'. This definition does not carry the same degree of prescription as the identification, placement and review process, and the appeal procedures since no delivery requirements are prescribed and the statement remains solely as a definition. We have argued elsewhere (Wilson, 1989) that the weight of the legislation favours a restorative interpretation of delivery requirements, and that the elements of a preventive approach, although characterized by the definition of a programme are more difficult to put in place. The law prescribes categories of exceptionality and their use, and requires annual reporting of number of pupils by category. Unlike the 1981 Education Act of the United Kingdom, or the 1975 United States Public Law 94 – 142, the only references to assessment are as quoted in the definition of the programme and in a statement that an identification, placement and review committee (IPRC) shall consider the results of an educational assessment and may consider a psychological assessment of the pupil. Written parental consent is required for psychological assessments and for placement of a pupil. Parents may consult with the IPRC, but no prescriptions are made about parental involvement prior to formal referral to the IPRC.

Thus, the Ontario legislation dictates those areas of delivery for inclusion in the interview that deal with the identification; referral and assessment of the pupil, the programming provisions for pupils after they have been identified as exceptional and placed, the annual review and evaluation of pupil progress and communication with parents. Because of recent literature on the consultative process within school staffs (Idol and West, 1987; Wang and Birch, 1984) and on the dynamics of effective schools and their application to special education (Bickel and Bickel, 1986), we included in the interview the topics of collaboration and communication within a staff, and between teachers and principals, school-level and school-board level resource staff.

The research was conducted over a four-year period, commencing in 1982, one year after the amended Ontario legislation was adopted. Only the final year (1986) data will be reported here, however. Each year, extensive descriptions were recorded of the beliefs, actions and reasoning of the interviewees. By the fourth year of the study a lengthy and comprehensive set of statements had been developed, refined by each year's analysis to represent features of the responses which were recurrent under each of the four topical areas. The need to train staff to analyze interview protocols also added considerably to the refinement process, until high inter-rater reliabilities were reached.

Statements about each topic could be grouped into one of four levels of response. Level 1 or non-compliant statements simply reflected lack of compliance with the minimum prescription of the legislation. Level 2 statements were grouped as being characteristic of a restorative viewpoint. Level 4 statements reflected preventive beliefs and actions. The Level 3 classification was reserved for statements that reflected elements of both delivery viewpoints but fell short of prevention. For example, a typical Level 3 example under the identification topic is a statement to the effect that pre-referral assessment and programme adjustments are conducted in the regular classroom for pupils who fail to keep pace with their peers, but these attempts are tried only for a period of two to four weeks, after which the child is referred for testing. Under the staff communication topic, a Level 3 response would be that consultation occurs between regular classroom teachers and a resource teacher who is designated to work directly with them, but in the absence of a designated meeting time, consultation occurs in the hallways, after school or whenever a teacher can be 'trapped'. Thus Level 3 responses suggest that teachers' beliefs are generally preventive and programme-focused, but insufficient priority is given in the school or by the staff member to allow such beliefs to be systematically and consistently carried into action.

The full series of statements cannot be included here. In Table 2, however, some examples are presented of statements which relate to each topic, grouped under the four levels.

Table 2: Examples of respondents' statements that reflect non-compliant, restorative, mixed and preventive statements

Non-compliant: 1

topic	–	communication with parents
subject	–	elementary school principal
question	–	'How do you seek informed consent from parents for psychological assessment?
answer	–	'We pin the permission form onto the child's clothes as they're going home. My secretary phones the mother the next day to remind her to send it back signed.'

Restorative: 2

topic	–	identification
subject	–	elementary regular classroom teacher
question	–	'How long would you carry out those in-class activities before referring?'
answer	–	'A very short time. I want the child to go to the (special education resource unit) as soon as possible.'

Mixed: 3

topic	–	programme modification
subject	–	elementary regular classroom teacher
question	–	'For a child who is of concern, how are you involved in programming for that child prior to the child being IPRCd?'
answer	–	'Peer teaching. The kid is paired with another child who is doing well. The curriculum itself is not modified.'

Preventive: 4

topic	–	evaluation of pupil progress
subject	–	secondary special education teacher
question	–	'How do you work with regular and resource teachers . . . in monitoring and evaluating these pupils' overall progress?'
answer	–	'We select which teachers fit our kids. We meet informally; try to keep the burden as little as possible:

– how to work with a particular kid; teaching ideas, behavioural goals, keeping track
– we negotiate modified exam writing.
We focus on how to deal with learning problems in the main class setting and how we can assist.'

By assigning each respondent's comments to a topic and level, a profile of viewpoints was established. The rating of level on each topic is reflected on an ordinal scale. For teachers, separate ratings were conducted for the eight topics described above, that is:

1 identification of pupils including referral and assessment
2 programming (a) prior to referral as exceptional
      (b) following placement in both mainstreamed and segregated settings
3 review (a) as a process of continuous assessment and ongoing evaluation
      (b) at the annual IPRC meeting
4 communication (a) with staff
      (b) with the principal
      (c) with parents.

Principals were rated on five rather than on eight topical areas. The topics of programming and review were not subdivided, since the principal was asked to describe his or her beliefs about how the teaching staff was or should be operating as a whole. The topics were (1) identification of pupils, including referral and assessment procedures; (2) programming for exceptional pupils (that is, following placement) in integrated, withdrawal and segregated settings; (3) review procedures (ongoing and annual); (4) communication with staff; and (5) communication with parents.

With the assignment of profile characteristics to respondents, the following questions could be addressed:

1 How valid and consistent is the grouping of belief systems into the restorative and preventive prototypes? Specifically, do the ratings for level assigned to each topic in an individual's profile correlate with the ratings assigned to all other topics? Is the rating scheme reliable?
2 Are there differences in the overall belief systems of different teaching roles; principals, regular classroom teachers, special education teachers and teachers in the resource role? Specifically, do the mean ratings of role groups differ?
3 Do members of a school staff share similar views about the delivery of special education? That is, is there a significant correlation in the ratings of principals and the three teacher groups when analyzed by school?

Method

Sample

In the first year of the study, seven children of 8 years of age and seven of 14 years of age were selected from each of two school board's enrollment lists to represent each of seven of the categories of handicap defined in the regulations. The principals and teachers, in whose schools these children were registered, became the subjects of the study. The children themselves were not a part of the study. As far as possible, subjects were followed for three or four years. When principals changed schools, members of their new staff were added to the sample. The replacement principal in the previous school was also interviewed. When teachers moved schools or roles, they were dropped from the sample unless they moved within the sample schools. By the fourth year of the study, some schools were dropped, reducing the sample size to thirty six schools. These schools were selected to maximize the number of long-term participants of the study, and the inclusion of three teaching roles in each shool. A school staff sample consisted of the principal (or sometimes the vice principal in a secondary school), a regular classroom or subject teacher and, where available, a segregated class special education teacher and a special education resource teacher. Depending on the school and school-board policy, in Ontario a special education resource teacher may have duties which range from teaching remedial groups on withdrawal to providing consultation and support to regular teaching staff, and to IPR committees.

The final year's sample consisted of thirty six principals and fifty four teachers.

Interviews

Interviews were conducted by four interviewers. Extensive training and joint interviewing sessions were held to familarize interviewers with the form of the interview and the recording sheets. Tape-recording of responses was abandoned early in the project because of their inhibiting effect on respondents. These were replaced by verbatim, written transcriptions which the interviewers selected from the responses and placed under topical headings on response sheets. Because this recording method resulted in some reduction of information, and because some respondents were less verbose than others, a system of probes was included in the interview to prompt respondents about topics which they omitted to describe or upon which they were encouraged to elaborate.

Individual, confidential interviews took place in respondents' schools during the school day, during time in which they were released from educational responsibility by agreement with the school boards. Interviews took from one to four hours with the majority lasting approximately two hours.

Rating

In the final year of the study, two raters assigned a numerical rating to the set of statements recorded under each topical heading on the response sheets. The ratings reflected the level of response on each topic on the scale of levels previously described, that is 1 for non-compliance, 2 for restorative, 3 for mixed and 4 for preventive statements. Half points were permitted for mixed responses, resulting in a final 7-point scale between 1 and 4. On a random sample of twenty four cases independently rated by both raters, the correlation was r = + .92.

Since the rating system had benefitted from four years of development, the first year responses were scored using the final year scales. The longitudinal results of the project are reported elsewhere (Silverman, *et al.*, 1987).

Results

Consistency of Belief Systems

Each topic on the response profile was treated as a subtest of the total scale, in order to estimate the internal consistency of the scale by applying Cronbach's alpha. The resulting reliability estimate was $\alpha = +.83$. The ratings for the teachers on the eight topics coded for year 4 and on four topics coded for year 1 — post-placement programming, pupil evaluation, communication with staff and with parents — were submitted to a principal components analysis followed by varimax rotation. The final solution displayed one factor on which five of the year 4 topics had factor loadings above .60 (see Table 3). These were identification, programming before referral and following placement, communication with the staff and with the principal. The three remaining year 4 factors had loadings of about .31. This factor accounted for 35 per cent of the variance. This factor substantiates the internal consistency of the preventive — restorative distinction as reflected in the alpha estimate. A second factor had loadings above .50 on each of the four year 1 topics, accounting for 23 per cent of the variance and distinguishes the results of year 1 from those of year 4. A third factor, with an eigenvalue marginally greater than

Table 3: Factor solution to the principal components analysis with varimax rotation of the topics included in the teacher interviews n = 112

		Factors		
Topic	Year	1	2	3
Identification	4	.80	.05	.15
Programme – pre	4	.64	– .06	.45
post	1	– .07	.91	– .00
post	4	.77	– .09	.39
IPRC involvement	4	.30	.13	.75
Evaluation	1	– .00	.91	– .03
Evaluation	4	.32	.03	.76
Communication – staff	1	.27	.53	– .46
staff	4	.60	– .09	.39
principal	4	.75	.02	.10
parents	1	– .10	.88	.08
parents	4	.32	– .12	.59
eigenvalue		4.21	2.74	1.01
percent of variance		35.1	22.8	8.4

one, accounted for 8 per cent of the variance. This factor suggests a collaborative or communications variable, indicating the topics that differentiate the hypothesized preventive from the restorative viewpoint, and that are beyond the strictly prescribed requirements of the legislation. Factor 3 correlates with factor 1 at $r = + .62$.

Mean Ratings of Role Groups

In order to address the question of whether staff groups differed in belief systems about exceptional pupils, a composite score was computed. Because of the evidence of internal validity of the scale, the composite was simply the mean rating for principals of all five topics, and for regular and resource teachers, of the five topics which matched those addressed by the principals. The special education teachers' composite was the mean of four scores, with identification excluded, since most special education teachers in the sample did not play a role in identification procedures. The mean composite rating for each group, and the proportions of members of each teaching role who were rated into each of the categories is reported in Table 4.

Table 4: Percentage of principals and teachers with composite ratings in each of four categories: 1.0–1.4 (non-compliance), 1.5–2.4 (restorative), 2.5–3.4 (mixed model), 3.5–4.0 (preventive)

		Rating			Percent of Respondents		
Role	N	Mean	S.D.	Non-compliant	restorative	mixed	preventive
Principal	36	3.06	.54	—	13.90	58.33	27.78
Special education teacher	8	2.76	.49	—	25.0	62.5	12.5
Resource teacher	23	2.81	.65	—	34.78	47.83	17.39
Regular teacher	23.	2.49	.60	.04	43.48	43.48	17.39

Influence on Belief Systems of Membership in a School Staff

In Table 5, the correlations are presented between staff groups on the composite scores across topics. The principals' ratings correlated significantly with the ratings of the regular classroom and resource teachers in their schools. The composite rating score of special education teachers also correlated significantly with those of the regular classroom teachers.

Table 5: Correlations (and number of cases) between the composite scores of principals and teacher groups

Teachers	Principals	Special ed teachers	Regular teachers
Special education	35 (12)		
Regular class	.56* (10)	.65** (11)	
Resource	.67** (10)	.17 (9)	.23 (10)

* significant at p<.05
** significant at p<.01

Discussion

The major finding of this study is the persuasive evidence that teachers and principals hold consistent and comprehensive belief systems about the delivery of special education to exceptional children. Furthermore, these can be reliably characterized as relating to two distinct prototypes with associated assumptions about exceptional pupils and about the teacher's role in practice. The prototypes were operationally defined as restorative and preventive for each of five main topics or phases in the delivery of special education in a school.

The operationally-defined prototypes stood up well on two tests of internal consistency. The first was the high level of correlations across all topics, as indicated by Cronbach's alpha. The second, the principal components analysis, suggested that about half of the variance in responses could be accounted for by a single factor which related to the scales in all of the topics on the year 4 interview. The third factor, which accounted for only a small percentage of the variance, was suggestive of a preventive focus in that it displayed loadings on those topics which were previously noted to be beyond strict compliance with the restoratively-based prescriptions of the law but which are characteristic of the preventive framework. The second factor clearly differentiates year 1 responses from year 4, and may indicate a change in frameworks that occurred over the four years during which school boards were developing policies and practices to fulfill the legal requirements of the amendments to the Education Act.

Recent literature (Hobbs, 1980; Gartner and Lipsky, 1987; Reynolds, Wang and Walberg, 1987) would indicate that the preventive framework represents a growth or development of teachers' thinking about exceptionality, away from the medical roots of the discipline. The rationale given by teachers for the beliefs which we have termed 'preventive' include an increased awareness of social, moral and professional obligations to consider the child in the larger context of the environment. If the differences between groups in the sample are indicative of different levels of growth, then it is not surprising that teachers with experience and formal training in special education rate higher than those in charge of regular classes.

The high ratings of principals is not explained, however, by formal training. Less than 10 per cent of the principals in this sample had taught exceptional pupils or had taken additional training qualifications in special education. They had received a considerable amount of in-service training in the legal and professional consequences of the new special education legislation, a possible factor in their ratings.

The correlations between staff groups could also be interpreted as evidence that staff within a school, and the principal in particular, have an impact on how teachers view exceptional pupils and their roles in working with them. The correlations of principals' with teachers' ratings is further support for the literature on effective school practices (Rosenholtz, 1985; Bickel and Bickel, 1986) which proposes that principals have a major impact on staff philosophy and practice.

In the special education literature, much is written about negative attitudes of teachers to exceptionality (Larrivee and Cook 1979), and about ways in which attitude might be made more positive by training or by exposure to exceptional children (Naor and Milgram, 1982; Gans, 1987). The results of this study offer a different perspective on the nature of teacher attitudes toward exceptional children. As shown in Table 4, the restorative viewpoint characterizes a significant number of educators in this study. In the fourth year of the study, 14 per cent of principals and 39 per cent of teachers subscribed to delivery systems with a composite mean rating below 2.5. People holding these beliefs do not express negative attitudes about or rejection of exceptional pupils, in the sense which is implied in much of the literature. Rather, they express a comprehensive and coherent viewpoint about the needs and treatment of exceptional pupils which to them is positive toward exceptional children and perfectly compatible with their duties as educators. Further, such views are commonly expressed by colleagues in the same school who hold similar assumptions about mental deficits, their identification and medical management. The restorative approach is negative in the sense that it is based on assumptions which have been widely challenged in the literature, in the testimony of court cases, and in society at large (Reschly, 1980; Gartner and Lipsky, 1987; Reynolds, *et al.*, 1987). As a framework for viewing one's professional responsibilites, the restorative vewpoint appears to be relatively slow to change. Yet is also appears to be susceptible to the viewpoints of colleagues, and it is inversely related to holding a teaching position with responsibility for exceptional pupils. One might tentatively conclude that interaction with colleagues in one's school is important in influencing the belief systems of a teacher. In-service mechanisms such as school-based teacher support groups might therefore be powerful in influencing attitudes.

In this study an attempt was made to operationalize the complex system of beliefs and actions of teachers and principals about exceptional and potentially exceptional children. One of the questions which remains to be explored is whether the differences in belief systems which characterize the teachers in this study also apply to educators in different teaching situations. It is possible that these results reflect the structure of the Ontario legislation, and the policies of the Ontario school system. A further, crucial question for policy makers is whether a more prescriptive, or indeed less prescriptive legislative requirement would affect teachers' viewpoints in different ways. The US and UK laws emphasize a less categorical, more programme-focused framework for delivering special education. This may be influential in establishing a more preventive viewpoint in American and British teachers.

Also important is the question of whether teaching practice is differentially affected by teachers' belief systems. Our preliminary attempts in this study to monitor practice through teachers' self-report was not conclusive. In interviews held six months after the interviews described here, teachers were asked how they worked with two exceptional pupils whom they had earlier nominated as having problems. The only variable which correlated significantly with the rating scale was the use of resources within the school system. The more preventive the teacher, the greater the number of resource people contacted by that teacher on behalf of the pupils. This finding is encouraging, since it provides a link between teachers' belief systems and their actions. Further evidence is, however, needed.

Despite these questions, the operational definitions of differing belief systems offer a tool for tapping the complex systems of teachers' beliefs and actions. While the focus of the study is upon teachers who work with exceptional pupils, the alternative belief systems are clearly applicable to all pupils, since they basically characterize a classroom teacher's responses to the diversity in behaviour and performance found in a typical classroom. If they are generalizable to other teachers, and if they have an influence on a teacher's actions, they constitute a descriptive system of the complex belief systems in the teachers' thinking, and of the considerable variation in teachers' assumptions and beliefs.

Author's Note

The research reported here was supported by a grant from the Ontario Ministry of Education.

References

BICKEL, W. E., and BICKEL, D. D. (1986) 'Effective schools, classrooms and instruction: Implications for special education', *Exceptional Children*, **52**, 6, pp. 489–500.

GANS, K. D. (1987) 'Willingness of regular and special educators to teach students with handicaps', *Exceptional Children*, **54**, pp. 41–5.

GARTNER, A. and LIPSKY, D. K. (1987) 'Beyond special education: Toward a quality systems for all students', *Harvard Educational Review*, **57**, pp. 367–95.

HOBBS, N. (1980) 'An ecologically oriented service-based system for classification of handicapped children', in SALZMEYER, E. ANTROBUS, J. and GLIAK, J., (Eds) *The Ecosystem of the "Risk" Child*, New York, Academic Press.

IDOL, L. and WEST, J. F. (1987) 'Consultation in special education (Part II): Training and practice', *Journal of Learning Disabilities*, **20**, 8, pp. 474–97.

LARRIVEE, B. and COOK, L. (1979) 'Mainstreaming: A study of the variables affecting teacher attitude', *Journal of Special Education*, **13**, pp. 315–24.

NAOR, M. and MILGRAM, R. (1982) 'Two preservice strategies for preparing regular class teachers for mainstreaming', *Exceptional Children*, **47**, pp. 126–31.

RESCHLY, D. J. (1980) 'Non-biased assessment', in PHYE, E. and RESCHLY, D. J. (Eds) *School Psychology*, New York, Academic Press.

REYNOLDS, M. C., WANG, M. G. and WALBERG, H. J. (1987) 'The necessary restructuring of special and regular education' *Exceptional Children*, **53**, pp. 391–8.

ROSENHOLTZ, S. J. (1985) 'Effective schools: Interpreting the evidence', *American Journal of Education*, **93**, pp. 352–87.

SCHON, D. A. (1983) *The Reflective Practitioner: How Professionals Think in Action*, New York, Basic Books.

SILVERMAN, H., WILSON, A. K. and SELLAR, W. (1987) *Phase III: The Education Amendment Act (1980) Bill 82 implementation study: Board policies and school level practices*, Report to the Ministry of Education, Contract no. MA–512–02–652.

WANG, M. C. and BIRCH, J. W. (1984) 'Comparison of a full-time mainstreaming program and a resource room approach', *Exceptional Children*, **51**, pp. 33–40.

WILSON, A. K. (1989) 'Ontario's Bill 82 in perspective', in CSAPO, M. and GOGUEN, L. (Eds) *Special Education Across Canada*, Vancouver, Centre for Human Development and Research.

YSSELDYKE, J. E. and THURLOW, M. L. (1984) 'Assessment practices in special education: Adequacy and appropriateness', *Educational Psychologist*, **19**, 3, pp. 123–36.

Part Two:
Integration and Early Years

6
Learning Together:
Practice in an Integrated Nursery Setting

Barry Carpenter and Mary Cobb

Introduction

Blythe School is a mixed day special school catering for children with special needs, particularly those with severe learning difficulties (SLD). At present there are eighty-six children on roll between the ages of 2 and 19. Few of the children live in the immediate locality of the school as the largely rural catchment area extends throughout a twenty mile radius. As will be noted later this has implications for parental involvement and integration opportunities for the children.

The School has a reputation for innovative practice in all aspects of special education. Parental involvement, early intervention and exploration of integration possibilities are just some of the issues that have been explored and utilized when establishing integrated nursery provision.

Development of Integration Links

Mainstreaming, normalization and integration are concepts that come from an increased concern for individual rights, and reflect the attitude that handicapped children are, after all, children first. In Britain the 1981 Education Act recommended the practice of integration but allowed each LEA to develop its own strategy. As a result integration initiatives have varied considerably throughout the country. This variation is apparent not only between LEAs, but also within them and even within individual schools. For example, at the school in which the integrated nursery discussed in this chapter is based, integration takes many forms.

Over the past seven years Blythe School has developed extensive integration links across all age phases (Carpenter, Fathers, Lewis and Privett, 1988; Carpenter and A. Lewis, 1989). Not only have projects centred on the Coleshill schools, but also in schools located in the villages from where the Blythe School children were drawn (Carpenter, Lewis and Moore, 1986; Lewis, 1986; Moore, Carpenter and Lewis, 1987; Roberts, in press).

A collaborative research partnership between the school and Warwick University has led to detailed investigations in the early years integration projects. The focus of this research looked particularly at language (discourse strategies) (Lewis, 1987; Lewis and Carpenter, 1988) and attitudes of young children towards peers with severe learning difficulties (Lewis and Lewis, 1987).

The appointment of an integration support teacher (IST) has greatly enhanced the integration links the school had already established. (A fuller account of the nature and function of this role can be found in Carpenter *et al.*, 1988; Carpenter and Lewis, 1989). Internally, the Blythe School staff have ensured that their children with profound and multiple learning difficulties have not endured a double segregation (Ouvry, 1987) by remaining solely within a 'special care' unit (Carpenter, 1987).

Gradually partial integration programmes (Carpenter and Lewis, 1989) have extended to all children with profound and multiple learning difficulties being educated for the whole of the school day alongside their peers with SLD (Carpenter, 1989). This initiative reached its ultimate goal with assimilation into the Further Education Department (16–19-year-olds) of four post-16 students with profound and multiple learning difficulties, enabling them to access the college of further education and, more extensively, community-based leisure facilities (Tompkins and Carpenter, in preparation).

Establishing an integrated nursery was one attempt to explore a means by which all children irrespective of ability (or disability) could benefit by playing and learning together. It was hoped that parents too would gain from the experience by raising awareness of their needs and the needs of others and offering mutual support. As Cameron (1987) has stated, integrated facilities for pre-school children aim to provide 'interaction, communication and parent-to-parent support and the start of disability awareness'. In order to achieve these aims it was necessary to establish opportunities for parental contact as well as integrating the children. Existing school-based support schemes and home–school link strategies were built upon and extended to include provision of a community playgroup and parents' centre. The notion of integration as a 'process' rather than a 'product' has been explored by Booth, Potts and Swann (1987). The integrated nursery at Blythe evolved as a process which responded to the changing needs of pupils, parents and staff.

Home Liaison Playgroup

Early intervention strategies for children with special educational needs (SEN) have offered a positive means of minimizing handicap and facilitating support for parents. Workers in the field responded with a variety of schemes aimed at supporting the early development of pre-school children with a variety of developmental handicaps or delays (Cunningham and Sloper, 1978; Gunstone, 1979; Hanson, 1977; Jeffree and McConkey, 1976; Revill and Blunden, 1979). The most notable of these home-based support projects being the Portage Project

(Bluma, Shearer, Frohman and Hilliard, 1976) originally founded in Wisconsin, USA (Boyd, Stanber and Bluma, 1976), but subsequently having its UK counterparts in the Wessex Project (Smith, Kushlick and Glossop, 1977) and the South Glamorgan Project (Revill and Blunden, 1979).

In 1978 the Warnock Report indicated the need for early intervention, envisaging this as an educative process with a key role for the parent as educator:

> education . . . must start as early as possible without any minimum age limit. (p. 73)
> In the earliest years parents rather than teachers should be regarded, wherever possible, as the main educators of their children. (p. 73)

It was recognition of the desirability for early intervention and parental support that encouraged the headteacher, supported by a multi-professional team to establish a Home Liaison Playgroup, based at the school, in June 1983.

The weekly meetings (for two hours each Friday morning) were attended by mothers and their children, many of whom were still babies, with a variety of handicaps including physical handicap, Down's Syndrome, mild disabilities and general developmental delay (Carpenter and Carpenter, 1989). Many parents transported themselves to the school: others were collected on the school minibus by a volunteer driver.

The playgroup was situated in the school toy library. The group was staffed by a teacher (the special school headteacher), a volunteer nursery teacher and two toy librarians, who were employed under the, then, Manpower Services Commission Programme to organize the school toy library. Siblings were encouraged to attend the playgroup also if they were not of school age. The focus of each weekly meeting would alter. A typical month's programme would be:

Session 1: Exploratory Play Activities (e.g., sand, water, play doh, etc).
Session 2: Art & Craft: finger painting.
Session 3: Home-Teaching Programmes (e.g., Portage, Makaton — Walker, 1978; P. I. P. charts — Jeffree and McConkey, 1976).
Session 4: Speaker: Speech Therapist. Topic — Feeding Programmes.

Ongoing play activities, using a variety of toys and equipment, were available at every session. Apart from the specific emphasis given to each session, ample time was set aside for mothers to sit and chat informally over coffee. The staff team would take responsibility for stimulating the children during this time, but as the children were in the same room as their mothers they did not get distressed at being taken out of sight of their mothers, and the mothers were able to observe their children at play.

Resources for the Playgroup

The toy library provided the play equipment for each session, and mothers were able to loan toys. The specialist toys such as pressure-switch adapted toys were very popular. Occasionally grants were given to the playgroup. Parents were encouraged, as part of their ownership of the group, to spend the money on improving resources for the playgroup. Toy manufacturers were invited to give demonstrations, and the parents recommended purchases suitable for the playgroup children. These toys were then bought, catalogued by the toy librarians, and made available to the playgroup families for loan. (Siblings attending the playgroup were always encouraged to borrow toys too).

The special school also made its parents' library available to the playgroup parents. An information sheet detailing the books was given for reference to each parent. Books were displayed weekly for parents to browse through. The early years of a handicapped child's life is a time for discovery and 'finding out' on the part of the parents. Eventually a supply of books specifically pertaining to early childhood was built up, and added to the parents' library.

An invaluable human resource were the many speakers who came along to talk to the playgroup mums. The speaker meetings were aimed at introducing the mums to a professional or organization that may be of use to them now, or at some point in their child's career. The speakers included a community nurse, a social worker talking about grants and benefits, a dietician, a representative from the Rowntree Trust, a clinical psychologist, a speech therapist, and many others.

The Portage Scheme was operated in an 'ad hoc' fashion from the playgroup: staffing resources were such that support to the home, other than initial or crisis visits, was not feasible. Parents were encouraged to act as the assessor of their child. They selected suitable targets, discussed them with the teacher, collected the necessary resources from the toy library (if they were not available at home), and monitored the implementation of the target. Often, the mothers selected targets that were too advanced for their child, but they came to this conclusion for themselves, and with no loss of dignity. It was a self-realization, rather than a passing of judgment by a professional.

The quest for learning and information became a significant aspect of this group. Two video courses designed for parents of young children with special needs were purchased. They were 'Let's Play' (McConkey and Gallagher, 1984) and 'Let's Talk' (McConkey and O'Connor, 1986). The former was particularly successful, and many mothers commented on the insight it gave them into the importance of play.

Community Playgroup

Blythe School's commitment to partial integration projects for its pupils had been explored successfully throughout all the class bases at Blythe other than the nursery. There were several reasons for this. At that time there was no local education authority maintained nursery in the immediate locality with which to foster contacts. Secondly, the policy throughout the rest of the school was to foster links with the *child's* local community. Since many of the children lived considerable distances from the school it was inappropriate to bus them into Blythe School and then transport them back to their neighbourhood nursery for several hours' integration. The Blythe School staff responded to the challenge of integration for the nursery children by establishing a community playgroup to be based at Blythe School. This notion of locational integration is a reversal of examples usually cited in which special needs children are integrated into mainstream settings (Lindsay and Desforges, 1986). It was foreseen that benefits would extend beyond integration experiences for the special needs children to include objectives concerned with 'parental integration' and increased family and community involvement.

These objectives can be summarized as follows:

1 Forging positive links with local pre-school children and their parents, which can be extended throughout the children's school careers via established integration initiatives with all the local schools.
2 De-mystifying special education: by 'opening up' the school to include the local community the aim has been to create awareness of the normality rather than the 'abnormality' of the school.
3 Promoting community awareness of handicap by dispelling the fear that is often linked to ignorance.
4 Utilization of resources available at Blythe School e.g., soft play room with ball pool, toy library etc.
5 To encourage and sustain parental involvement in their children's education.
6 To provide the opportunity for all parents particularly those having children with special educational needs, to offer support to one another.
7 To establish much needed pre-school provision for local children.

The target group for the community playgroup were the special needs children and their parents in Blythe Nursery and up to twenty local pre-school children of two and above and their parents. Recruitment of local pre-schoolers was explored through two avenues: the health visitor recommended children and parents who would benefit socially from meeting and playing with other children and the Blythe School headteacher visited the local clinic, distributed information leaflets and talked to mums about the proposed playgroup's aims and the facilities available. The response was overwhelming with the result that the playgroup now has a waiting list for the next two years with parents registering children even before birth!

The community playgroup was established in 1987. The original group consisted of twenty-one local children and their mothers and twelve special needs children, six of them with mums. The large number of local compared with 'special needs' mums is explained by their compulsory attendance whereas the structured part-time or full-time placement of the special needs pupils in the nursery has allowed many of their mums to gain employment and hence restrict their attendance at playgroup. Several fathers attend the playgroup when they are available to do so and have offered their support in other ways e.g., donating toys, making equipment and filming the latest Christmas production.

The playgroup has continued to run along its original lines. Meeting every Tuesday afternoon during term time the children are divided into three mixed groups of special needs and local non-handicapped children. There is a weekly rotation of these groups in the three areas used by the playgroup, namely the toy library, soft play room and nursery, offering opportunities for development in the areas of play, gross motor skills and creativity.

The Parents Room and an adjacent kitchen act as the venue for the parents to join discussion covering a variety of topics. In the playgroup's early sessions, staff planned and implemented a disability awareness course with the parents of children with special needs acting as co-tutors, often quoting personal anecdotes to illustrate information presented on video, etc. Parents were asked to suggest ideas for future sessions; these were all acted upon and included Makaton signing, talks from external speakers and active parental participation with all the children in movement and aromatherapy sessions. A typical termly programme would be as follows:

Blythe School Community Playgroup

Programme for Autumn Term

Session

1	Toy demonstration by Mr Voas from the NACRO workshop.
2	Introduction to 'Let's Play' course.
3	Video: exploratory play.
4	Toy making: exploratory play.
5	Video: social play.

Half Term

6	Toy making: social play (You will need 1 shoe box & lid, 1 sock or arm of old shirt.)
7	Video: energetic play.
8	Toy making: energetic play. (You will need 2 pieces of material 12 cms × 18 cms, needle and thread.)
9	Video: skilful play.
10	Toy making: skilful play. (You will need 1 washing up liquid bottle.)
11	School concert.
12	Christmas party.

Integrated Nursery

Following the success of the community playgroup it was decided to extend this provision to include part-time placements for pre-school local children in the nursery. A pilot study using four children, two boys and two girls who were regular community playgroup attenders, took place during the Spring/Summer Terms 1988. The children and their mothers continued to attend playgroup and the children joined the nursery for three additional half days per week. Success was measured in qualitative rather than quantitative terms. Attitudes of parents became increasingly positive. At a nursery parents' evening one couple (parents of a non-handicapped child) described how they had become integrated as a family into Blythe School, their son setting them an example by accepting the special needs children as his friends with no preconceived ideas of 'handicap' or difference. The part-time nursery provision also served as a beneficial introduction to full-time education when the four children were admitted to local first schools in September 1988. Records of progress were supplied to the first schools by Blythe School. The nursery staff had a well established system of evaluating the performance of the special needs children which was readily adapted to the more experiential based learning of the non-handicapped pre-schoolers. From September 1988 nursery provision was extended to include part-time placement for twelve local non-handicapped children aged 3 + years who had attended the playgroup and would be transferring to local first schools in the following September. Arrangements continued as before with the children and their mums attending the weekly playgroup sessions plus three additional half days per week. At that time the total number of special needs children was twelve and so it was decided that the non-handicapped children would be divided into two groups (Group A and Group B) — each group attending the nursery for different sessions so increasing the ratio of special needs to non-handicapped children. In the Anson House Project, Sebba (1983) reports a similarly large proportion of special needs children. Results of her study not only showed no significant differences between special needs and non-handicapped children in their overall patterns of interaction but also no preferences in choice of playmate in terms of distinguishing between special needs and non-handicapped peers. Thus, to maximize the potential for interaction and to restrict the number of highly mobile non-handicapped children within a fairly limited area, it was decided to integrate the twelve special needs children with alternating groups of six non-handicapped children to be supervised by one teacher and three nursery nurses.

Out of the ten half day sessions the attendance was organized as follows:

Pattern of Children's Attendance

	Mon	*Tues*	*Wed*	*Thurs*	*Fri*
a.m.	Special Needs	Special Needs + Group A	Special Needs + Group B	Special Needs + Group B	Special Needs
p.m.	Special Needs	Playgroup = Special Needs + Group A + Group B (children & parents)	Special Needs + Group A	Special Needs + Group A	Special Needs + Group B

Since the special needs children attend the nursery on a part-time basis from the age of 2 it has been essential to provide sessions for them to adapt to leaving parents on days when less children are present. Furthermore, in these circumstances the staff have more time to reassure parents and children. Therefore all day Monday, and Friday mornings, have been set aside purely for the special needs children.

Although similar play activities and experiences are offered to all the children, the special needs children follow a carefully structured curriculum based on the needs of the child as perceived by staff in consultation with parents. Throughout a school day special needs children are withdrawn to work with staff on a one-to-one basis. Progress is carefully monitored and daily feedback is given to parents via the 'chatterbox' book — a home school diary — which encourages two-way communication between home and school. Apart from this individual work the special needs and non-handicapped children work and play in a 'normal' nursery environment which has the added advantage of resources available in the special school e.g., soft play room, sensory garden, computer equipment, etc. The nursery is not purpose built and space is restricted. Therefore with increasing numbers of children it has been necessary to adapt another room in the school for use by the nursery children. Formerly the toy library and now the resources room, this room provides the space and equipment for an integrated group and two members of staff to work away from the nursery. As it is situated in the main school building it also provides a gentle introduction to the older special needs pupils in a non-threatening environment.

The Development of the 'Parents' Centre'

Blythe School already had strong links with its parent community. A Parent Support Group met fortnightly in the Parents Room. Termly workshops were held for parents for them to share in the range of curriculum developments in the school, or negotiate their child's plan of learning.

The school's 'open door' policy meant that parents were regular visitors to classrooms. A toy library offered a loan service of play equipment for use in the home. A popular vehicle for parents exploring a range of issues surrounding the upbringing of a handicapped child was the parents' library. Books on a variety of topics would be loaned by parents, often those describing other parents' experiences of life with a disabled child were the most frequently requested. Joint staff/parent in-service training was a recent successful innovation which improved the collaboration between home and school.

The Parents' Centre, linked to the integrated nursery, was not a separate building, as such, but a collection of facilities that would support parental participation in their child's education (Carpenter, 1989a). The Parents' Room acted as a venue for parents to meet informally. Tea and coffee were always available in this room. Particularly in the anxious early days of wondering if their child had separated successfully, parents would collect in the Parents' Room until they felt it was safe to depart. Throughout the academic year this room could be used by parents as a 'drop-in' base, or for consultations with the class teacher.

As the parents' library is housed in this room parents could browse, at their leisure, through the range of books on offer. Daily they were encountering children with a wide variety of handicapping conditions: their curiosity was aroused, and many parents were eager to find out more. They loaned books on Down's Syndrome, physical handicaps, sensory impairments, and many others.

The toy library proved popular too, not so much for its loan service, but as a base where parents could observe mainstream and special needs children actively engaged in play, often using some of the specialized play equipment and resources. On several occasions local toy manufacturers provided a display for parents who were then invited to purchase toys on behalf of the toy library. This ensured 'consumer commitment' to the items purchased.

The Response of Non-handicapped Children's Families

Attitudes of parents have become increasingly positive. One teacher at Blythe School carried out a comparative study of mainstream parents' attitudes at the beginning and end of their contact with the Integrated Nursery. This small-scale survey (part of a postgraduate course of study) indicated that, over a twelve month period, parents of mainstream children became more informed about disability, more realistic in their expectations of children with special needs and generally more positive in their approach to those children.

Rarely have the mainstream nursery children questioned the disabilities of the children with special needs. However, one parent reported that she had observed her son constructing a long tube by fixing plastic straws together, and then putting the end of this tube up his nose. She enquired as to why he was doing this and he retorted 'to help me breathe'. The mother concluded that her son was 'acting out' a situation from the integrated nursery, where a child with lung damage wears an oxygen tube linked to a cylinder for most of the day. Subsequently when her son became breathless through running he would rush out to put on his 'oxygen tubes'. From first hand experience this child was investigating for himself the implications of disability.

Similarly another parent reported that when out shopping one day, her daughter encountered one of her nursery peers with special needs. She introduced him to her family by saying 'This is my friend, Danny'. She saw none of his physical handicaps or unusual mannerisms; she saw only the child.

This child's acceptance of her disabled school friend has also been reflected in the response of our families. All children are invited to birthday parties; there is no exclusion of children with special needs, but rather a positive inclusion of these children for the many qualities they offer.

Development of the Integrated Nursery Curriculum

Upon admission to the nursery every child undergoes a period of baseline observation. The observation records may be of a general nature (e.g., the actions of the child, his language etc., in the playground), or of a defined learning experience (e.g., in the sand/water play area, what outcomes were displayed by the child?). Indeed, where the teacher needs to probe more deeply into a child's response in a key experience area a specific intervention may be planned (e.g., sorting objects by colour), and the outcome noted as a 'task response'.

Using these various observational strategies cumulative records are built up on each child, reflecting relevant and pertinent needs and attributes. A profile emerges of the child from these records. The challenge then to the nursery situation is to provide a framework for supporting child development.

In providing a challenging learning environment for the young child the problems of ensuring continuity and progression, relevance and differentiation appear. The obvious solution to this is to document the range of activities and experiences the child receives through his nursery education.

A tradition of school-based curriculum development existed at Blythe School (Carpenter, 1984; Blythe School, 1986). Whilst there were several published schemes or commercial materials available which could be helpful in the nursery classroom, our situation differed because of the range of children attending the nursery, and their widely varying learning needs.

Thus, any curriculum documents *had* to reflect the specific needs of this diverse group of children, and the physical, human and material resources available to our particular nursery. Our starting point was the children. From the observational records it became evident as to the key experiences being presented to the children, and the skills they were displaying in the various learning situations. It was possible, from this initial analysis, to predict on a continuum, a progression of experience which the children may (or may not) participate in as they progressed through the nursery.

Curriculum Development Working Party

A Curriculum Development Working Party was established comprising of the head of nursery, the three nursery nurses, the integration support teacher, and the headteacher. This group set about reviewing the seemingly arbitrary lists of experiences and skills that had been composed from the observation records. Discussion took place to clarify terminology, tighten up descriptors and ensure that the requirements being placed upon the learning situation by the children were clearly understood by every member of the team.

Three functions were demanded of any record-keeping system devised for use in the nursery:

1 to accurately reflect each child's nursery experience, and to inform classroom staff of progress;

2 to inform parents of their child's experience and attainments;
3 to act as 'feeder' records to the receiving mainstream first schools.

Could any one system meet all these requirements? What should the presentation format be? Was a 'list' satisfactory?

Consultation Process

As our desire was to use the records for parents and receiving schools we consulted both. By now our 'lists' were becoming quite unwieldy and were certainly unattractive. We wanted the records to tell the parents and receiving teachers something meaningful about the child that would enable them to continue the monitoring of the child's understanding, and extend the child's learning.

From an idea by Waterland (1987) we developed a pictographic means of presenting the records. Simply these were line drawings of a house or flower, and on each part of the design a skill or experience was written. Immediately, the attractiveness of this presentation appealed to parents and receiving teachers alike, as well as to the nursery staff themselves. At a parent workshop, parental opinions were sought as to the language used on the records. Was it jargon-free? Could they conjure up a picture of their child from each statement?

If possible we wanted the record to be a profile of the child. To achieve this goal it had to be a profile of the whole child, in his home as well as school setting. Therefore, parents were asked to share the kind of experiences their child may receive in the home which they felt able to contribute to the profile record. Parent-initiated statements appear throughout the profile records:

'Enjoys music and singing at home'
'Likes painting at home'
'Likes using scissors at home'
'Enjoys active play at home'

The ownership of statements of experience which did not include the words 'at home' could equally belong to the parents too. Many nursery-based activities may be covered in the natural cycle of family life. The child, because of his confidence and intimacy with his family, may demonstrate skills in their presence that he does not display in the school situation. All teachers are familiar with the plaintive cry of parents 'Well he does it for me at home!' (This statement is also uttered by parents who are teachers!) Therefore statements that have not been observed in the profile at school, may be completed by the family when they note them:

'Throws ball to adults'
'Sings and dances to music'
'Intensely curious regarding environment'
'Puts on coat'

Some statements are deliberately school-focused to check the transfer of skills from one environment to another:

> 'Enjoys music and singing at school'
> 'Likes painting at school'
> 'Enjoys active play at school'

Or, the school situation, its structure and numbers of adults and children may be conducive to extending the child's range of abilities:

> 'Works with teacher and group of peers to accomplish task'
> 'Likes being with others at school'
> 'Shows concern for peers in distress'
> 'Experiments with wet and dry sand'

The Profile Records in Practice

Observation sheets were used to collect information on the child. This information was then matched, by the nursery teacher, to a statement on the profile record. The statement would be coloured in. It is planned for the next intake of nursery children to use a different colour for each term to indicate broadly when the child demonstrated the particular skill, and also to highlight progression through the school year as new skills are acquired or new activities experienced.

Throughout the academic year the profile records are available to any member of the nursery team, parents or teachers/headteachers from the receiving first schools. Regular termly visits were made by the latter to increase their understanding of the nursery, and to familiarize themselves with the children.

At the end of the academic year a parents' evening was held. Each parent was presented with their child's profile. After a time studying the profile informal discussions were held with the nursery staff. It was stressed to all parents that the profile was incomplete without their contribution. Some parents had proffered information throughout the year; others wished to reflect in their own home on the statements which pertain to their child but had not been observed in the nursery. The general discussion that followed reflected a high level of understanding amongst the parents of the content of the nursery profile. Our goal of 'shared ownership' of the profile had been achieved.

The National Curriculum and the Nursery Profile

During the period of time that the profile record was being compiled (the academic year 1988/89) three National Curriculum documents (N. C. C.) appeared, namely mathematics, science and English. The nursery teacher, in writing up the profile statements endeavoured to ensure that they dovetailed with Level 1 statements of attainments in the three core National Curriculum subjects. Revisions to other areas of the nursery profile record will have to be made as other National Curriculum documents appear.

The compatability of the nursery profile record with the National Curriculum was seen as particularly advantageous by the receiving first schools. Not only would this afford continuity of curriculum experience but it would ensure progression from one school to the next. It would be possible also for the First schools to utilize the profile records themselves for those children in the reception classes who were as yet, year group 'R' and not year 1. However appropriate learning foundations for transition to level one at the age of 5 were being presented and documented through the profile document.

At the end of the academic year 1988/89 each receiving First school was given a copy of the profile record for each nursery child about to enter their reception class. Our hope was that the records would help the receiving teacher to understand something about the child which would otherwise take weeks to find out. In that the statements reflect observable child behaviour they are not a vehicle for passing on anecdotal information, but clear, factual informative statements. At a glance simple, objective records are available which can tell interested people something useful about the child's understanding and behaviour.

Present and Future Issues

Undoubtedly the formation of an integrated nursery has maximized the potential of integration, not only for the children themselves but also for their parents and the community. It has also reinforced the notion of integration as a process which involves changing not just the organization of the school but also attitudes of pupils, parents and staff.

Using the special school as a base for integrated provision has achieved the objectives of early intervention and parental involvement whilst enabling non-handicapped children as well as their special needs peers to benefit from the resources that the special school can offer. Within the nursery setting the special needs children are withdrawn for individual work but have the added stimulation of non-handicapped children working with them for group and play activities. The integrated nursery fulfils criteria outlined in a model of interaction proposed by Carpenter and Lewis (1989). In this model the uniqueness of the curriculum for children with severe learning difficulties (SLD) is emphasized whilst acknowledging the shared curricular areas appropriate for SLD and non-handicapped children. The benefits of basing integrated provision in the special school are that the needs of all the children can be met in a familiar environment by offering shared experiences in enrichment curriculum areas and setting individual curriculum targets pertinent to a specific child's priority learning needs.

Inevitably there have been problems associated with the establishment of integrated nursery facilities. However these difficulties have been met and dealt with as they have arisen. Open enrolment for special needs children has meant that numbers tend to increase throughout the year, thereby necessitating the introduction of an additional class base for the nursery children. The organization of the nursery environment and activities that take place need careful consideration if play skills and interaction are to be encouraged. The needs of the parents must also be met. Some parents of special needs children have felt that the secure, supporting environment established in the home-liaison playgroup has been threatened by the influx of large numbers of parents of non-handicapped children. Their fears have been allayed by encouraging them to act as co-tutors, promoting handicap awareness. Any issues that have arisen have been discussed openly by the people involved and solutions sought.

Concluding Perspective

The process of establishing integrated nursery provision is ongoing with constant evaluation and adaptation of resources to suit each child's individual needs. One thing that is certain is that through its concern with similarities rather than differences the integrated nursery has achieved a major role in the early stages of normalization for its pupils. It is hoped that for these children the process will develop through continuation of integration initiatives with local first, middle and secondary schools.

References

BLUMA, S., SHEARER, M., FROHMAN, A. and HILLIARD, J. (1976) *Portage Guide to Early Education Manual*, Wisconsin.

BLYTHE SCHOOL (staff of) (1986) *Working with Makaton at Blythe School*, Surrey, Makaton Vocabulary Development Project.

BOOTH, T., POTTS, P. and SWANN, W. (1987) *Preventing Difficulties in Learning*, Oxford, Basil Blackwell/Open University Press.

BOYD, R. D., STANBER, K. and BLUMA, S. M. (1976) *Portage Parent Program*, Wisconsin, C. E. S. A.

CAMERON, J. (1987) Families and the Services They Want. Paper to a Lambeth Conference.

CARPENTER, B. (1984) 'Curriculum development using the Skills Analysis Model: A practitioner's viewpoint', *Mental Handicap*, 12, pp. 58–9.

CARPENTER, B. (1987) 'Curriculum planning for children with profound and multiple learning difficulties', *Early Child Development and Care*, 28, 2, pp. 149–62.

CARPENTER, B. (1989) 'The Curriculum for children with profound and multiple learning difficulties: current issues', *Early Child Development and Care* (June).

CARPENTER, B. and CARPENTER, S. A. (1989) 'The Blythe Home-Liaison Playgroup: An example of early intervention for children with special educational needs', *Early Child Development and Care* (November).

CARPENTER, B., COBB, M. and HAWLEY, P. (1989a) 'Make room for parents', *Child Education*, October.

CARPENTER, B., FATHERS, J., LEWIS, A. and PRIVETT, R. (1988) 'Integration: The Coleshill experience', *British Journal of Special Education*, 15, 3, pp. 119–21.

CARPENTER, B., LEWIS, A. and MOORE, J. (1986) 'Integration: A project involving young children with severe learning difficulties and first school children', *Mental Handicap*, **14**, 4, pp. 152–7.

CARPENTER, B. and LEWIS, A. (1989) 'Searching for solutions: Approaches to planning the curriculum for integration of SLD and PMLD children', in BAKER, D. and BOVAIR, K. (Eds) *Making the Special School Ordinary?*, Lewes, Falmer Press.

CUNNINGHAM, C. and SLOPER, P. (1978) *Helping Your Handicapped Baby*, London, Souvenir Press.

GUNSTONE, C. (1979) *The Anson House Pre-School Project Research Papers*, University of Manchester.

HANSON, M. J. (1977) *Teaching Your Down's Syndrome Infant*, Baltimore, University Park Press.

JEFFREE, D. and McCONKEY, R. (1976) *Parental Involvement Project: Developmental Charts*, Kent, Hodder and Stoughton.

LEWIS, A. (1987) 'Modification of discourse strategies by mainstream six and seven year olds towards peers with severe learning difficulties', *Proceedings of the Child Language Seminar*, University of York.

LEWIS, A. and LEWIS, V. (1987) 'The attitudes of young children towards peers with severe learning difficulties', *British Journal of Developmental Psychology*, **5**, pp. 287–92.

LEWIS, A. (1986) 'Their face is different — Integration and the "handicapped"', *T. A. C. T. Y. C.*, **7**, 1, pp. 76–85. (Journal of Tutors of Advanced Courses for the Teaching of Young Children.)

LEWIS, A. and CARPENTER, B. (1988) 'Discourse, in an integrated school setting, between six and seven year old non-handicapped children and peers with severe learning difficulties', *Proceedings of Ninth International Congress for the Scientific Study of Mental Deficiency*, Dublin, Ireland.

LINDSAY, G. and DESFORGES, M. (1986) 'Integrated nurseries for children with special educational needs', *British Journal of Special Education*, **13**, 2.

McCONKEY, R. and GALLAGHER, F. (1984) *Let's Play: A Video Course*, Dublin, St. Michael's House.

McCONKEY, R. and O'CONNOR, M. (1986) *Putting Two Words Together: A Video Course*, Dublin, St. Michael's House.

MOORE, J., CARPENTER, B. and LEWIS, A. (1987) ' "He can do it really" — integration in a first school', *Education 3–13*, **15**, 2, pp. 37–43.

OUVRY, C. (1987) *Educating Children with Profound Handicaps*, Kidderminster, British Institute of Mental Handicap.

REVILL, S. and BLUNDEN, R. (1979) *Home Training of Pre-School Children with Developmental Delay: A Report of the Development and Escalation of the Portage Scheme in South Glamorgan*, Mental Handicap Research Unit (Wales), Cardiff.

ROBERTS, P. (in preparation) 'Integration and Information Technology: a case study involving pupils with severe learning difficulties and Middle School'.

SEBBA, J. (1983) 'Social interactions among pre-school handicapped and non-handicapped children', *Journal of Mental Deficiency*, **27**, pp. 115–24.

SMITH, J., KUSHLICK, A. and GLOSSOP, C. (1977) *The Wessex Portage Project*, Winchester, Hampshire, Health Care Evaluation Research Team.

TOMPKINS, A. and CARPENTER, B. (in preparation) 'A post-16 education project for students with profound and multiple learning difficulties'.

WALKER, M. (1978) 'The Makaton Vocabulary', in TEBBS, T. (Ed.) *Ways and Means*, Somerset Education Authority.

WARNOCK, M. (Chairman) (1978) *Special Educational Needs: Report of the Committee of Enquiry into the Education of Handicapped Children and Young People*, London, HMSO.
WATERLAND, L. (1987) 'For the record', *Child Education*, February, 1987.

7
Meaningful Curriculum in an Integrated Primary Assessment Unit

Pamela Wotton

The Assessment Unit

The Assessment Unit, situated in an Oxford City first school, provides a resource for the city and its immediate surroundings. The Unit was established to provide long-term assessment for children with special educational needs. Referral is through the school psychological service and pupils tended to remain in the Unit until a 'correct' placement could be made for them. A placement, prior to the implementation of the 1981 Education Act invariably meant in one of the special schools or occasionally in a residential special establishment.

Initially the Unit had been accommodated in an ESN (M) special school and it was expected that pupils from the Unit would remain in the special school system. It was when extra room was required for an expanding population of ESN (M) children that the Assessment Unit was moved. At that time the re-location to a site of an ordinary school did not entail that the Unit pupils would have access to a normal curriculum in the mainstream school. The parents of the pupils did, however, see this move in a positive light because they were happier to see their children attending what was known as a ordinary school compared with the previous special school. Unfortunately, this small step in progress was balanced against the LEA practice of using the Assessment Unit within the mainstream school as a way of softening parents' attitudes towards special schools, and opening up an easier path for parents to accept the special school placement. This illustrates in a very simple way, but one that is very commonly experienced by teachers attempting to promote integration practices, the problem of how an education system 'balances' progress so that progress in one area is nullified by a change of policy and practice in another.

The Assessment Unit was re-housed to its present site in 1974. At that time the Unit was seen by the headteacher and staff of the ordinary school as part of its facilities, and not a separate entity. There was the expectation that the pupils would participate in as many activities and school events as possible. The acceptance of the pupils, as well as the presence of a number of children with physical handicaps, learning or behaviour problems in mainstream classes, was instrumental in my own change of attitude towards segregated education. Progress had been made, however, and the pupils' future education was no longer just a decision of a visiting educational psychologist whose judgment was based on and linked closely to testing procedures. Previously parents were seldom consulted and only informed of decisions that had been made. The contribution to placement by the special needs teacher was very limited, sometimes almost negligible, and the possibility of placement in mainstream schools was not an alternative that was taken on board. I make these observations on past practice as if these were the only changes that have taken place over the past twenty years. These changes are really of emphasis, providing as they do, the background climate for any movement forward for an integration policy. But without this shift in attitude, by teachers and support services, little progress can be made in other significant areas, such as the curriculum and the actual management of the integration process itself.

Pupils

At the time this chapter was written, there were eleven children in the Assessment Unit, five girls and six boys, with ages ranging from 5 to 9 years. Indira has been with us the longest, having a language disorder compounded by the fact that she has to use both English and Punjabi. She has little competency in either and it was her language problem coupled with disruptive behaviour that were the main reasons for her referral to the Unit. Carniz is a placid, lethargic child, the youngest of a large family. Both Punjabi and English are spoken by all members of the family. She is competent in neither. When admitted to the Unit, Carniz had restricted language, using single words and phrases, and in a very stereotyped way. It took a herculean effort on the teacher's part to get her to look at something and there were periods when she would stare steadfastly out into space. Carole's mother wanted her to go to a school for children with severe learning difficulties where it was thought she would be looked after. In school, Carole was found to be very slow responding, both physically and verbally, but usually responded if given time.

Sharon has a degenerative neurological disease which impairs her speech and motor functions. At the moment she is being integrated into the mainstream system with some support so she is able to spend part of her day in the Unit and part in a junior class.

Maria is Brazilian and Portugese is spoken at home. She is poorly coordinated and has strange flapping and waving movements when she is not involved in an activity. Her language is poor and often difficult to understand. She often mixes English and Portuguese. Dominic is emotionally disturbed and his behaviour includes staring into space with a strange grin on his lips, running about aimlessly, climbing on furniture and making noises. Later in this chapter, I have described Dominic's problems and needs in more detail to illustrate in a little more depth some of the problems a teacher is faced with in providing appropriate curriculum for children in an Assessment Unit.

Rajiv has a range of bizarre behaviour and frequently runs wildly around, giggling and slapping people, or crawling across the floor grabbing at their legs. He will drape himself over another person and finds it almost impossible to sit on a chair that is not occupied by someone else. At home the family speaks Punjabi but Rajiv speaks neither Punjabi nor English well.

Michael has poorly developed language and will repeat what has been said or just nod if he does not understand. Whenever he cannot do exactly as he wants he has tantrums, spitting, screaming, kicking, biting and swearing. These continue until he has tired himself out, but can occur more than once a day, on a bad day.

Jonathan was suspended from his local mainstream school for violent and disruptive behaviour. His behaviour alternates between very affectionate and sulking which normally deteriorates into a tantrum similar to Michael's. Jonathan's language skills are good, but he will attempt nothing he is not sure he can do, and reacts aggressively if another child is able to do what he cannot do.

Peter is an anxious quiet boy, with poor motor and language skills. Dennis, on the other hand, is wild, noisy, uncontrollable and races about the room, shouting and making lightening attacks on other children. He is very destructive and spoils his own as well as other people's possessions. He rips his clothes and never has any shoe laces. He eats anything and scours the floor and bins for tasty morsels. If he cannot do what he wants he becomes more violent and destructive and punches, bites and kicks. He has perfected the technique of chewing the leads from colouring pencils and spitting coloured saliva at whoever happens to be within range. Books are the only thing that Dennis really likes. He will sit for long periods looking at books and enjoys being read to. He has good vocabulary and wide general knowledge as well as a vast store of obscenities and abusive language, both racist and sexist.

During this term there have been some disruptions in the lives of three of the children. Maria spent four days in a paediatric assessment centre for medical tests. These in outcome proved singularly unilluminating. Jonathan's father is refusing to allow his mother access, and is himself, with Jonathan, about to be made homeless, because he cannot keep up mortgage payments. Dennis is having psychotherapy sessions once a week. These are to be increased to two or three times a week as soon as possible.

It can be seen from these vignettes of the pupils needs and problems that their educational needs are not only severe, complex and persisting, but there is a continuing aggravation of home circumstances long before they reach the classroom and which affect their emotional state and capability for learning. I would like to consider Dominic's needs as a pupil in the education system and to do this by describing this in the form of a case history.

Dominic: A Case Study

Dominic was referred for admission just before his fifth birthday. According to the speech therapist, his language was stereotyped, comprehension limited, there was evidence of echolalia. His foster parents had noted his very obsessional play and how he held his Donald Duck toy against his face for long periods when he would just stare into space. They said it was impossible to break into Dominic's thoughts when he was engaged in 'telepathy' as they called it. He also seemed to be indiscrimate in his affections for adults, would do nothing for himself and demanded attention of all five members of the foster-parent family. At the age of three, Dominic had been referred to the children's psychiatric hospital because he was withdrawn, had little language, he was unresponsive, regularly soiled himself and had a tendency to stare at the ceiling for long periods. The paediatric investigation revealed no physical basis for his symptoms. At four years Dominic was placed in a children's home as his foster parents were showing signs of emotional and physical stress.

In the Assessment Unit, Dominic's behaviour was odd and unpredictable as he alternated between being very active and very passive. He wanted to be carried about during break-times, and given the opportunity, would sit on an adult's lap for long periods in a very unresponsive way. Both teaching and non-teaching staff were unable to resist him, or perhaps their response to Dominic satisfied a need they had. It was several weeks before I managed to wean the staff away from him. At other times Dominic would race around the room, climbing on furniture and people with total disregard for their feelings. He had tantrums and destroyed everything he got hold of, except his drawings. He also ran. He would be through the door or out of the window, and off.

When Dominic had been in school for a relatively short time, although it seemed like eternity, both the nursery nurse and I began to experience feelings of dislike towards him. We would watch the taxi arrive, hoping he was not in it, and when his smiling face appeared at the door, and he ran in leaping at us, it took tremendous willpower to greet him with a smile. Fortunately, we were able to talk about these feelings to each other and present a united front to the rest of the staff, who thought us heartless monsters. Thankfully these feelings of dislike did not last too long.

Dominic was quiet and calm only when he was drawing. He drew houses, singly and in rows, everywhere. They were three dimensional and through the windows were flights of stairs. Occasionally his grandmother was drawn looking through a window or appearing out of a chimney. Sometimes I would occupy another window or chimney. Then Dominic drew other buildings, roads, bridges and roundabouts. He began to name the places he drew and to include the land around. Dominic drew only in black, he would not use colour or paint. Dominic called his pictures, maps, until we explained that they were landscapes and showed him that maps were different. He then began to draw a map of the UK remarkably accurately and from memory. He named the places he knew or had visited. Later the outline of Western Europe appeared and the maps bore a remarkable resemblance to the television weather maps. He then began to concentrate on drawing maps and trying to write the names of the countries. When Dominic began to paint, he did not attempt the detailed drawing he was doing at the time but covered the paper with a muddy brown. He never enjoyed painting, preferring to draw. Later Dominic began to colour his landscapes, using greens, browns and yellows to produce very attractive pictures.

Following his fifth birthday, Dominic was moved from the children's home and went to live with his grandmother. Since then he has drawn pictures of her. They have become more detailed but retain the characteristics which seemed to capture a likeness of her, as seen from his viewpoint, looking up at her. Dominic can reproduce these pictures by the score and during periods of anxiety, he will carry one about with him, tucked up his jumper or down his sock.

Dominic's language development was very poor when he first came to school. He spoke in a strange monotone, like a voice synthesizer. As his language developed and he used longer sentences his intonation changed to a two note sing song which was extremely irritating, especially as he was speaking continually, repeating everything that was said in the classroom. It was, I believe, this irritating voice more than anything else that led to the feelings of the hostility I felt for a time.

It has always been necessary to use Dominic's current obsession in an attempt to gain his interest. To encourage him to read, he began to recognize words which meant something to him: nanny, bridge, road, for example. He chose the words and illustrated them and it was not long before he had acquired a large sight vocabulary. As Dominic's reading and writing were beginning to improve, he discovered numbers. For some months his life was full of numbers. He wanted to work with numbers, to write them to a million. He counted in ones, and twos, fives eights, anything. Numbers were written everywhere and he seemed to understand how they worked with little or no explanation. His poor expressive language made it difficult for him to explain his problem-solving techniques.

After four terms, Dominic had made sufficient progress in his behaviour and learning to allow us to arrange for him to spend time in one of the infant classes. He would spend the afternoon in the infant class listening to stories and doing number work. The other children were impressed with his ability and managed to refrain from laughing at some of his odd remarks and bizarre behaviour. By the end of the summer term Dominic spent a considerable portion of each day in the mainstream school, his behaviour became better, he became more confident. Dominic was now aged 7 years and this coincided with the arrival of a visiting American teacher who was responsible for a junior class in the mainstream school. The teacher agreed to take Dominic into the class and made preparation for his arrival. The pupils in the junior class were more reserved in their welcome than the infants had been. Dominic had to prove himself again and the teacher helped him to do this by involving Dominic in a project which required him to do a lot of drawing. This impressed the children who thought the pictures exhibited in the school corridor were done by me, not Dominic. They were further impressed by his maths ability. As their liking for Dominic increased, so they wanted him to succeed. They missed him when he was not there and tried to protect him from his teacher when he was being obnoxious. They tried to get Dominic to conform to their standards but found his unpredictable behaviour exciting. They were, however, outraged when

Dominic swore at the teacher and decided that he should return to the Assessment Unit to show him that this is not how juniors behave.

Dominic's early life provided him with a variety of problems which affected his learning: his obsessiveness and anxiety, his need for reassurance, his bizarre behaviour and poorly developed language. Particularly worrying was Dominic's inability to form relationships. Except for his obsession with his grandmother, Dominic took very little interest in other people except when their actions affected him. The effect these actions had on Dominic decided whether he hated or liked them at that moment. This may be the result of poor parenting, but, I think, it also has something to do with the way in which Dominic had been passed from person to person, from place to place, with little regard to the harm it was doing him. The period he spent living with his grandmother is for Dominic the longest period of stability in his life so far. In spite of the progress he had made in school, he was still extremely vulnerable to change. Dominic experienced another occasion when he discovered that people were not permanent, they appeared and disappeared without his understanding why. On this occasion it was when his mother had returned to live with him for a while and then decided to depart to live elsewhere. At this time, he was spending most of his mornings in the junior class. Suddenly everything changed and Dominic was again showing some of his bizarre behaviour that he had exhibited when he first came to school: screaming, running about, climbing on furniture and people, walking about with his head stuck up the back of my sweater, while I was wearing it, and swearing almost continually. This was a period when Dominic was unable to go into the junior class for almost two months because of his erratic behaviour. He gradually began to spend short periods again in his junior class without support from a nursery nurse, but there were times when he refused to go in knowing that he would not be able to conform.

Over the three year period that Dominic had been in the Assessment Unit there had been changes in the nursery nurse and other children. This change in population did not seem to affect Dominic, and while it could not be reassuring to him, this coming and going of people was part of his life. His permanent reference points apart from myself were the school secretary, the headteacher, dinner ladies and other members of staff. The two mainstream classes that Dominic had joined had visiting teachers, again a temporary experience for Dominic, but they had been chosen because they had experience with working with children with special educational needs.

In the Assessment Unit, Dominic is one of a small group and gets a great deal of individual attention and space to work out his problems. There are, however, some extremely disruptive children, who, at times, demand the attention of all the adults in the room. Dominic sometimes imitates this behaviour. The behaviour of the children in the mainstream is more positive and has a beneficial effect on Dominic. There are also drawbacks for Dominic in the mainstream class. He misses a great deal because of his obsessions. For Dominic to participate in the work in the mainstream, he needs to be encouraged to approach the work through his own interests and this would have required a more individualized curriculum. With his literacy and numeracy skills as well as his creative ability, it should have been possible to provide Dominic with access to the curriculum by selecting the activities which would assist him to attain the curriculum aims. This would be done in the context of his interests, obsessions, emotional and learning problems. It would seem that Dominic's behaviour cannot change unless he is feeling secure.

It is clear there is an immense gap between Dominic's behaviour and that which most teachers consider acceptable. His junior class teacher believed that Dominic should be in the mainstream, and wanted him to succeed, but found Dominic extremely difficult and at times impossible to cope with. Because the Assessment Unit and the mainstream school are on the same campus it is fairly easy to maintain a flexible approach to the integration issue. Pupils with behaviour as bizarre as Dominic's are not usually educated in the mainstream school and will perhaps, continue to attend special schools. But if children like Dominic are to benefit from mainstream education, a radical change is needed in teacher's understanding of what constitutes progress in education. Removing children with special needs from ordinary schools means that we have come to expect certain standards of behaviour from pupils and everything outside is deviant. Dominic's behaviour may be deviant, but with more support, a curriculum relevant to his needs which takes account of his abilities, he could be integrated.

Dominic is certainly the most disturbed child I have tried to integrate, but the difficulties he faces are the same as for other children from the Assessment Unit. The small number of hours allocated to allow these children to move from a very small unit to a large group ensured that they will not succeed. Teachers accept the children with the best of intentions. They believe that they can provide for them, but the nature of their problems, lack of resources, large classes, the organization of the school and the curriculum, all militate agains this. The onus is on the child to fit in with the existing school arrangements. If the child fails to make progress it seems as if the child is at fault.

Pupils like Dominic have been removed from mainstream education because their learning problems cannot easily be identified so their needs cannot be met. Once their problems have been identified and their curriculum needs described, there are two options open: they can either move to a mainstream school with minimal, temporary support, or they can be the beneficiary of a multi-professional assessment and go to one of the special schools in the areas. If we choose the former then the likelihood is that the child will make little progress, since staff in mainstream schools have not had to provide for children with such diverse learning problems. These have been put in the hand of 'experts' in special schools. Now teachers in mainstream schools are expected to develop appropriate programmes of work and possess the teaching skills and strategies to cater for a wide range of abilities and needs. They often feel unable to provide for these children when the support is withdrawn.

Dominic and other pupils from the Assessment Unit, need more specialized support than is available from peripatetic advisory teachers, they need support over a long period, perhaps for most of their school life. There are many activities in which Dominic can participate without extra support, so he needs a support teacher whose time is flexible enough to allow her to give him the help he needs, when he needs it. If this kind of long term support is not available to Dominic then we fail him.

Devoting so much time and thought to one small child, gave me some idea of how Dominic must feel about his grandmother. He is obsessed with her as I had been with him, but his obsession is to reassure himself that she is there. My obsession allowed me to see more clearly what Dominic's needs are and how I respond to them. It allowed me to understand that for Dominic to overcome his enormous emotional problems, he needs stability, security, an opportunity to work out his feelings through his art and the understanding of the adults who are part of his life. Watching Dominic I was aware of how many times he was censured, reprimanded, his energetic racing about curtailed, and how often he was expected to be quiet, to conform to what we, as adults expected. And this in a school in which the staff are particularly accepting and used to children like Dominic. The following passage struck a chord when I read it:

> Mustn't hold hands, mustn't make a noise, mustn't play up;
> mustn't make a noise, mustn't play up, mustn't sleep in the day;
> mustn't make people laugh, mustn't make a noise;
> mustn't play up, mustn't roll your eyes, mustn't be naughty;
> mustn't play with your penis, mustn't make a noise;
> mustn't stay still, mustn't eat too fast, mustn't make a noise;
> mustn't fart too loud, mustn't make faces, mustn't make strange noises
> mustn't make people cry, mustn't play up, mustn't play with fire;
> mustn't look at girls, mustn't make a noise, mustn't roll your eyes;
> mustn't be a nuisance, mustn't make a mess on the floor, mustn't make a
> noise. (Caddy 1985)

Language Curriculum

The Bullock Report (1975) stressed the importance of language and the role it plays in generating knowledge. First as an intellectual process which becomes integrated with other intellectual areas to enhance and extend the process of thinking, and secondly, through the aspect of concept formation so that we can represent the world to ourselves. Children learn to use language through their experiences, the use of language by other people and the expectations other people have of them. The pre-school language experiences of children differ considerably, and it is important for each child to develop adequate language skills to facilitate the process of organizing events, experiences and interactions to produce an inner and more complex model of the world.

The language curriculum used at present in the Assessment Unit is the most recent and detailed I have written. The starting point for developing all curricula in the Unit is individual needs. Although concentration on individual needs may lead to children following a narrow programme of work, I have tried to avoid this pitfall by using a variety of activities and topics to widen their experiences, and so achieve the criteria required for the stated objectives. It is essential for the pupils to have an adequate grounding in language skills to ensure needs are correctly assessed and appropriate future education provided. It is difficult to assess learning potential if language is poorly developed, and this is a further consideration in the development of a language curriculum.

Another consideration is the importance of acquiring competence and social skills to allow integration into mainstream schools to be as smooth and successful as possible. For the pupils in the Unit certain skills must be learnt if they are to be integrated into mainstream schools. In addition to the acquisition of the basic skills of numeracy and literacy, important in the eyes of teachers in the mainstream, they need to acquire language skills which will enable them to relate to people, events and conversation in a manner acceptable to other people, and within the broad social spectrum not solely in the unusual confines of a special class. The more restricted their ability and knowledge, the broader and more important their linguistic skills need to be if they are to be successful in their everyday lives. These pupils often fail socially because they are unable to relate in an acceptable manner to everyday behaviours and topics. Some of them may acquire only fundamental linguistic skills, but they should still be given the opportunity to listen, watch and participate in the broader range of language used by other children and adults.

It has always been a problem providing a workable curriculum for the children who attend a unit of this kind. This is due in part to the diverse and complex range of their learning and behavioural problems; to the variable length of stay, and to the fact that children may arrive or leave at any time throughout the term. The arrival of a new child, part way through the term can have a devastating effect on the dynamics of the group, particularly as these children are usually transferred from other schools after being suspended for very aggressive and disruptive behaviour. The curriculum must allow for this, cater for each child's special educational needs, and provide a method of assessing progress in each area of learning. For these reasons an objectives model seems to be appropriate.

Objectives Curriculum

Many children who come to the Assessment Unit need to be taught skills which other children acquire naturally. The objectives model curriculum is based on the principle that all behaviour is learned and that children can be taught those skills which they may lack. This model concentrates on aspects of learning and teaching which can be observed. Each area of the curriculum is identified and a terminal goal for each area is described in the form of a behavioural objective. Each terminal objective is analyzed into a sequence of intermediate skills which are written as behavioural objectives. The behavioural objectives describe what the pupil has to do to demonstrate that the skill has been learned. It describes the pupil's task, the conditions in which it is presented and the criterion for successful performance. The acquisition of these intermediate goals is essential for pupils to master the terminal objective.

The base line for each pupil is identified in each area of language and the child is introduced into an appropriate grouping for each specific language skill covered by the curriculum. To discover the base line, the child works through the tasks until he or she no longer achieves the required criteria. Testing then stops and the child is introduced into a working group at a similar level, and one in which the child is likely to have some success. Each child may belong to several different groupings, so allowing him or her to interact with different children for different language activities.

The curriculum is divided into eleven discrete areas based on the sub-tests of the Illinois Test of Psycholinguistic Abilities. The language areas covered are: receptive and listening skills; auditory figure-ground; auditory closure; auditory memory and sequencing; body image; spacial awareness; general sensory perception; visual discrimination; visual figure-ground; visual closure; and visual memory and sequencing. Terminal objectives are identified for each area and appropriate intermediate behavioural objectives are specified. The intermediate objectives have been determined by task analysis and are organized in sequence which accords with the development of pupils and their acquisition of skills. Objectives are defined to achieve the aims of the curriculum and their precise definition allows the teacher to assess, through observation of the child's response, whether they are established. As the learning experiences are selected through appropriate objectives, the recording system is designed for the child's progress to be monitored. This recording system is precise and each child must achieve specific criteria to ensure a skill is learnt. Criteria may be modified for some pupils who have specific physical and sensory disability. Ideally, this system of selecting learning experiences through appropriate objectives and recording outcomes, should allow for modification of objectives, content and teaching methods, where necessary.

This objectives approach has allowed for considerable success for a number of pupils in the Assessment Unit. Many of the children have meagre experiences and linguistic skills and a concentration span which is measured in micro-seconds.

An integrated approach, where a topic is used to generate interest sufficient to ensure that basic skills are learnt, is almost impossible to obtain with pupils in the Unit, and its use in the past demonstrated that, not only were skills not learnt and language not developed, but near nervous breakdown produced in the teacher.

In the Assessment Unit the objectives approach has advantages both for pupils and for the teacher. It allows each pupil to work in small groups with different members depending on the activity. This ensures that each pupil will relate in some way to every other pupil in the Unit, under supervision with guidance to encourage appropriate responses. It also gives each child the opportunity to be praised and encouraged by the others to obtain some success in some areas of language. Each child is also sure of individual attention from the teacher, focused on specific needs. For a teacher the objectives model has several advantages. It allows the teacher to find out what each pupil can and cannot do, and so allows teaching strategies to be planned, and tasks for the pupil to be set at the correct level. It ensures that classroom help can be used effectively for consolidating and practising skills. Criterion referenced tasks give the teacher an objective means for deciding whether skills are established and are, therefore, suitable for evaluating learning. Objectives also deal with specific learning problems and so are informative for parents and allow for their involvement in their child's learning.

The objectives model also has its disadvantages. Behavioural objectives may establish precision only in a narrow band of activities where the task presented may have little in common with tasks presented in other situations. The curriculum may be narrow and relevant only to the teaching of basic skills which, when established, may not transfer to other situations. The situation in which skills are taught may be artificial and seem to have little relevance to skills needed outside the classroom. This curriculum is based on the belief that children have deficits and this places them in a position of one who responds, rather than one who initiates.

Group Activities

To overcome some of these disadvantages, activities involving the whole group of children were arranged to allow and encourage them to use the skills they have acquired. Working in a group often stimulates the child to talk more frequently and spontaneously. The variety of language experiences, however, may be more restricted without skilful management by an adult. Group activities give pupils the opportunity to respond appropriately and may reduce any anxieties they feel about the correctness of their response. There are, however, drawbacks here too. The louder, more vocal pupils, are more likely to respond and dominate the conversation. The pupils with poorly developed language skills often do not fully understand or know what to say or do and would often respond by taking their cue from the others, and repeating as much as they could recall of the voluble pupils' responses.

The objectives model curriculum shows how the child uses the language to respond in a particular situation but does not seem to carry over to group activities or conversation. It may add to the language he or she has but if it is not used appropriately in ordinary conversation then one important aim of the curriculum, social competence, is not achieved. This suggests that a new, or at least different, approach may be in order. It is this different approach that I used as the basis for modifying the language curriculum.

An Experiential Curriculum

All of the pupils in the Assessment Unit have some language skills in common. They are all able to use language to protect their own interests; to open and to maintain to some extent relationships with other pupils and adults, to report on their present experiences and direct their own actions and those of others. The extent to which pupils use their language skills differs considerably. Those pupils with poor language tend to use words to place labels on objects, actions and people, and each word may have several meanings for the pupil. The precise meaning of the word, at a particular time, may be understood by the listener taking into account non-verbal cues and any information that can be gleaned from the situation. The pupils with good linguistic skills, in addition use language to describe, report, reason and predict. At times they can maintain a conversation with an adult, but apart from Jonathan and Sharon, were unable to do so with another pupil. To provide the pupils with common experiences may enable them to use their language skills, however limited, to talk to each other. Where the objectives model failed in one of these aims, namely, to enable the pupils to relate to other people in an acceptable manner, it was possible that an experiential curriculum would be more successful. For this reason I chose to concentrate on the area of general sensory perception.

A broad aim of the curriculum would be to improve the pupils' language abilities by providing them with a variety of experiences and media. By using the senses: visual, auditory, tactile, olfactory, gustatory, the precise aims of the curriculum may be stated:

1   to improve the childrens' general sensory perception and awareness;
2   to encourage them to acquire accurate information through their senses;
3   to encourage them to explore the environment;
4   to encourage them to use their senses to identify and describe familiar sights, sounds, tastes, smell and textures in their environment.

To enable the pupils to achieve the aims of the curriculum they should first be aware of the parts of the body associated with the sensations. They should also be able to identify and name them and their functions. The pupils would need to develop each sense individually and concentrate on the information received through that sense in isolation. This would involve the pupils experiencing a wide range of sensations with which they must become familiar. The pupils should understand, and if possible, use appropriate descriptive language. Pupils would be encouraged to explore various environments and use the skills they have acquired to describe them.

To achieve these aims, tasks would be set which require the pupils to recognize and interpret the sensory information they receive. Identification of various sensations received through the sense organs, concentrating on one sense at a time and using, where appropriate, other senses to interpret the stimulation transmitted by the sensory organs, resulting in appropriate responses to the environment, events, situations and conversation.

Creative, practical and exploratory experiences would give the pupils opportunities to identify various sensations and learn the terms to describe them. Play experiences would give them the opportunity of extending these experiences in their own way. A structured programme of sensory stimulation to clarify the sensory experiences and ensure they are established, would form the basis for recording whether skills are learnt. For example, visits would be arranged to give the pupils the opportunity to experience a variety of environments which may already be familiar to them. They would be encouraged to explore these environments through their senses and to look, touch, listen, smell and where appropriate, taste, as much as possible. The visits would not be restricted solely to the acquisition of the sensory experiences and should give the pupils the opportunity to gain as much as they can from them. They would also form the basis for some creative work. The visits would be to country and town environments.

Certain skills are already possessed by the pupils. All are able to identify and name eyes, ears, nose mouth / tongue, hand / fingers; match and identify a variety of shapes and name at least three; match and identify a range of colours and name at least nine; identify and name a number of common objects and animals. Indira, Sharon, Jonathan, Dennis and Dominic are able to demonstrate they understand the concept of big and small, but only Dominic and Dennis understand long and short, thick and thin, and are able to order more than two objects by size. All of the pupils can describe at least one attribute of an object correctly. All the pupils recognize the others by the sound of their voices alone and can recognize a limited number of other sounds. Dennis can identify most sounds he hears and knows the correct term to describe the sound.

This was the base line from which to start and all the pupils are able to do what is listed above: they also had other skills which would become apparent as we progressed. The first consideration was to discover whether the pupils knew what function certain parts of their bodies performed. To open some discussion on this, I read the story of Little Red Riding Hood. Talking about the story, we discussed the wolf's eyes, ears, teeth and what he said they were for. Although the story had been a very simple one, only Dennis, Jonathan, Sharon and Indira had followed it. The others had, as usual, been gazing into space, fiddling, annoying their neighbour, for example. Only Jonathan and Dennis could tell what the wolf used his eyes, ears and teeth for. We talked about bodies in general, identified all the relevant parts and discussed their function. So that all the pupils were aware of what we were doing I spent some time ensuring they were pointing to the correct organ, I then said: 'We see with our . . . We hear with our . . . ?'. We used eyes, ears and hands to look listen and touch. We sang songs and said rhymes concerned with those parts of the body.

In the afternoon I wanted to know which of the pupils had retained any of the information on the uses of their sensory organs. Dennis, Jonathan, Dominic and Indira identified the parts of the body associated with each sense. Rajiv repeated whatever I said; Carniz said 'mummy' each time; Peter said the first word that came into his head, for example; (We hear with our . . .) 'Music'; (We see with our . . .) 'house'. Michael, Maria and Carol responded in similar ways. When asked the use of the sensory organs, none of the pupils was able to give the correct response to each. Maria and Rajiv just repeated what I said; Carniz said 'sleeping' each time. The rest of the children responded as follows:

PW: Our eyes are for . . .

Dominic: To see. Dominic can see further than you. Got big enough eyes. Got eyes wider than Nanny. If you were looking through binoculars the River Thames would only be about ten feet down. It would be ten feet down.

Peter: For eyelashes.
Michael: Eyebrows. Shut.
Carol: See out.

Dennis, Jonathan, Sharon, Indira said 'looking'.

PW: Our ears are for . . .
Dominic: For tissue, so you can't have earache.
Peter: Poke in. Eardrops.
Michael: Ear 'oles.
Carol: Talk.

Jonathan, Sharon and Dennis said 'hearing' and Indira nothing.

PW: Our mouth/tongue is for . . .
Dominic: Swearing.
Peter: Toothpaste. Eating.
Dennis: Biting. Shouting.
Indira: Opening. Speaking.
Michael: Poking out.

Sharon, Jonathan and Carol all said 'talking'.

PW: Our nose is for . . .
Dominic: Put tissue on it.
Peter: Picking.
Michael: Sneezing. Tissue.
Carol: Tissue.
Dennis: Blowing.
Indira: Blowing.
Jonathan: Smelling.

PW: Our hands/fingers are for . . .
Dominic: Thumping in things.
Peter: Clapping. Hide them.
Indira: Eating dinner.
Dennis: Picking up things.
Jonathan: Eating.
Michael: Read the paper.
Sharon: Don't know.

These responses, elicited in a number of ways, indicated not only the particular preoccupation each pupil had with certain organs, but that most of the pupils needed to be aware of the sense they were using as they were using it, and to be reminded which words were associated with each sense. To remind the pupils which sense they were using, activities were prefaced with a statement drawing their attention to that part of the body: we are going to listen to some sounds with our ears, we are going to look at some pictures with our eyes. Some useful props were brought from the local party shop: a large pair of glasses, a false nose, a pair of 'Prince Charles' ears' and some face paints. A pair of fingerless gloves accentuated the pupil's fingers. The relevant prop was used by the pupils for particular activities. Once they got over the fits of laughter that wearing them produced, the props did focus their attention. Another reminder was through pictographs. The words were incorporated into pictures, for example the words 'look' and 'see' had the 'oo' and 'ee' made into eyes, the words 'touch' and 'feel' were written into the pictures of hands. The pictographs were put on the walls with examples of the pupils' work, illustrating the use of the sense.

Using the model of Advent calendars we made a wall picture of a house of horrors, in which the pupils hid self portraits behind doors and windows they could open. Dennis who manages to reduce almost every communal activity into a riot, was placated by helping to make a book for himself, with flaps to lift up. I hoped that, given Dennis's interest in books, and the limited vocabulary needed in these 'look books' as he calls them, he may begin to read.

During the three weeks leading up to the mid-term break, two trips were arranged, one was a walk to the river and parks, the other to a wild life park. The trips were arranged to encourage the pupils to use their senses and widen their experiences. The pupils were excited and as the walk was along the footpaths, fields, the river bank and finally the parks, I hoped there would be some linguistic gains from it. We took some bread for the ducks and a bag for interesting finds, which the children later used to make a collage. Despite the families of ducks on the river, Carniz still seemed unable to look at them, or at anything else we pointed out. She marched steadfastly on seeming oblivious of everything around her. Rajiv, however, was tremendously excited, and learnt two new words, one from Dennis, which I hoped he would forget, and the other, 'babyducks' which he now used to describe all water birds. Indira probably had the most exciting experience: she slid down the bank into the river! After that the rest of the time was spent ensuring that neither Rajiv nor Dennis helped anyone else to have the same experience.

The visit to the wild life park was a limited success for some of the children. Dominic, who does not know the names of many animals, was expected to benefit from this trip; but only wanted to run and talk about the contours of the land: 'It goes up here, and if you go on that path it will be like a hill. Dominic knows that'. He and Carniz needed to be held, looking into the animal enclosure, and questioned on what the animal was doing, what colour it was, to be sure they had seen it. Rajiv again was very excited and saw a large number of 'babyducks', which he refused to believe were called flamingoes. Maria and Indira learnt to recognize a tiger as distinct from other large cats. Michael was interested only in what might be in his packed lunch and Peter spent as much time as he could in the lavatories. Dennis shouted at all the animals and tried to climb over the barriers into their enclosures. And it rained! Despite the limited success of the trip we did get some interesting creative work from it. The pupils made pictures using a variety of material to experience different textures. Maria began to recognize and understand the meaning of 'soft' when she made a picture using feathers. Classroom activities backed up the few gains made on the trips. Indira wrote about falling in the river and had learnt the meanings of the words wet and dry, through experience. We used tapes to illustrate animal sounds, and the photographs I had taken at the wildlife park were put in a book to remind the children.

So far, it seemed, nothing had inspired Carniz to look. When the weather became windy we made a kite, using the basic shapes the children knew. Indira used the sewing machine to make the tail and we took it to the middle of the field to fly. It took some time to get the bridle exactly right and Rajiv became very excited and kept shouting 'Oh, my darling, my darling'. We rounded up the pupils and Carniz's head was inclined in the direction of the kite and she actually saw it and became quite animated. On subsequent occasions when we flew the kite she would stand gazing up at it saying 'kite, kite, kite, Pam'.

During the three weeks it became obvious that if the pupils were to gain anything from this curriculum, I would have to remove Dennis from the group. Activities involving the whole group just did not work. At first a lot of time was wasted getting Dennis to sit down. Then his behaviour was so disruptive that it was not possible to complete anything. Separate activities had to be arranged for him. Michael, Indira, Sharon and Jonathan thought he was getting preferential treatment and complained and sulked. Even when they were quite happy to let Dennis do something else, they were still disturbed by him. The shouting, screaming, disgusting noises, the racing about and the constant invasion into what the others were doing, hitting them, spitting, snatching their things and answering their questions, made it almost impossible to accomplish anything.

A classroom activity was used to explore sound. The general aim of the activity was for the pupils to identify common sounds. The pupils sat grouped around a large picture of a street scene, which had earlier been used for general discussion. There was a selection of smaller picture cards which depicted some of the objects shown in the large picture. A tape was played and each sound was played twice; once softly and once loudly. The main objective was for the pupils to match the sound to the correct object in the picture. A matching card was then placed on the picture. The simple activity of identifying the sounds, locating the object and putting the card in the right place was what was expected of Maria, Rajiv, Michael, Carol, Peter and Carniz. The other pupils were also required to distinguish between the loud and soft sounds.

Maria, Rajiv and Carniz were able to identify most of the sounds by using the visual clues and selecting the picture card to put on the large picture. They were able to name only a few of the more common objects. Peter, Michael and Carol could name more of the objects, and Carol and Michael were able to use the correct word to describe some of the sounds. Indira, Jonathan, Sharon and Dominic could identify the sounds, and only Dominic needed the small picture to prompt him. They could describe only a few of the sounds in sentences. They had more success with discriminating between loud and soft sounds. Sharon found this more difficult than the others, who, once they understood what was meant by the terms 'loud' and 'soft', were able to distinguish the difference.

Evaluating the successes of those three weeks: Carniz looking at the kite; Rajiv learning two new words, one obscene; Maria and Indira discovering that a tiger had stripes; I did not feel that the curriculum was working. Not enough gains were being made to justify its continuation. The time taken to arrange activities which involved all the pupils; the stress felt during and after the activity, caused by trying to contain such an assortment of volatile pupils, was disproportionate when compared with the little they gained. I felt that they could have made much greater progress using different methods. It was as the mid-term break loomed that I realized that I could not justify this curriculum. I decided to abandon it at the end of the week, after the party which the pupils had been awaiting.

Dominic and Sharon had birthdays and spent the morning with one of the helpers, making cakes. Indira had been growing cress and it was just right for harvesting. Dennis, to prevent his raids on the cake mixture, was taken shopping to buy bread for sandwiches. When he returned he helped to boil eggs to go in the sandwiches with the cress. The pupils made party hats and the table was prepared. I hoped that the three weeks of communal activities, all my exhortations not to shout, to wait your turn, to talk to one another, would have had some effect. We sang Happy Birthday, clapped the right number of times for each child's age and tried to start up a conversation about the food; what Dominic and Sharon were having as birthday presents and topics of general interest. Indira, however, was sulking and refused to have anything, or to speak, because it was not her birthday until September. Jonathan was complimenting Sharon on the cakes. Dominic was complaining that he did not like cress. The rest of the pupils were concerned whether there was any more to eat, and Dennis was creeping about, under the table eating the crumbs and the cake papers. Fortunately it was Friday afternoon and the end of the first half of term and I abandoned the experiential curriculum.

Integration

Over the past four years nineteen pupils have moved from the Assessment Unit into mainstream schools. While all of these pupils have learning problems and some behaviour problems, all were considered to be within the ability range usually accepted for the pupils to be appropriately placed in the mainstream schools. The learning problems were diverse but are not of the kind that would make these children more suited to being educated in a special school. Parents, educational psychologists and I all believed that they should be in mainstream schools. The first group of five pupils who were integrated received no extra support for the simple reason that the LEA administrator maintained that if the pupils were considered to be placed appropriately then the school must be providing the kind of education suited to their needs! One pupil who moved to a middle school was provided with a part-time temporary welfare assistant due to a visual impairment and vulnerability, but only after she had been integrated. This was at the insistence of the headteacher of the middle school who felt he could not be responsible for her safety.

A precedent was created when Craig, who had been in the Assessment Unit for a longer period than most children, was to be transferred to the local middle school. Craig had learning and behaviour problems, was an anxious pupil and had language difficulties. He is dyslexic. Craig's parents wanted him to attend the local school and the headteacher agreed if support could be provided. Reports describing Craig's learning problems were sent to the Area Education Officer requesting support for him. It was pointed out that if this support was not provided then the only alternative would be a special school for dyslexic pupils. These are few and far between and are usually expensive. This produced an agreement that some teaching hours would be made available and this was to come out of the home tuition budget which then was the only means of financing it. It emerged that support for integration would be made available if the alternative was unacceptable to the LEA because of the cost. Although this was a minimal amount of support, five hours teaching support a week for two terms, this became the basis for supporting all pupils integrating into mainstream schools. This is now considered a right for all the pupils providing as it does a base on which to build for future planning and financing.

Integration of pupils with special educational needs from the Assessment Unit into maintream schools seems to occur in the following ways:

Integration with no support;
Gradual integration with the support of the Unit staff.
Integration with the support of a home tutor;
Gradual integration with the support of a home tutor.

The first group of pupils to move from the Assessment Unit into the mainstream schools was placed without any support in spite of the fact that they had to adjust to a move from a small unit of ten pupils to a large class. Two of the pupils moved to a large middle school which was in the process of reorganization. The teachers in the schools were expected to provide for the pupils' very complex learning problems, and the pupils were expected to adjust to the new situation. Neither pupils nor teachers were prepared. The time allowed for liasion between all concerned was inadequate and it was impossible to follow up any problems which subsequently occurred. The gradual integration of these pupils with support of the Unit staff was made possible only in the first school in which the Assessment Unit is situated. This involved one pupil who lives locally and for whom it was his local school, and two pupils whose parents requested they remain in the school. Integrating pupils in this way allowed them to spend periods in mainstream classes and to use the Assessment Unit as a base which provided support in the form of materials, teaching and curriculum planning. The length of time the pupils took to integrate fully, and to require the support of the Assessment Unit, varied according to each pupil's needs.

Six pupils were integrated with the support of a home tutor. The pupils were moved from the Assessment Unit into middle schools and were allocated five hours home tuition a week for two terms. The home tutor worked in the school with the pupil, helping to adjust to the new situation and preparing work and materials to be used when the home tutor was not there. While the home tutor was with the pupil problems were reduced but this minimal level of support is inadequate for most of the pupils. The gradual integration of five pupils with home tuition was used in first schools and teachers welcomed the gradual introduction of the pupils into their classes together with the home tutor. It began with a pupil spending one day a week in the mainstream school with the home tutor, and the other four days in the Unit. Over a period of about half a term the amount of time the pupil spent in the mainstream increased, and the home tutor organized her time with the pupils in the most appropriate way. Integrating pupils in this way has the advantage of giving the pupils a complete day in a new setting with support, and as the time spent in the mainstream increased and the pupil gains in confidence, so the support is rearranged to spread over this longer period.

Each pupil integrated into mainstream school had complex learning problems and the staff were apprised of these problems in discussions with the headteacher and class teacher. Where home tuition support was provided schools welcomed the extra teacher as this reduced the pressure on the class teacher and the pupils. Staff in all the schools expressed their concern when the support was withdrawn and in all cases felt that the level of support should have been greater and for a longer period.

Two pupils returned to schools that had referred them. Simon was allocated no support and the behaviour problems he had exhibited, and were partly the reason for his referral, reappeared on his return. Benedict was reintegrated gradually with the support of a home tutor but his progress was not maintained when the support was withdrawn. Returning pupils to the school which referred them seems, at first sight, to be a sensible move; the staff know the pupil, and with the progress made in the Unit, detailed reports and suggestions on teaching strategies, it might be assumed that the patterns of behaviour and progress acquired during their stay in the Unit, would transfer to the mainstream classroom. This proved not to be so. Teachers retained the notion of the pupil as at the time of referral, and since the referring school had not changed, the original problems reasserted themselves. These problems may be alleviated temporarily if support is available but if there is no support, or when support is withdrawn, the problems reappear.

Pupils who move on to the different schools encounter different problems. Staff often are unaware of the complex nature of the pupils learning problems and assume that they can provide for the pupils without taking too much account of the information available from the Assessment Unit. For example, pupils who move to middle schools have to contend with many bewildering problems. They are moving from a small unit in a relatively small school to a large class in a bigger school. Gone is the integrated day: they have different lessons with different teachers. They have to find their way around a new school, with bases and years and departments. They have to be in a specific room at a specific time and to have the correct books for the lesson. They have to copy or follow directions written on a blackboard; they may have to cope with dinner tickets; lockers with numbers larger than those they recognize ; with timetables. Bruce, who despite his good reading and maths ability, found it almost impossible to overcome his distaste for, and difficulty with, writing and was expected to copy his timetable from the board on his first day at middle school. Fortunately, the home tutor was there to help him, but her presence did not prevent him from spending most of his first week in the lavatory being sick. Mandy could never find her dinner tickets, she lost her gym shoes, swimming gear and on a trip to the ice rink, which is near her home, wandered off and went home. She was not missed and it was her parents who informed the school of what had happened. All of these problems had been discussed at length with the teachers in the schools, but it is not until they experience them that they really understand just how difficult these pupils' problems are.

Brian, who had been integrated into the first school with the support of the Unit is now in the middle school. He is a rather odd looking boy, whose behaviour and responses are often inappropriate. During his time in the Unit he made some progress and began to concentrate. In the mainstream in the first school he made considerable social progress and had one or two close friends. During the summer term of this third year in the middle school, Brian's mother came to see me. Brian was arriving home with his legs covered in bruises and he had started to wet the bed, something he had not done since he was 2- or 3-years-old. His mother was worried and Brian was persuaded to tell her that he was being teased and bullied at school. Brian's greatest concern, however, was that he did not see himself making any progress; he was worried more about his poor reading and maths than about the bullying. Brian was seen at the local Children's Hospital and again by the educational psychologist. A meeting was arranged at school and Brian's problems were discussed and strategies devised to help him. It is unfortunate that it took so long for this to happen.

Craig was the first child to receive support on moving from the Assessment Unit into the mainstream. His anxiety, dyslexia and often confused language, together with some odd mannerisms, made him a lonely boy. In addition to his two terms home tuition, Craig had a variety of other forms of support, all temporary and part time, and granted after considerable haggling. The uncertainty of this support and the lack of consistency, make Craig more anxious. When anxious, Craig needed to talk, and because the middle school and first school share a site, Craig would come to see me to talk about his numerous problems. Through his third year in the middle school Craig's visits became more frequent, almost daily. He usually ate his lunch in my room, telling me what was worrying him, often in tears. He referred to himself as someone with 'special needs'. He worried about his lack of progress, of which he was aware, despite good school reports each term. He felt that he was not making enough progress to allow him to fulfil his ambition to work in a hospital. He was not so unrealistic as to believe he could be a doctor or nurse, but he wanted to have a job taking people down to the operating theatre. He had worked hard for, and succeeded in getting, first aid badges in the scouts, but believed that he would not learn enough at school. With his mother's permission, I met Craig's headteacher to explain what Craig felt was happening. Some of Craig's concerns were easily dealt with: he was to be allowed to read to a teacher during the compulsory silent reading time; he would no longer be expected to do the class tests since he could not read the questions; the PE teacher would, in future, choose the teams and not leave the choice to the children, because Craig was never chosen. Craig said, 'They think because you're special needs you can't play games and they don't want you'. Craig continues to visit me to talk but no longer seems so anxious. It is, however, unfortunate that he did not feel able to talk to an adult in his own school.

James moved into the first school with support from the Unit staff. His behaviour had improved and he was making some academic progress. His move to middle school uncovered a number of problems. James had tantrums, made no progress and the teachers were finding him very difficult and disruptive. When I happened to meet James he told me he liked the school, was being good and getting on well.

One recurring theme, which these pupils serve to illustrate, is that those pupils whose behaviour is not overtly difficult are often seen to be doing well by their teachers. They may not make much progress but are deemed to be working hard, whereas the loud, disruptive children are referred back to the educational psychologist because of their behaviour and lack of progress. This, however, is not necessarily the view of the pupils, yet they are rarely asked how they perceive their school career.

Despite the problems there are some advantages for the schools into which children are integrated, although these advantages sometimes need to be spelt out. Having these children in the schools meant that the school was more representative of society, made up of a wide range of individuals, with different abilities and needs. When a school opens its doors to pupils with very complex problems there is often an unexpected bonus in the effect the pupil has on other children. In the middle school into which Mandy was integrated, two girls who were considered by their teachers to be difficult took Mandy under their wing and were very concerned that she had everything she needed and was in the right place at the right time. It does also, unfortunately, allow some pupils scope for bullying and teasing, but this is something with which most schools have to deal, and it is because these pupils are noticeably different that they often bear the brunt of the bullying.

Discussion

In this chapter I have described briefly my experiences of attempting to plan and follow through a curriculum for a group of pupils with severe developmental problems aimed at maximizing their re-introduction to mainstream schooling. I have explained the use of both a highly structured behavioural objectives approach, geared to individual needs, and a more experiential approach utilizing group activities. It became apparent that there could be gains to be made using either approach but for whatever curriculum is utilized there are considerable constraints arising not only from the severity of each pupil's needs but the interaction of these needs within the small group environment of an Assessment Unit.

The major problem in providing curricula for the pupils in the Assessment Unit is the difficulty of working as a group. Each pupil needs a separate programme of work, some parts of which may coincide with another pupil's, consequently groups tend to be very small. Another problem is the disruptive behaviour of most of the pupils. It is almost impossible to complete any activity without an outburst of some kind or other disrupting it. None of this particular group of pupils is able to consider the others and the effect their behaviour is having on anyone else. Although the objectives model worked better for me, and is certainly less stressful for me to implement, it may not be particularly stimulating for all pupils. It was, however, effective in some respects with this particular group. I also observed some positive effects ulitizing the experiential curriculum. Rajiv was much more animated, and he was now more inclined to try to communicate. Of all the pupils he seemed to enjoy the trips most. He was very excited and full of wonder at the things he saw. I think I enjoyed taking him out more than I did the others. Subsequently, when I returned to working in small groups, and to the objectives curriculum Rajiv began to use some descriptive language. For example, he no longer always gave single word answers, but occasionally expanded them to two words: 'red car' instead of just 'car' or 'red'. I cannot be sure that this results from the experiential curriculum, it may be something that was about to happen anyway, or it may be that the pleasure he got from the trips made him more responsive, and stimulated him to use language he already had but did not bother to use. It is important, however, that they have experiences which encourage them to explore their environment in a positive way, but to maximize those experiences it is necessary to have more time with individual children at the time they need it. Also for pupils to improve in their social skills they need to work together as a group over a long period, and in as many different situations and ways as possible.

It may be useful to consider other methods of providing for the needs of the pupils in the Assessment Unit and trying to reach a balance between the two curricula I have described. It may be possible to adapt the objectives curriculum, which does ensure that all the pupils made some progress, and apply it to a wide framework which would make it more relevant and would transfer to other situations. The linguistic skills which the pupils develop must allow them to communicate in an effective way and help them to achieve some competence in basic skills. This may also give the pupils a range of language skills needed in the classroom. By using a more holistic approach, and not dividing language up into discrete areas, as I did with the objectives curriculum, the pupils might well develop language skills in a more natural way. I do not believe that it is possible to write a specific curriculum for a group of children whose needs are as disparate as those whom I teach and I must return to individual needs as a starting point.

Perhaps of more significance, in relation to issues on integration, is not the specific nature of the curriculum, but other matters, such as LEA policies and practices. It is these that at the end of the day, determine whether an integration programme will go forward for a particular pupil. There are major obstacles at this stage in the integration process long before a pupil actually appears once again in a mainstream school.

References

CADDY, D. (1985) 'Copious notes on how to conduct one's behaviour by a precocious nobody', in DURY, I. (Ed.) *Hard Lines*, London, Faber and Faber.
BULLOCK REPORT (1975) *A Language for Life*, London, HMSO.

Part Three:
Integration in Secondary and Further Education

8
Physically Disabled Pupils:
Integration at William de Ferrers Comprehensive School

Mary Field

Introduction

William de Ferrers School is a community comprehensive school with 1400 pupils aged 11–18 years. It opened in 1982 as part of a centre in which the school shares many facilities with the community. The district sports centre, public library, community education and community association all share the facilities. The centre houses the police station and area educational psychological service; it provides offices for the Town Council and a variety of organizations such as the Citizens' Advice Bureau, Probation Service, Relate and the Careers Service. At one end of the building is the Youth Wing and playgroups are held in the community association's social area.

This concept of total provision for the community of a new and expanding dormitory town made it easier to integrate physically handicapped pupils than in an older, more traditional school. Everyone came to the William de Ferrers Centre, so why not have handicapped pupils too? A disabled toilet area had been provided by the architects and a lift had been installed to get barrels of beer up to the bar in the social area. The lift has been very useful for children in wheelchairs and on crutches but the toilet area was useless for anyone in a wheelchair until it had been extended and re-equipped.

The first of our handicapped children was Lee who has a rare form of muscular dystrophy which is not degenerative. He also has a severe spinal curvature which is getting worse. Lee can walk for short distances without crutches but he has great difficulty with stairs. He was an ideal introduction to the problems and rewards which come with integration because he sorted out most of the problems for himself, helps everyone else and is always cheerful, polite and hard-working. When it was suggested to some of the staff that three more handicapped pupils were soon to arrive, they immediately thought of Lee and assumed that there would be few difficulties. That attitude has been carefully fostered so that pupils who are far more severely handicapped have been accepted by teachers and pupils and have been happy at school. Lee is now in his fifth year and shares his taxi to school with

Nicholas who is in the first year. Nicholas also has muscular dystrophy but he is rapidly losing the use of his muscles, is confined to a wheelchair and can do very little for himself. Lee is Nicholas' hero.

Physical Handicaps

Very few physically handicapped children use wheelchairs, while pupils who look completely normal and can use all their limbs may have severe problems such as epilepsy, diabetes or hearing problems. There seems to be a tendency to automatically assume that handicapped pupils will have wheelchairs and mobility problems. In practice, wheelchairs may not be a severe problem and dealing with severe epilepsy or providing facilities for hearing-impaired children may be much more difficult.

Wheelchairs are no problem at all when it comes to external examinations. Much greater difficulties are created when a pupil needs to use a word-processor because the keyboard makes a noise and disturbs other candidates or when a partially-hearing pupil cannot cope with a music examination which involves listening to a tape and then answering questions.

Without experience, it is difficult for teachers to understand that the same medical conditions can result in widely varying disabilities. Ellie, David and Martyn all have spina bifida. Ellie is paralyzed below the waist and uses a wheelchair, David is able to walk using crutches and can ride a bike while Martyn shows no sign of disability. However, all three pupils are doubly incontinent. Some diabetics and epileptics have their condition almost totally controlled by medication so that no evidence of any problem is ever seen in school, while other pupils with these conditions frequently visit the medical room and, occasionally, their parents, or even the doctor or ambulance, may have to be called.

Any definition of 'physically handicapped' or 'disabled' must be artificial. Many children have some physical problem ranging from a tendency towards colds, hay fever or sore throats, through conditions which have been diagnosed and treated in infancy, to severe congenital disorders which may create problems throughout life.

Mainstream or Special Education

The 1981 Education Act has abolished categories such as ESN or maladjusted and replaced them with a single category of 'children with special educational needs' including children with a disability that makes it hard for them to make use of ordinary schooling in the area. The Act states that children with special needs should be integrated into an ordinary school so long as parents' wishes have been taken into account; the child's needs can be properly provided for; other children in the school are ensured an efficient education; and resources are being used efficiently. Parents should be involved, children's feelings and perceptions should be taken into account, and the parents have right of appeal.

However, few parents know enough about mainstream and special education to make a reasoned choice without heavy reliance on what they are told by the doctors, educational psychologists and local schools. Neither mainstream nor special education provides everything that a child needs. Many special schools are large enough to provide facilities for nearly every subject so that the pressure to integrate handicapped pupils into mainstream schools is social rather than educational. Parents, especially young ones, tend to feel they are failing their child by allowing him or her to go to a special school or they may feel there is some social stigma attached to special schools. One headteacher of a special school said that 'to use the argument that the children must learn to cope is facile'.

The child's needs are given in the 'Statement of Special Educational Needs' but this limited list is only a tiny fraction of the real needs of a child. Any school which does not wish to admit a handicapped child can claim that it cannot meet the child's needs but this claim may be overruled by the LEA. It is almost impossible to estimate in advance what effect a new handicapped pupil will have on the education of other pupils or on the use of resources. Extra facilities for such pupils are often promised but do not always materialize. We may sympathize with an LEA which is not prepared to spend a lot of money altering toilet accommodation or installing ramps until the child arrives at the school in case the child does not come and the money is wasted. However, the child needs those toilet facilities and that ramp on the day of arrival and cannot wait until months later. Such situations upset the child and parents and create a sense of frustration and lack of support among teaching staff before the child has been allowed to settle into the school.

Physiotherapists often argue that the social gain for a handicapped child in attending a mainstream school is more than counter-balanced by the lack of opportunity for regular physiotherapy. Even in a situation where a physiotherapist visits our pupils two or three times each term, works out a programme for them and teaches the welfare assistants how to supervize it, she remains convinced that Nicholas does not have enough physiotherapy or spend sufficient time in his standing frame. Giving him more physiotherapy, which he dislikes, would mean missing lessons and he can only use the standing frame at lunch time because it is too heavy to carry around. In a special school his physical needs would be better provided for but socially he might be less well catered for. It could be argued that the purely educational element is irrelevant since his life is likely to be short. His mother's arguments are more practical. If he went to a special school, he would either spend several uncomfortable hours travelling each day or he would have to be a boarder. She wants him at home where she can care for him. Nicholas wants to go to school with his friends and enjoys a fifteen-minute taxi ride with Lee.

How Much Integration?

The Spastics Society defines integration as:

The opposite of segregation! It is educating children with or without special educational needs together, in ordinary schools for some or all of the time... Segregation restricts our understanding of each other's needs. Familiarity and tolerance can reduce fear and rejection. Integration contributes to a greater equality of opportunities for all members of society.

A particular child may be integrated for two lessons per week or for the full timetable. He or she may spend weeks, months or years in a special school and then return to a mainstream school. Whatever is best for the child should be made possible. Most special schools aim to send any pupils who are capable of benefiting from the experience to a mainstream school for at least one or two subjects. However, some teachers in the mainstream schools who receive these pupils tend towards an attitude of 'I can't see why they bother'. The children often seem to attend the lessons for one subject such as typing and return to their special school without having any real contact with the mainstream children. In some cases the child only attends some of the lessons for that subject and never becomes an accepted part of the group. Such arrangements are counter-productive but are probably inevitable while we are still experimenting with collaboration between schools.

Within a mainstream school, there may be a special unit for pupils with a particular disability. Units for partially-hearing pupils are often very successful in that they are able to arrange for their pupils to attend mainstream lessons for most of the day but can provide support when it is needed. However, most mainstream schools have no special accommodation for physically handicapped pupils. Too many of them are ready to boast that all pupils are integrated for the whole week and do not realize that the child is sitting watching for several periods each week and does not have access to the special facilities that he or she needs.

The biggest problem in successful integration is PE lessons. The pupil can usually physically attend them but an alternative to outdoor PE is needed. Pride in a handicapped pupil attending all lessons seems misplaced if that pupil is standing watching football or sitting in a wheelchair scoring for netball while getting cold and bored. However, PE lessons provide an ideal opportunity for the pupil to carry out a physiotherapy programme, although supervision will be required from a welfare assistant. Handicapped pupils may become tired very easily and PE lessons spent lying quietly on a PE mat may be a very productive way to spend the time. Nicholas and Lee both need to spend periods lying flat with their feet over the edge of a PE mat in order to stretch the tendons of their legs. Daniel, who has night epilepsy, goes home in order to rest for an hour and Ellie, who has spina bifida, is allowed to come to school an hour later instead of attending PE. David does weight-lifting and Lee has a physiotherapy programme as well as a variety of extra activities. In other local schools, there are keyboard skills classes, word-processing sessions and extra craft lessons. Children in wheelchairs enjoy competing for the Royal Society for the Prevention of Accidents Wheelchair Proficiency Awards and can practice for their test with the help of volunteer sixth formers during PE lessons.

It is no use providing open access to a school if that access is not complete and adequate compensation is not made. Too often handicapped pupils have to leave lessons early and arrive late because of problems with mobility, safety and toiletting. Sometimes they have restricted options due to access or are told that they will not be able to attend one subject. Taking children out of special schools because they are segregated is not a solution if we immediately re-segregate them by having a system in an ordinary school which separates them from their peers.

Some children may only be physically capable of coping with three days a week or five mornings or 30 instead of 40 periods in the week. This should be accepted. We should be aiming to provide what is best for the child and not trying to 'prove' that all children can be integrated for the whole week.

For some children, the best system seems to be for them to spend a period of time in a special school and then to transfer to a mainstream school. A further period in the special school might be necessary at a later stage or the special school could be used as a resource by the mainstream school. Robert arrived in our third year after attending a small boarding school for pupils needing speech therapy. He receives some help with reading and writing from the Supportive Education Department but otherwise is no different from any other pupil. At the same time Julian joined the sixth form from a special school for delicate children. He had been a boarder at the school, which had only 45 pupils, since he was 8-years-old. Both boys must have suffered from culture shock when they arrived in a large comprehensive school, but they had received the individual care and attention at their special schools which has enabled them to cope with the transfer. Both boys are confident, hard-working and keen to make progress; both are determined to compensate for anything that they think they might have missed in the past.

Preparing for Integration

There is a tendency for the staff at any school which is to admit a physically handicapped pupil to believe that a medical report will provide guidance as to the physical needs of that pupil. That belief has resulted in showers being installed that were not needed and equipment that was essential not being available. Only two of the physically handicapped pupils in this school have statements of special educational needs and these statements would do little to help another school which did not know the children. The safest course of action is to meet the parents and the child, determine basic priorities with regard to essential facilities and then use commonsense. If the teacher responsible for the child at the previous school can be contacted, many potential problems may be solved for the cost of a telephone call. However, physically handicapped children do not often accompany parents on fleeting visits to the new house and the first appearance in school may be on the day that the child expects to attend classes. Parents often manage to persuade schools that, despite the medical records, the child can cope with anything and will be no problem at all. To some extent, this is because the parent honestly no longer views the disability as a problem but it is also because the parent is anxious that the child might not be admitted to the school. Fathers, in particular, seem to be convinced that their children in wheelchairs have no special needs at all!

Contacting advisers, the educational psychologist, the LEA, the physio-therapist, occupational therapist, speech therapist and the previous school takes very little time compared with persuading the 'Buildings' section of the LEA that a disabled toilet area needs alteration. Most important of all, the teaching staff should be informed of the nature of the handicap, its educational implications and any special arrangements that are being made. Teachers should be given as much information and support as they feel they need in order to teach the child without detriment to the rest of the class.

Physical Needs of the Child

It is relatively easy to gain advice from an occupational therapist, nurse or doctor about aids to mobility and toiletting needs; most LEAs have someone who will advise on ways of overcoming the problems of stairs. Catalogues of special tools for Home Economics and CDT can be obtained and there are adjustable tables and endless gadgets available. Handicapped children have learning needs which are additional to those of other children and they need to be aware of all the gadgetry which is available to ensure that they are able to have access to the curriculum. The teacher must not do everything for them or put them in a group where other children will do it. A child with the use of only one hand is unable to hold a potato and peel it so he needs a gadget to hold a potato while he peels it. Ellie, in her wheelchair, could not reach the cooker but she could cook in a microwave oven and an electric frying pan if these were placed on a coffee table. David, Lee and Nicholas have problems with taking down homework at the end of each lesson so each of them uses a dictaphone. Such equipment is expensive but costs less than a place in a special school.

Many of the physically handicapped children will be regularly visited in school by the physiotherapist, occupational therapist, nurse, doctor, adviser for partially-hearing or partially-sighted pupils or the speech therapist. A place which is reasonably private is needed; no child should be expected to describe his or her problems in a medical room where other children with minor ailments can overhear the conversation. A welfare assistant may be needed to help some pupils. Michelle has epilepsy and is unwell most afternoons and needs someone with her until she is well enough to return to lessons. Nicholas needs supervision between lessons, toiletting, putting in and taking out of his standing frame and supervision during his physiotherapy. Both Nicholas and David need help in the classroom; Nicholas is unable to fetch necessary equipment and David needs constant encouragement to make an effort and not spend his time dreaming while using his legs as an excuse for not using his head.

The main aim of the welfare assistant must be to encourage independence. Ultimately, she has succeeded if she makes herself redundant! However, the welfare assistant is there to enable the school to cope with the child equally as much as to enable the child to cope with the school; one of her functions is to support the teacher whenever help is requested. All the handicapped pupils in this school share four part-time welfare assistants whose hours are arranged so that, for almost all of the week, we are able to have two assistants on duty at a time. Sharing the assistants avoids the problem of one of them 'belonging' to a particular child and reduces the dependence of the child on a particular 'slave'.

School outings, trips, field work and course work outside school need not be a problem if there is cooperation between the parents, pupils, welfare assistants, teachers and the LEA. Lee rarely uses a wheelchair but sits in one when he goes out of school on visits so that he does not delay other children. David was persuaded that he could go on the French trip if he went in a wheelchair on the boat and used his crutches, as usual, at other times. He was accompanied by a welfare assistant who was paid by the LEA. Michelle took part in work-experience despite her epilepsy because we were able to find a sympathetic employer. Electric wheelchairs are often best left at school overnight because they are not easy to transport; this means that they need their batteries recharging at school. Alternatively, electric scooters used for transport to and from school may be exchanged for hand-propelled wheelchairs in the daytime; the scooters need their batteries recharging too. Our caretaker takes great pride in keeping wheelchairs and scooters in running order.

Uniform may seem unimportant but most handicapped children want to look like everyone else. Ellie wore a jersey instead of a blazer because the blazer sleeves wore out so quickly on the wheels of her wheelchair. Nicholas wears black tracksuit trousers because ordinary trousers will not go over his calipers. Robert, who has had many operations on his legs, delights in being the only pupil who has permission to wear Bermuda shorts and trainers in school.

Academic Needs of the Child

It is difficult to distinguish between physical and academic needs in many cases because physical needs may create academic problems and vice versa. Pupils who are incontinent usually have to be toiletted about every two hours and often leave a lesson early or arrive late as a result. Missing part of the lesson creates an academic need and also draws attention to the physical disability. It is often unavoidable but lateness can be minimized if the welfare assistants are well organized. Conversely, the academic problems suffered by pupils with spina bifida or cerebral palsy may be alleviated by provision of a welfare assistant, dictaphone, word-processor or special gadgets.

Most handicapped pupils have an even greater need to learn to use a computer, especially a word-processing package, than other pupils. As Nicholas becomes less able to hold a pen, he will be able to use a word-processor. David dislikes writing because it is physically difficult but he is enthusiastic about word-processing. It is also necessary to consider the special needs of handicapped children which are additional to those of other children. Word-processing and physiotherapy have already been mentioned; personal hygiene has to be taught, especially to incontinent pupils; independence training is necessary; and children in wheelchairs need to be taught to maintain them. Diabetics, epileptics and asthmatics need to understand their condition and may need help with medication. Most handicapped pupils have spent periods in hospital and need the help of the Supportive Education Department when they return to school. Pupils on restricted timetables need constant monitoring or they find endless excuses to not complete classwork or fail to hand in homework.

Pushing children academically when they already have physical problems may seem unkind but their parents are often only too well aware that the children have to be able to cope in the outside world when they leave school. Life will be easier if they get some qualifications and have the self-discipline to find and keep a job. What seems like cruelty now may prove to be kindness later.

Social Needs of the Child

Socially and emotionally, handicapped pupils need support. Even able-bodied children who have been brought up with handicapped pupils and who are usually helpful and considerate can be thoughtless and hurtful at times. It helps if the handicapped child knows that he or she can retreat to the medical room for a friendly chat with the welfare assistant if it becomes necessary.

However, the real need is for social contact with the peer group. Breaks spent in the disabled toilet, lunch times spent in the library when the others are playing football, and travel to and from school by a lonely taxi do not encourage social integration. If teachers and welfare assistants are aware of the problems, they can be minimized. A warm place like the library is needed at lunch time but why not allow three or four friends in there with the disabled child? Toileting need not take all of breaktime and it may be possible to reorganize taxi routes so that two or three children share a taxi. Time spent in a standing frame or lying on a PE mat is less soul-destroying if there are two children to talk to one another even if they are of different ages.

Often children do not verbalize their needs and adapt to situations in the easiest way. One boy in a Further Education Centre had a lecture on the top floor of the building immediately before lunch. He was unable to get downstairs fast enough to join his friends in the canteen so he started to bring his own sandwiches. When the others went off at lunch time, he did not go with them and so, gradually, he became isolated from his friends and eventually dropped out of his course. Somehow, we need to organize lunch times so that handicapped children can mix socially even if they fail to attend all the extra sessions that specialists arrange for them. Success is watching Nicholas chase the girls in his electric wheelchair!

Coordination with Other Agencies

Inevitably, coordination involves numerous telephone calls and letters and a great deal of frustration. It is worthwhile if it means that the children are happy because they have the facilities that they need. Sometimes, there are amusing situations. Attempting to demonstrate to an LEA representative that a pupil in a wheelchair could not transfer from the wheelchair to the toilet led to a great deal of hilarity. The problem was solved by the caretaker who suggested that, if his cupboard were added to the toilet area and the cupboard contents put elsewhere, there would be room to put the wheelchair beside the toilet.

Each term a report is required by the area office to determine whether we still need our welfare assistant hours. It is a necessary but time-wasting chore since the needs of the children rarely change. Recent legislation means that the governors need an annual report on pupils with special needs. At irregular intervals, the community paediatrician and educational psychologist ask for reports. It never seems to be possible to use the same report for all of them.

The community physiotherapist, occupational therapist and educational welfare officer are all very helpful and we have established a friendly relationship with the lady on the phone at area office who helps with unusual problems.

Coordination with Parents

Ellie's mother came into school about once each week and had a chat and a cup of tea with the welfare assistants. She knew what was happening in school and kept the school informed as to progress at home. The system worked very well. For example, Martyn's mother knows where his spare clothes are kept and comes in, checks the cupboard, replenishes stocks and leaves without feeling she is bothering anyone. Nicholas' mother is so worried that she might be a nuisance that she avoids coming to school, with the result that Nicholas tells us one story and tells her a different version. Chaos results! One strategy that has helped has been a contract which stated that Nicholas had agreed to go in his standing-frame at certain times until a given date. It was made to look very formal, was signed by Nicholas, his mother and the welfare assistant, and copies were given to the physiotherapist and deputy head. The idea seems to have worked.

A student who had epilepsy was determined to do a nursery nursing course at the local Further Education Centre. She was advised by the school's careers staff that she ought to think of something else but she did not tell her mother. She had an interview with a careers officer who told her mother that the FE Centre would not accept her. The student and her mother were upset. Better coordination would have helped but it is very difficult if the pupil cannot or will not accept advice.

Information and Support for Teachers

Evidence suggests that the amount and quality of the information that teachers have had about handicapped children is only one factor in producing a favourable attitude among class teachers. Equally important is experience of having handicapped children in the classroom. Provision of help from a welfare assistant will make teachers feel more favourable to the presence of a handicapped child in the class and more confident of their ability to cope. Subject teachers are more likely to have positive attitudes towards a handicapped pupil if they can make a contribution towards his or her educational development. Warnock (DES, 1978) emphasized that: 'Staffing ratios... were considered to be the most important factor contributing to successful integration'.

PE teachers need detailed information concerning the handicaps of children together with their educational implications. Some doctors have suggested that, because epilepsy still carries a social stigma, parents should not tell schools when a child is diagnosed as having mild epilepsy. Most teachers and nearly all PE teachers are outraged at such a suggestion and consider it to be a criticism of their professionalism. In this school, the PE department, the Supportive Education Department and tutor usually want to be informed of everything that is known about the child and his or her problems. Other subject teachers are content to learn whatever might affect them and their lessons. As long as all teachers know that they can have access to as much information as they want, we are able to avoid the 'Nobody-ever-tells-me-anything' syndrome. As a result, the children have been successfully integrated. Some teachers who were apprehensive at first have found a new interest in providing for the handicapped children and have become very proud of their achievements.

Epilepsy remains as the condition that is feared. Many teachers still do not realize that it is almost always controlled by modern drugs; the teachers still have fears about safety and not knowing what to do if a child has a fit. Gradually, our teachers have come to realize that Michelle is the only one of our six epileptics who is ever ill in school and she can be taken to the medical room in the early stages of her attack. The knowledge that a welfare assistant can be fetched to the classroom and will remain in class with a child if this is necessary alleviates many teachers' fears concerning disabled pupils.

It has been noticeable that, in the last two years, new teachers who arrived in the school have been less afraid of having handicapped children in class. Integration is becoming more usual and comments from teachers such as 'It's alright. We had children like that in my last school' are much more common.

Fire, or a fire practice, creates a problem. Lifts must not be used so handicapped pupils must be carried downstairs. Our children are all fairly light in weight and, so far, we have always managed. No one has the solution to this problem but certainly it should not be used as an excuse for excluding handicapped pupils from mainstream schools.

Attitude of Other Pupils

Children who have grown up with handicapped children in their class accept the situation naturally and expect equal opportunities to be available. Handicapped children who have attended mainstream schools for many years do not expect to be treated differently. They have to be persuaded that, at times, they must be treated differently so that they can be taught all the extra things that they need to know.

Able-bodied pupils who come here from schools which have no handicapped pupils find it strange at first and may make a few thoughtless comments but they soon realize that such behaviour is not acceptable. Handicapped pupils who arrive from special schools try exceptionally hard to be the same as everyone else.

Nicholas has been with four members of his class since they were all 4 years old and he was able to run and play with them. As he has become more disabled, the others have become more supportive. They are aware of the deterioration but have never openly asked questions at school. We have often discussed whether there should be some open discussion with Nicholas' tutor group but the general consensus is that we should not initiate the discussion. When the children, who are now 12 years old, ask for information openly they are more likely to be ready to accept the truth.

Sometime in the future we may have to discuss death with a disabled pupil's class and, perhaps, with a disabled pupil. Other children have died who attended school, but their deaths have been accidental and, after the initial shock, a period of talking has resulted in acceptance. The expertise of the special schools will be helpful and we shall certainly be asking them for advice.

Sex Education

Pupils who have little or no feeling below the waist are unlikely to know what their sexual response might be. They need considerable counselling in the whole area of adult relationships before and after any lessons which might be provided for the peer group. Coordination with parents and teachers is necessary but another adult may be the best choice as counsellor. One of our welfare assistants is a qualified nurse and is happy to take on this role.

External Examinations

Examination boards like to be contacted around October concerning any pupil who has special needs that may affect examination performance. Provided that the school clearly states the problem and a possible solution and sends a medical certificate, the examination boards seem to be prepared to agree to any reasonable request. Last year, in this school, we were allowed to add an extra ten minutes to the times allocated for GCSE exams for several pupils, large print papers were provided for a partially-sighted pupil, an exemption from a music examination was allowed for a partially-hearing pupil, the script of a French tape was provided so that a teacher could read it for a pupil to lip-read, a boy was allowed to dictate his papers, and handicaps were taken into account when papers were marked.

Careers and Career Education

Many pupils with minor ailments such as colour blindness have to learn to accept that some career paths are not open to them. It seems that working with children and anything involving driving are among the occupations which are not open to epileptics. If the handicapped children are treated in much the same way as other pupils but given a little extra help and counselling, there should not be too much of a problem.

We have a sixth form and students can, therefore, stay here until they are 18 years old. Only one handicapped pupil has left school so far. She left after GCSE and went to a residential college where she is happily continuing her education while being given intensive training in independence. The college congratulated her and the school because she was much more independent and socially confident when she arrived at the college than other students who had come from special schools.

The Burden on the Handicapped Children

Ordinary children in mainstream schools sometimes suffer from stress-induced illness. Our physically handicapped pupils, who have a full curriculum including homework, have physical problems of varying intensity which make them tire easily. In addition, we expect them to do physiotherapy, learn to use word-processors and look after wheelchairs. In between they must fit in periods in hospital and then catch up the work they have missed; and, more regularly, they may have to catch up on the first few minutes of some of their lessons, which they may have missed because of mobility and toiletting problems.

Sometimes, we need to sit back and remember that no child can cope with this amount of pressure indefinitely. Then we need to do something about it. All these activities are necessary but the child also needs an opportunity to rest, to think and to take part in the normal social activities which are the right of every child.

References

ILEA (1985) *Educational Opportunities for All?* (Fish Report), London, Inner London Education Authority.

LYNES, W. (1986) *Integrating the Handicapped into Ordinary Schools*, Croom Helm.

MALE, J. and THOMPSON, C. (1985) *The Educational Implications of Disability*, Royal Society for Disability and Rehabilitation.

DEPARTMENT OF EDUCATION AND SCIENCE (1978) *Special Educational Needs* (Warnock Report), HMSO.

A variety of fact sheets published by the Centre for Studies on Integration in Education (for Spastics Society) (1986/87).

*David is the subject of a book for children by Brenda Pettenuzzo called 'I have Spina Bifida', Watts (1987).

9
Negotiating Science with Disaffected Pupils

Mollie McPherson

Practising teachers will recognize the sinking feeling in the pit of the stomach when next year's timetable reveals that they have drawn the 'short straw' — the disaffected, undisciplined, uninterested, non-examination group. They are those who remain after options have been made, and class lists drawn up: the residue left behind who are lumped together to do courses with ubiquitous names such as the 'interest science group'. A rough translation for the 'interest group' is — those who have no interest or desire for learning about a subject. One's reaction to such a group will vary depending on the ethos of the school and its catchment area.

The year I received the 'interest science group' I was teaching at a school with a fine academic record, traditional teaching methods, firm but caring discipline and a supportive staff. The pupils came from a varied background and this pattern was evident in the 'interest group'. The school would call them the well off but wayward, the socially disadvantaged low ability, as well as the quiet well behaved but disinterested pupil. This mixture of pupils was alloted a slot on the timetable to do 'interest science' last thing on Friday afternoon. A daunting prospect! However, life is nothing if not a challenge and having been served a 'bitter pill' it simply remained to analyze the needs and meet them to the best of my ability. The situation amounted to teaching twelve disaffected pupils for seventy minutes every Friday afternoon.

These pupils were very varied, at least two actually took physics as an examination subject but couldn't or wouldn't choose another area of study for this option grouping. These two boys were therefore more able and more interested in the subject and in many ways set the learning tone for the group. However, both pupils had behavioural problems one having been expelled from kindergarten for aggression! Several of the group had passed most of their school years in a 'remedial' class and showed signs of social as well as academic problems. They were generally from disadvantaged homes, some were being helped by the educational psychologist. The kinds of behaviour they exhibited were attention seeking and aggression towards one another. One fairly bright boy had chronic anti-social tendencies coming to us after expulsion from another school and a period of time in a Remand Centre. Many had home problems such as coming from one parent families and one child had to cope with the knowledge that his grandfather murdered his grandmother. This no doubt is the typical mix of an 'interest group'. Its one odd feature was the fact that it contained only one girl who suffered socially from the presence of eleven boys because of their attitude towards her.

What Was to be Done with this Mixed Group?

Several things militated against a traditionally taught course:

1 this was a mixed ability group — therefore the setting of task with graduated demands would be a problem;
2 the pupils had varied experience because of previous streaming;
3 the nature of the group meant they were NOT interested in the work;
4 Friday afternoon was a poor time to motivate the disaffected;
5 the brutal approach that would be required to keep order and sanity by traditional teaching was distasteful.

On the positive side of the situation, I realized that I had good laboratory facilities and a free hand with equipment as this was the only science lesson timetabled for the period. Furthermore the head of department was perfectly happy for me to do any course I felt fit with a non-examination group. Thus, I was able to do what I thought was suitable and had access to whatever apparatus I needed.

My experience of counselling and teaching personal and social development had taught me that giving pupils responsibility for themselves and what they did was highly motivating for them. Consequently if I could hand the running of this lesson to the pupils and become a 'facilitator' perhaps I could solve some of my problems. For example:

1 If the pupils were choosing what they wished to do there was a commitment to the work. Since this lesson was a non-examination class I could risk allowing them a completely free choice, and then help them to achieve their aim.
2 Choice and small-group work would overcome the mixed ability problem of the class since each pupil could decide what they were interested in doing and work to his own level in that area.
3 If pupils were doing what they wanted rather than what I wanted the coercion and discipline problem would no longer exist.

How does one go about setting up such a utopian situation? Short answer — 'with difficulty'. More to the point — How does one provide the pupils with the skills which allow them to take responsibility for themselves and the lesson, as well as facilitate the achievement of the goals set by the pupils? The answer to these two questions is subjective. It will depend on the pupils and their reactions, the teacher and her/his sensitivity and skill, the school and its tolerance. The processes used with these pupils was a mixture of activities to help them cope with the social and personal demands of the lesson and facilities to help them solve the science problems they had set themselves.

Beginnings

At the start of term the pupils expected to come to the laboratory and be told what they would do and when they would do it. These expectations needed to be broken down if the work was to proceed. Consequently on the first encounter we sat in a circle and did an activity to relax the group. We then started to explore what the pupils felt was good and bad about science lessons. This was done anonymously by completing the sentences:

> What I like about science is . . .
> What I dislike about science is . . .

and placing them in a hat. Each child retrieved someone else's note and read it out and commented. This made it possible for ideas and suggestions to be forthcoming that would otherwise have remained unsaid (for replies see Appendix). Since this was a disaffected group the comments were extreme and I needed to be able to accept them and ask the group how they felt about them. Thus the responsibility for the 'tone' of the lesson rested on the group, who generally would not endorse the more extreme comments. In this way we stepped from the traditional science lesson and began to assess it in terms of what the pupil thought was good and bad and the reason why. The class were then assured that they would not have to do the things they disliked and we would concentrate on what they did like. There was shock and disbelief on their faces when they first heard this and they waited for proof.

Choosing our Work

Having established a somewhat more relaxed, accepting and questioning atmosphere within the group it was possible to ask what they would like to do in the lesson (bearing in mind that it was a science lesson) and what they would not like to do. The 'Brainstorming' activity that followed was a work of fiction.

The pupils were testing me. 'Will she really write down all the things we suggested we would like to do'. The answer was 'YES' regardless of the unacceptability of any comment, because the group had themselves to take responsibility for what they had said. Once all the suggestions were recorded the group was asked. 'Which of these ideas could be used, given the resources we have and remembering that this is a science lesson?'. Every contribution was valued. Pupils soon rejected the inappropriate and usually accompanied the rejection with a terse comment to whoever had made an outrageous suggestion. On this occasion, the final list included:

a	Projects	g	Eating sweets
b	Films	h	Dissection
c	Party	i	Birds
d	Outing	j	Games

e Experiments   k Electronics
f Computer   l Drinks

The list was not very inspiring but reflected four things

1 The level of ability of the group
2 The lack of experience in guiding their own learning
3 Level of interest in science
   e.g., a), f), h), i), k)
4 A testing process — ('How far can we go before teacher says "no"?')
   e.g., b), c), d), g), j)

The pupils' lack of experience and knowledge about science meant that under the heading of Projects and Experiments, I needed to feed in ideas that might interest them. A teacher would need a considerable awareness of the suitable material available in a school at this point in order to fulfil the facilitating role. Introduction was made to such schemes as 'Science at Work' — where the pupils could work at their own pace in an area that interested them.

The request to eat during class seemed quite reasonable since it would harm no-one. However the request for drinks was soon dropped when the class established that organizing and clearing up would be their responsbility. They were most realistic when they realized how much of the running of events was being given to them.

Films, games and outings were also acceptable and needed to have a scientific aim.

Having established what was going to happen, pupils then chose what they would do. The computer was a popular option and since we had only one machine a rota was necessary. This job was given to a less able, social outcast. It gave him status and with guidance he coped well. Two pupils decided to do electronics but this too became very popular when the others saw what fun it was making buzzers work and lamps light. Two pupils wanted to order films, and having consulted the catalogues and discussed the situation with the group, the range of free films was decided upon. They ordered a series of films on motor cars which everyone wanted to see. Thus for four weeks, part of the lesson was set aside for a film. The pupils who ordered the films organized the dates and also produced a project on cars which seemed a highly commendable outcome from an initial request for films.

Dissection proved to be a problem. My expertise was limited to dissection of fish and that I found distateful. The Biology Department had ethical objections to just doing dissections not linked to a course and consequently the individual concerned had to rethink his work. The reasons for this pupil's choice were uncertain. However, when I subsequently heard of the nature of the murder committed by the child's grandfather the request seemed to have macabre overtones.

The 'Games' request was in fact referring to activities to help develop social and personal skills and it was decided that I as teacher should prepare these. It was then an enjoyable activity that everyone could participate in. I was grateful for this opportunity because it made it possible to tailor the activity to provide the skills which I perceived were necessary to help pupils cope with this style of lesson.

It was during these sessions that I attempted rather unsuccessfully to integrate the one girl into the group. She was a fairly quiet but puposeful individual whom the boys set up as a sex object. She became the butt for many sexist remarks. Despite all efforts to value individuals for what they contributed rather than what they requested. I was unable to get the group to accept the girl as an individual. It remained eleven boys and one girl and I wondered if perhaps the girl was party to the conspiracy — preferring that distinction. She may well have enjoyed the attention although towards the end of the year she was the one person whose attendance became irregular.

Those pupils who did not like writing and experiments were the most disaffected — they tended to opt to do something and then wonder aimlessly about achieving little apart from when they spent time on the computer. However, occasionally such pupils did find something riveting e.g., an electronic balance was left out from a previous lesson. One pupil showed interest in this and consequently was shown (a) how it worked, (b) the two scale ranges, and (c) how to read the vernier scale. This pupil became so engrossed, weighing everything he could find that he did not want to leave at the end of FRIDAY afternoon! This enthusiasm encouraged an equally disaffected pupil to join in. This small success must be treasured because such incidents happen rarely with the truly disaffected.

The computer was so popular that it became a source of controversy. Who would use the machine when the scheduled person was absent? Who would help those who had a problem? Such arguments were put to the group, who seemed so personally involved as individuals that eventually the teacher had to be arbiter. Fortunately this was the only occasion which warranted such action. Generally the group administered its own discipline.

The Visit

Settling upon a venue for outings proved to be a long decision-making process. It was the subject of weekly interest and many of the members had ideas which the group rejected on the grounds of cost or distance. Finally an afternoon visit to the Science Museum was agreed. I was delegated to organize the mini-bus and negotiate extra time from other teachers. The latter was easily done. No-one was eager to teach this group. The group also produced a check list of things required:

1 Mac	5 Sensible walking-shoes
2 Money	6 Pencil and Paper
3 Can of drink	7 Bag
4 Sandwiches	

Item 6 is interesting because although 'report backs' were to be spoken not written the group recognized the need for some notes to help the organization of thoughts.

Sandwiches and drinks were to be consumed en route as we went during lunch in order to get a longer stay at the Museum. The pupils were excited by this picnic idea and reacted to the whole event as if it were a treat.

It was with some misgivings that I set off with a minibus full of pupils to the museum. We had discussed how to behave — what we would expect to see — how we would report back on the event. Not unnaturally the verbal report back received everyones support. There were three reactions I observed in the museum:

1 Enthusiasm, followed by long careful study of certain areas in the museum.
2 Enthusiasm, followed by hurried, short investigation of every area.
3 Little interest and general boredom.

The first reaction was a delight to watch — certain boys had considerable interest and knowledge about specific things. One of the least able but hard-working boys was thrilled to explain all about an exhibit of bullets, showing almost encyclopaedic knowledge of the age, use and type.

The second group enjoyed their visit but found the report back a problem because of the speed with which they had taken in a mass of exhibits. However, anything that they could make work themselves, attracted and held the attention of these pupils and they were enthusiastic to demonstrate to their 'mates' how apparatus worked.

The latter group styled by the school as 'no hopers' were a sad bunch. They were the two who had failed throughout school life and now seemed to have little self-respect because they were resigned to failure. Nothing seemed to motivate or make them enthusiastic. They took a cursory glance at the museum — they were happpier drinking squash but didn't mind being shown by others how to press buttons to make things work. Perhaps they did gain something.

It was the following week before pupils could sit down and discuss what had gone on at the museum and individually report back what they had discovered. Each pupil's report was then graded by the group (a procedure which will be fully explained later). One less able boy, usually the butt for everyone's humour, was highly commended for his report by the group, which gave him a great boost and increased his standing considerably. Two people who always had problems organizing themselves (though they were not without ability) were told quite categorically by a remedial member that they had not got enough out of the visit and had produced a poor report. This met with the approval of the rest of the group and had a devastating effect on the culprits — one assumes that they will be unwilling for such peer comments to be levelled at them again. The boys who had been classed as 'no hopers' gave reports which just managed to avoid the displeasure of the group and so presumably were satisfied with themselves.

The general feeling of the pupils was that they had enjoyed themselves, wanted to go out again and were aware that this was one of the few outings they had had because of who they were.

Assessment

It became clear that if pupils were working on projects and topics of their own choice and no two people would necessarily cover the same ground, assessment was going to be difficult and an examination irrelevant. However, all 'interest subjects' in this particular school could be awarded 'Leaving Certificates' and thus it was vital to have some way of meaningfully assessing the course.

The only logical way to do this was to give the pupils responsibility themselves. If they had been responsible for deciding what they would do, then they should be allowed to judge how well they had done it. This was organized on a weekly basis. Firstly we sat as a group and decided what aspects of work were important and then we agreed to score everyone each week, on each aspect, using a 10 point scale. Each child had a grid as shown below which acted as a termly record of achievement that could be submitted to the head of upper school as proof of worth for a final leaving certificate.

NAME						
WEEK	1	2	3	4	5	6
ATTENDANCE						
STANDARD OF WORK						
ATTITUDE						
ABILITY TO COMPREHEND AND CARRY OUT WORK						
EFFORT						
VOLUME OF WORK						
CONTENT						

In order to complete this record, work was brought to a suitable finishing point ten minutes before the lesson ended. Since we were a small group everyone individually presented his work to the group and we then gave a grade on each criterion. Having gone through the process on one week the subsequent occasions took little time and pupils quickly and fairly graded their colleagues. Peer group pressure had been built up and pupils accepted without argument a poor grade when it was realistic. However, if I felt too harsh a mark had been given as a group member, I would point out where I saw improvement or effort and was aware that I could sway the whole group. I tried to avoid this but when necessary I did contribute. I did not abdicate my responsibility as final arbiter, though this was tempting.

Enabling Exercises

Central to all of this work were the personal and social skills pupils needed to carry it out. The school did not do P.S.E. on the timetable and to start developmental group work with 15-year-olds who were used to silent classrooms with little movement was a risk. However, I planned to build the social skills into the lessons as and when required.

The first thing that had to be learned was that if something interesting was going to happen 'you' had to be quiet so that 'teacher' could begin. This was achieved by waiting for some time in a relaxed manner until quiet was obtained and declaring 'I am playing "the waiting game" now we can start'. Since the lessons were enjoyed and the pupils wanted to start, a mention of 'the waiting game' brought quiet, thus the tone was set — teacher did not shout, pupils cooperated because they wanted to.

It must not be imagined from the above statement that all was then simple and without problems. Pupils could decide an activity was 'not for them' and cause problems for others who wished to participate. This difficulty was neatly overcome by doing an activity called 'I could sabotage this game if I... '(*Gamesters Handbook*, Brandes, D.). The outcome of the activity was that the pupils were confronted by the ways they said they could ruin a lesson. To my surprise the memory of this game remained with the class all year. One pupil could be heard accusing another — 'you're sabotaging this' and the accused generally refrained from his activity and let the main lesson continue. He realized that the group had recognized his intent.

If disputes arose during the lesson it was policy to call the class together, discuss it and let the peer group be the arbiter. In order to help pupils to be articulate and clearly make their point in such discussions other P.S.E. games were played. Other exercises were carried out to help with cooperation, concentration, observation, self-image and confidence.

Clearly the pupils ended pieces of work at different times and I had to make sure that they could then be moved on to something else which would fill the end of a lesson, to avoid proving the truth of the saying 'the devil makes work for idle hands'. Some pupils, for example, were set problem-solving activities (like egg-race problems). These were done in pairs and judged by the group. They were popular and more were requested. Consequently at appropriate points in the term such activities were undertaken together with tasks such as: 'What would you place in a time capsule to let people thousands of years hence know what science and technology are like now?'

Other extra activities included end of term parties — planned, organized and enjoyed by the group.

Observations

Central to this style of work is 'teacher as facilitator' and pupils taking responsibility for their own learning. In order to achieve this the pupil has to be valued. It is essential that they have sufficient confidence and self-respect to make decisions and judgments using suitable criteria. They must be able to organize themselves, to set goals and have appropriate strategies for achieving them.

These specifications are difficult to achieve with pupils who are used to didactic teaching. It has already been explained how the first steps were made to change the ground rules in the classroom. Pupils said what they liked to do and were listened to. It was essential that the pupils' wishes were given due regard. Having stated what they liked and disliked, it was necessary to make sure that the likes received maximum attention and the dislikes minimum attention. In this way trust built up between teacher and pupil. This trust and respect were very important in the work. Pupils had to develop trust and respect for each other and for the teacher in order to negotiate the events which were to be carried out. The pupils therefore arrived at the lessons with expectations about the content and the teacher. I suspect that the pupils saw me as a person who demanded a high standard of work and expected no nonsense from pupils (similar to most of the other staff in the school). It was from this base that I had to develop trust. The keys to being trusted seemed to be:

1 listening as well as hearing;
2 maintaining confidentiality when needed;
3 adopting behaviour consistent with the rules established by the group at the outset.

Thus, if a class is told it can choose, pupils must believe that their choices have been met and that the teacher has fulfilled, as far as she is able, her part of the bargain. Choice however cannot be unlimited, and the parameters on this class were:

1 suitability to a science lesson;
2 availability of material;
3 constraints of school ethos.

Having been able to comply with pupils demands in a way that they accepted as fair and reasonable we began on the road to self-directed learning.

Listening skill activities were incorporated into lessons as well as self-image exercises to enable pupils to be better at helping each other. Clearly it was important to listen carefully in order to negotiate, be it over the work to be done, the assessment of that work, or the setting of group standards. Furthermore the closer the group became in terms of understanding what they and others were like, the more sympathetic their behaviour was likely to be. Knowledge of self sets both limitations and targets for the individual, and knowledge of others gives greater understanding tolerance and power in a given situation. Thus when assessment of work was carried out pupils were aware of one another's faults and clearly took this into consideration when scoring. However, this was not always the case and pupils did take the opportunity to use deeper understanding of others in a malicious way. This had to be dealt with firmly. For example, a very cutting statement with sexual overtones was made about the only girl in the group. It was done to hurt the individual and shock me. I asked the girl if she minded and we discussed the statement. She did not, so in as relaxed a manner as possible we, as a group, explored the statement.

Why had it been said?
Was it appropriate?
How did the girl feel about it?
What did the group think about the supplier of the statement?

How would they have felt?

What was to be done?

This left the girl with a clearer picture of what the statement was really about. The group supported her and the statement was seen in its true light — a malicious attempt to embarrass the girl. The boy who supplied the statement felt duly chastened by peers — a very powerful tool, and the girl was left in no doubt about the integrity of the group.

On another occasion one boy was challenged and told in very crude terms he was useless and no-one liked him. This incident was handled in a similar manner to the previous one. The statement was explored and the feelings of all the group were taken into consideration. The outcome was that the boy realized many of his limitations and the exasperating effect he had on others, but also received massive support from group members who labelled him 'a good mate'.

These crises had to be dealt with by the group because they were responsible for what happened in the lesson. Consequently the outcome was always unpredictable but in my experience members were honest and caring. I never felt after such incidents that a pupil had been left unsupported by some members of the group, and it was never necessary to intervene or privately counsel a pupil who had been hurt by the group pressures.

The pupils had to organize themselves to a large extent, deciding what they would do and how they would do it. They shared experiences so that a pupil finishing one activity would ask to move on to something that someone else had done because he had been told it was interesting. It was possible to engineer situations that would help individuals gain status, or face realities through the organization of the lesson. Thus the less able could successfully do an important but simple job like organizing a rota for the computer. The activity was simple, but it also had power since the person concerned was responsible for choosing the order in which pupils had a turn on the computer. The boy earned respect from the group and self-satisfaction. His self-image was undoubtedly more positive and he seemed more self-assured when making a point in group discussions. Furthermore his contributions were more favourably accepted.

A situation also arose where one of the most 'macho' of the pupils felt sufficiently secure and supported to share his feelings of loss whilst in a Remand Home. At the end of one lesson, the discussion had been about how it felt to be away from home for a long period. After contributions from several pupils, some expressing pleasure and some loss, this individual said he had missed his parents, especially his mother, whilst in custody — because his mother cared about him. The statement was met with silence. Presumably the group were surprised that such a 'hard man' could express such feelings. He had in some ways lost face with the group but in others gained it. There were those who would have liked to say that their mothers 'cared' but they clearly did not dare to. The revaluation had a calming effect on the boy: he seemed less obstructive and aggressive for a while. Perhaps the exploration of feelings had a temporary civilizing effect upon him.

The request to watch films was an obvious ploy to see how true to my word I would be. It seemed that for trust to develop we had to watch films. Fortunately the proviso of science films to fit with the objectives of a science lesson were accepted as reasonable. The pupils wanting films were not very amenable to participating in science lessons. They had hoped for a 'drop out clause'. However many organizing skills were developed:

1 negotiating with the group over titles;
2 deciding upon the sequence;
3 setting the dates;
4 filling in forms,

Having become involved with the subject area, they were quite enthusiastic about extending the film viewing into a project. Thus social learning went hand in hand with conventional school learning thanks to the supportive attitude of other pupils and the teacher.

The course was not without conflict. When the rota system for the computer broke down because the designated people were absent, the status of the producer of the rota was not sufficient for him to instigate a rearrangement: tempers were lost and order was only restored after some effort. Everyone felt aggrieved and the organizer of the rota sulked for the lesson because he did not get his own way. (His status was much lowered for such childish behaviour.) The group finally decided upon a compromise for use of the computer but everyone left a little bruised. There were no winners. Fortunately, this happened only once. The group managed to avoid the situation on future occasions, being more flexible over the arrangements. Thus a lot of learning about cooperation had been done, but in a rather painful way for the individuals.

Assessment of work was one of the most successful parts of the activity. It was taken seriously by all members and, since comments were constructive and fair, pupils accepted what was said by their peers and often tried very hard to improve their attainment level. It was also a device to ensure that enough work was done to the best possible standard and made sure of the total involvement of the pupils. This class also negotiated what was written on their reports at the end of the year. It seemed entirely appropriate that they should be involved in the whole of the assessment process.

Clearly the pupils assessed the lessons 'with their feet'. They attend on FRIDAY AFTERNOON!

Personal Standpoint

It seems to me that the course has been a worthwhile experience for the pupils. They learned science which interested them and developed social interactive skills which they previously did not appear to have. I hope that these skills will be used in other areas of their lives. Unfortunately they are not provided with the right environment for this in many normal school lessons. Nevertheless I feel that given the right circumstances, the pupils will use these social skills. Certainly other staff commented that the pupils were better at expressing themselves in discussions, but expected to be listened to and demanded certain levels of respect. This sort of child can seem very threatening if you are not used to 'teaching through the counselling mode'. However they do make more thinking, caring and responsible citizens. They will be the ones who ask the questions, solve the problems and are sensitive to feelings. They will be the individuals who respect those who respect and help them. It makes the pastoral role of the teacher reach right into the lesson. The pupils's need is central — not the subject.

The knowledge curve is exponential — we cannot hope to know everything. Thus, subject matter must take second place to process. The process of learning is closely linked with what an individual is like, how socially skilled he is and how well he can work in a group to solve a problem. This involves all the social skills of listening, interacting and negotiating. Gone are the days when people work quietly alone learning great truths. Most progress is made by teams pooling facts, sparking off ideas and cooperating over skills. It would be unrealistic if schools did not function in the same way. Self-direction and monitoring will be lasting because pupils 'own the learning'. It is meaningful and not imposed.

Appendix

Don't Like:

Writing	2 Votes
Tests	5 Votes
Teachers talking	2 Votes
Homework	5 Votes
Work that is too hard	6 Votes
Experiments	1 Vote

Do Like:

Computer	4 Votes
Experiments	5 Votes
Talking	2 Votes
Films	4 Votes
TV	5 Votes

10
Hearing Impaired Students: A Student-Teacher-Class Partnership

Susan Foster and Thomas Holcomb

Introduction

Picture yourself as a teacher entering the classroom on the first day of school. Now expand this picture and find a hearing-impaired student in your class and an interpreter sitting next to you translating everything you say into sign language. How comfortable would you be? What are your thoughts and concerns? What questions would you want answered about the needs of hearing-impaired students or the role of the interpreter? Who is responsible for making this class fully integrated, you or the hearing-impaired student? Would you be able to include all your students in the learning experience, hearing and hearing-impaired alike?

Now, put yourself in the place of the hearing-impaired student. You want to fulfil all the criteria established by the teacher for success, including participation in class discussions, presentations to the class and group work. How do you feel? What are your concerns? What would you want your teacher, interpreter and classmates to know in order to make the experience positive for all? Is it your responsibility to approach your teacher? Is he or she approachable?

The authors had the opportunity to experience this kind of situation first-hand. Mr Holcomb, who is hearing-impaired, was a student in Professor Foster's graduate class at a local university. By openly discussing our feelings and concerns about the class, we were able to learn from each other as well as from our successes and mistakes. Our purpose in writing this paper is to describe what happened to us, and the ways in which our discussions shaped our thinking and actions regarding integration of hearing-impaired students in a class of hearing peers. This is not a research paper, nor is it a comprehensive review of the literature on integration. Rather, it is a story based on personal experience.

The paper is divided into two parts. In the first we provide background information on educational models for hearing-impaired students as a way of setting a context for our experience. This involves a description of recent trends for educating hearing-impaired students in the United States, including the current emphasis on moving students from separate to integrated environments. Additionally, three levels of integration are explored, including institutional, individual and group. This section is concluded with a discussion of the terms 'accessibility' and 'accommodation' and their potential interpretations as they relate to the integration of hearing-impaired students within educational settings. The second part of the paper begins with a presentation of our thoughts and concerns as teacher and student as we prepared for the graduate class. Using our experience as a starting point, central issues in classroom integration are described and suggestions offered for making the integrated class a successful experience for everyone.

Setting a Context for Our Experience

Integrating hearing and hearing-impaired students within educational settings is a complex and challenging task. Our experience within one class setting is only a small piece of the total picture. In this section, background information is presented in an effort to describe the larger picture and how our experience fits within it.

Educational Models Serving Hearing-impaired Students

Most educational programmes serving hearing-impaired students in the United States today fall into one of three models. The first involves the use of *totally separate programmes*, often referred to as schools for the deaf or centre schools. These institutions may be residential or day programmes, but are usually self-contained and serve only hearing-impaired students. The second kind of educational setting is the *separate programme for hearing-impaired students within regular schools* (that is, schools which serve primarily hearing students). Hearing-impaired students in these programmes go to the same school as their hearing peers, but are usually taught in separate classes for part or all of the day. The third type of educational model is the *totally integrated programme*, in which the hearing-impaired student attends all classes with hearing peers.

While hearing-impaired students have been educated within all three kinds of settings over the years, recent political and philosophical trends in the United States have emphasized integrated over separate settings for all students with disabilities, including those who are hearing-impaired. For example, the passage in 1975 of the Education for All Handicapped Children Act (PL 94–142) has been interpreted to mean that children with disabilities should be educated within the mainstream of the educational system whenever possible. As a result, hearing-impaired students are more likely to attend school with hearing peers today than they were twenty or thirty years ago. The focus of this paper is on the third educational model described above, that is, *totally integrated settings*.

Levels of Integration

Within educational settings, efforts to integrate hearing-impaired students can occur at three levels: institutional, individual and group. At the root of every integrated educational programme is an *institutional* philosophy, which sets the tone for that programme. The institution hosting or providing the programme is responsible for implementing the integrated programme, which includes articulating the services to be provided, hiring staff and providing support services. Concerns at this level may involve policy development and are usually administrative or fiscal. Depending on how the service is designed, it may be costly to integrate the hearing-impaired student. It is therefore important that financial support for the programme be comprehensive and secure. Often, steps must be taken to involve participants internal to the institution as well as critical external groups (such as parents, local, state and federal agencies, and professional licensing groups), and to consider their perspectives and agendas. In addition, institutional commitment to the stability of the programme, in the form of policy statements and internal funding priorities, can be critical to its success.

On the *individual* level, hearing and hearing-impaired students interact informally. These interactions, which have been referred to by Garreston (1977) as 'the unwritten curriculum', occur during such routine situations as walking down the hall, riding the bus and chatting in the lunchroom. Reasons for such interactions vary — necessity, curiosity, common interest and/or a desire to broaden one's perspectives. Often, these interactions occur as a matter of chance — being at the right place at the right time with the right person. Research suggests that individual interaction may be especially challenging to hearing-impaired students in integrated settings, since involvement is voluntary, sporadic and usually unstructured (Foster, 1988 and 1989). Furthermore, these kinds of informal and incidental interactions are likely to present the greatest communication challenges, and success depends on the resourcefulness and motivation of participants.

Most interaction between hearing-impaired and hearing students within educational settings occurs on a *group* level, for example a classroom, club or athletic/social event; these are the settings in which students are in regular proximity to one another, with a shared goal and leadership in the form of a teacher, club president, coach or other facilitator. The quality of such interactions often depends on the structure of the activity, the attitude of participants and the philosophy and skills of the group leader. Educators who want to facilitate interaction between hearing and hearing-impaired students within group settings need to create an environment in which meaningful interaction between participants is encouraged. All members of the group must be involved in the implementation of such a plan, which should include commitment to and strategies for equal participation. The focus in this paper is on integration at the group level, and within this level, on one kind of group setting — the classroom.

Accessibility and Accommodation: Working Definitions

As a teacher and a hearing-impaired college student who shared a classroom for one semester, we were faced with many of the dilemmas and concerns which teachers and hearing-impaired students face daily in a range of integrated educational settings. Much of what we did was an outgrowth of our interpretations of the concepts of accessibility and accommodation. What is accessibility? How can it be accomplished? What exactly do we mean when we say that the individual should be accommodated within the integrated class?

One way of thinking about accessibility and accommodation is to consider the first a goal and the second a way of implementing or achieving that goal. That is, specific accommodations are made in order to operationalize a particular definition of accessibility. However, there is more than one way to define accessibility and, depending on the definition, the accommodations will be very different. For example, *one definition* is that accessibility means physical access to or presence in the environment, whether that be the school system, building or classroom. According to this definition, accessibility does not necessarily imply or require any specific accommodations (for example, changes in the physical environment, support services such as interpreters or modified teaching strategies); all that is required is that the hearing-impaired student be permitted to attend school with normally hearing peers. Unfortunately, research has shown that placing a hearing-impaired student in a class with hearing peers does *not* insure interaction (Antia, 1982; Gresham, 1986; Mertens and Kluwin, 1986). Hearing-impaired students who are integrated without support services are often completely isolated from the educational process as well as from hearing teachers and classmates.

A second definition is that accessibility involves access to formal classroom instruction in the most traditional sense. Usually, this is taken to mean access to the teacher during explicitly pedagogical interactions such as lectures and advisement, and access to the curriculum and instructional materials. Accommodations *are* required to implement this definition of accessibility; sometimes they are quite basic, for example, seating the hearing-impaired student at the front of the class or having the student review material with the teacher outside of class. More often (at least in the United States) accommodations at this level involve additions to the class environment in the form of specialized services such as interpreters, notetakers and tutors. This second definition of accessibility and accompanying accommodations is perhaps the most prevalent today. In this vein, the most recent issue of the *Guide to Post-Secondary Programs for the Hearing Impaired* (Rawlings, Karchmer and DeCaro, 1988) listed 150 universities and colleges that provide specialized support services for hearing-impaired students in the United States and Canada. Accommodations for hearing-impaired students enrolled in these programmes vary widely and may include one or more of the following: sign language and oral interpreters, counsellors who can communicate in sign language, notetakers, speech therapists, audiologists, tutors, remedial courses in subjects such as English and maths, and teachers who can sign.

One of the most serious limitations of this second definition of accessibility is grounded in the assumptions about classroom learning, and most especially the belief that such learning is limited to the formal curriculum and direct instruction by the teacher. Learning that results from informal conversations among students and teachers is frequently overlooked, as is the opportunity for personal and social growth through student interaction within class.

Another limitation is related to the accommodations generally associated with this definition of accessibility, and the distinction between *provision* and / or *tolerance* of support services and the *full utilization* and *acceptance* of such services. For example, teachers who are unfamiliar with visual learning modes may believe that if an interpreter and notetaker are provided, they need do nothing different; that is, all elements of their pedagogical style, including interactions with students, class management strategies and evaluation procedures can (and in fact should) remain unchanged. The assumption is that the presence of the interpreter and notetaker have made hearing-impaired students equal to their hearing peers and further accommodation unnecessary. However, the services of an interpreter do not necessarily make the hearing-impaired person a full participating member of the group (Foster and Brown, 1989; Saur, Layne, Hurley and Opton, 1986). Teachers who assume that such services are sufficient may misinterpret the behaviour of hearing-impaired students. For example, hearing-impaired students may appear passive or withdrawn in class when in fact they are unable to participate in class discussion because the teacher has failed to consider and correct for the lag time between verbal communication and the completion of the interpreter's translation into sign language. As a result, the teacher who is unaware of the implications of hearing impairment for participation in class discussions may jump to the conclusion that students who do not participate have not completed the assigned reading, are shy, or simply have nothing to offer.

There is yet a *third definition* of accessibility which has received less attention but which is perhaps the most challenging. Within this definition, accessibility is interpreted to mean complete involvement in both formal and informal dynamics of classroom learning, including participation in class discussion, group work and equal access to the range of informal conversations and interactions which routinely occur among students and between students and the teacher in class. The provision of services such as interpreters, notetakers and tutors is necessary but not sufficient to implement this third definition of accessibility. For example, having an interpreter in the classroom is one thing; understanding that there is a lag associated with using an interpreter and changing the rules of class discussion to insure the hearing-impaired student equal opportunity to participate is another. Using written or other visual materials is important, but will not help if the teacher points to the board while speaking, since hearing-impaired students cannot watch the interpreter and the board at the same time. Accommodations at this level involve the use of special classroom management techniques, modifications of instructional materials and enhanced awareness on the part of all class participants about strategies to improve communication for everyone. In short, the teacher and students need to become partners in the creation of an educational setting within which each member has equal opportunities to join in the learning process.

This last definition of accessibility is guided by two assumptions or beliefs about the nature of classroom learning. The first is that learning within the class setting is a dynamic process involving dialogue among students as well as between the student and teacher. The second is that, since all students are valued members of the class, it is to the benefit of the class to insure everyone access to all class activities.

The college experience of Mr Holcomb prior to his enrolment in Professor Foster's class includes examples of both the first and second definitions of accessibility; the university enrols hearing-impaired students and interpreters are provided upon request for all classes. However, these accommodations had proved insufficient for his full involvement in the learning process within class. In order to enable him to be a truly equal and comfortable participant in class, accommodations which go beyond the provision of basic support services were necessary.

Learning from Experience

In this part of the paper we present our thoughts about the creation of integrated educational settings, and how such settings can be established and maintained to the greatest advantage of all participants, hearing and hearing-impaired alike. Although neither of us is new to the professional and / or personal arena of deafness, our experiences in class presented each of us with opportunities for personal and professional growth. For example, Professor Foster has worked for five years as a researcher at Rochester Institute of Technology's National Technical Institute for the Deaf (RIT's NTID) and knows some sign language. However, she had never before had a hearing-impaired student in her graduate class (offered through another local post-secondary institution). As a hearing-impaired student enrolled in a PhD programme, Mr Holcomb has proven academic skills combined with years of experience in a range of classroom settings, but he had never been asked by a teacher to help design and implement a plan for creating a totally accessible class. In order to work together, we were required to think not as experts, but rather as learners who make mistakes and work through difficult situations. Although we would not generalize from our experience to those of all teachers and students in integrated class settings, we feel that some of our experiences may not be unique to us or the college environment. Having said this, what were some of the central questions and issues we faced as we prepared for and then moved through the semester? What did we do? Where did we start?

Professor Foster initiated contact by asking Mr Holcomb if they could meet to discuss communication and other issues related to class participation. Mr Holcomb agreed, and they met. As a result of their discussion at this meeting, Professor Foster drafted a class handout on the topic of communication. Together we reviewed and revised this draft until it was satisfactory to both (see Appendix: Communication Courtesy). However, we discovered that this was only the beginning. We also learned that discussions of accessibility and accommodation are only part of what must take place in order to insure all participants equal involvement in class activity; implementing these ideas is equally important. Through collaboration, we attempted to create an educational environment in which all students were fully integrated. In the following pages, we describe some of the challenges we encountered to integrating hearing-impaired students in class, as well as the steps we took in an effort to make the class accessible for everyone.

We identified eight areas in which hearing-impaired students may experience barriers to full participation; these are barriers associated with:

1 interest and awareness of teachers and hearing-impaired students;
2 willingness of both teachers and hearing-impaired students to adopt new (and frequently nontraditional) roles;
3 confidence of hearing-impaired students;
4 visual obstructions;
5 use of interpreters;
6 instructional style;
7 attitudes and behaviours of hearing classmates; and
8 unspoken rules and expectations.

Our format is to describe the barrier in a general way, then discuss more specifically how we addressed this barrier. General descriptions of barriers appear in ordinary print. Personal accounts of our responses to these barriers appear in italics; the speaker is indicated by beginning a personal account with either **SF** (Susan Foster) or **TH** (Thomas Holcomb).

Barriers Associated with the Interest and Awareness of Teachers and Hearing-impaired Students

While extensive physical accommodations are often required to allow disabled individuals to participate in the academic arena, 'true access' can't be achieved if they are faced with teachers who are unwilling to work with disabled students (Wright, 1980). Research has shown that, because they are considered difficult to teach, hearing-impaired students are sometimes identified by college teachers as the least desirable group with whom to work (Fichten, Amsel, Bourdon and Creti, 1988). This places them at a clear disadvantage to other students with disabilities as well as to hearing peers. Even with extensive and often costly accommodations such as interpreters and notetakers, the quality of experience for integrated hearing-impaired students is not optimal if they are taught by teachers who have little interest in having them in their classroom or are unprepared to incorporate them into class interaction. This problem is compounded by a lack of comfort on the part of both the student and teacher in dealing with deafness in the classroom. Discomfort can lead to a rather typical response of ignoring the problems or minimizing the differences between hearing-impaired learners and their hearing peers.

Inadequate awareness on the part of both teachers and students with disabilities has been cited by many as a key problem (English, 1971; Gresham, 1982; Hirshoren and Burton, 1979; MacDougall, Munhall and Destounis, 1981; Rauth, 1980; Reynolds, 1980). For example, a common approach to disabled students has been to treat them like any other students. This may be a poor solution to such situations. However, the decision that special steps *should* be taken does not insure that such steps *will* be taken, nor is it always clear *who* should take the first step.

Who's responsible? This is a central question which came up in our experience. What are the student's responsibilities? The teacher's? Should students be expected to become experts in environmental engineering simply because they are hearing-impaired? Should teachers be expected to become experts on deafness? These are all sticky issues, not easily resolved and certainly not amenable to a blanket solution which would cover every situation and all students or teachers. Fichten, Amsel, Bourdon and Creti (1988) suggest that both teachers and students with disabilities need to assume responsibility for making the experience work. Instead of minimizing the presence of disabled students in class, teachers should address specific needs of the disabled student by being open about them. Strategies suggested include student initiated behaviours such as establishing dialogue with the teacher before the term begins and sharing their special needs. The teacher must take the initiative if the student seems unwilling or hesitant to initiate contact. Such discussions should assist the teaching / learning process and make the experience more positive and comfortable for both the teacher and student.

SF: *My initial reaction when I learned that Mr Holcomb was taking my course was excitement mixed with concern. I looked forward to the challenge of having a hearing-impaired student in class. My concern stemmed from worries about how communication would occur in class, and some doubt as to whether I would be able to facilitate equal participation by all students. I decided to take action before the term started. As noted earlier, I initiated contact with Mr Holcomb for the purpose of learning more about accommodations which I should make in order to facilitate his participation in my class. However, I recall feeling unsure of whether this move on my part was appropriate, and worried that my actions might seem patronizing. I went ahead because I was more worried about avoiding difficult or counterproductive situations in class than I was about how I might be perceived by Mr Holcomb.*

TH: *I was surprised and pleased when Professor Foster asked to meet with me to discuss strategies for effective communication in class. I was surprised because none of my previous teachers had made any effort to establish this kind of dialogue, even though they were in most cases completely unfamiliar with the needs of hearing-impaired students. I was pleased that Professor Foster did not assume that her research experience in deafness was adequate preparation for managing an* integrated classroom. I welcomed this opportunity to collaborate with her in creating an accessible class environment.

Barriers Associated with the Willingness of Both Teachers and Hearing-impaired Students to Adopt New Roles

One of the most difficult steps we encountered involved the task of assuming new roles. Usually, hearing teachers who have a hearing-impaired student in class for the first time are unaware of what should be done to create a fully accessible class environment. In order to accommodate the hearing-impaired student, the teacher must assume the role of learner; sometimes this involves acknowledging the hearing-impaired student as expert/teacher as well as a willingness to collaborate with and accept correction from the student when necessary.

SF: *I learned most of the strategies I used to make my class more accessible from Mr Holcomb. Sometimes I made mistakes, in which case I learned to accept correction. For example, as mentioned earlier, I assumed the responsibility for drafting the 'Communication Courtesy' handout in which I described how communication could be facilitated in class. However, in my first draft I stated that 'the hearing-impaired student would be using an interpreter to communicate'. Upon reviewing this handout, Mr Holcomb suggested that it would be more accurate to state that* **everyone** *in the class would be using an interpreter to communicate; that is, hearing students would be as dependent on the interpreter as the hearing-impaired student for communication, since the latter used sign language and the former had to rely on the interpreter to translate the signs into voice so they could understand their hearing-impaired classmate. My original statement of who would be using the interpreter was not only incorrect, but also revealed one of my assumptions about deafness, which is that interpreters are used only by hearing-impaired people. While such an assumption might seem irrelevant and harmless, it may have significant ramifications; for example, if it is assumed that the interpreter is there solely for the convenience of the hearing-impaired student, then it is only a short step to the conclusion that the student should take responsibility for hiring, supervising and possibly even paying the interpreter.*

Conversely, the student must be willing to become a teacher and assume the role of expert in providing information to the teacher and classmates about what works and what doesn't. Sometimes this means that the student must be assertive and even aggressive when necessary in pursuing accommodations.

TH: *While I am in total agreement with the notion that hearing-impaired students must be assertive in pursuing accommodations, it is more easily said than done. With my other teachers, I found myself unable to initiate dialogue similar to the one I had with Professor Foster. Instead, I opted for a 'safer' approach in which I waited until the end of the first class before approaching the teacher. Even then, I tended to be conservative with my suggestions out of fear that the teacher would not take them kindly. I suspect that my experience portrays a dilemma faced by many hearing-impaired students. The questions of what approach to take with teachers and how aggressive one needs to be to ensure optimal accommodation need further investigation.*

Barriers Associated with the Confidence of Hearing-impaired Students

The goal of full participation cannot be realized if the hearing-impaired student lacks self-confidence. Often, hearing-impaired students express uncertainty about the appropriateness of their discussion questions or comments in integrated class settings. Previous negative experiences may contribute to their passive behaviour; for example, the student may have been ridiculed for past attempts to participate. The importance of positive and sustaining feedback as a means of enhancing disabled students' confidence in the classroom has been discussed by Larrivee (1985). Lack of positive feedback may be another reason why hearing-impaired students are sometimes hesitant to join in class activities; in this vein, students who have actively participated in class discussions in the past without receiving cues from other students or the teacher may become less confident that their remarks are timely or appropriate.

TH: *I explained to Professor Foster that hearing-impaired students often miss out on the subtle yet critical feedback given by teachers to students. For example, the teacher may say things like 'Hmm' or 'I see' while listening to a student's comment. There are ways of giving similar feedback to hearing-impaired students, and I suggested that such strategies would be very helpful to me. As a result, I received both verbal and sometimes more subtle reinforcement from Professor Foster about the appropriateness of my comments and questions. This was accomplished through various visual means — nodding her head, offering brief feedback statements in sign language such as 'Interesting!' or 'I see', or raising her eyebrows to indicate uncertainty or a need for further clarification. In other instances she would speak with me after class, letting me know that I had raised a valid question during the discussion. I finally was able to enjoy these reinforcements, which were probably taken for granted by my hearing classmates.*

Barriers Associated with Visual Obstructions

Accessibility for hearing-impaired students depends primarily on visual accommodations. Lack of participation is not necessarily a direct result of the hearing-impaired student's communication style, but rather the degree to which the physical environment makes such communication possible.

The first and probably most apparent obstruction involves the physical characteristics of the classroom. For example, reflections behind windows and barriers to direct visual contact with the teacher (such as posts) can make it difficult for hearing-impaired students to follow the teacher. In addition, if students are seated in rows, the hearing-impaired student won't be able to see (identify) every speaker. These kinds of obstructions may cause even more problems for hearing-impaired students who are not using interpreters and instead rely on residual hearing and lipreading to acquire information.

> **SF:** *Since the class was a seminar, it was important that students be able to see each other and me clearly. Based on Mr Holcomb's advice, I selected a well lit room in which the furniture could be arranged in a semicircle. The interpreter was strategically placed next to me, providing all students with a visual line to the teacher, blackboard, screen and interpreter. The window had curtains and blinds which could be adjusted to allow more or less light into the room. Overhead lighting was controlled selectively; that is, part of the overhead lighting could be turned off without plunging the entire room into total darkness.*

Another consideration involves the use of media. While it may be a common practice for teachers to use media and speak simultaneously, it can be difficult for hearing-impaired students to absorb information from the media and the teacher at the same time. For example, a teacher may introduce new material by putting a transparency on the overhead projector and begin speaking. The hearing-impaired student will need to deal with several different things; reading the information on the overhead, writing down notes from the transparency, lipreading the teacher or watching the interpreter and making notes of the teacher's comments. Trying to do all these tasks simultaneously is a frustrating experience. Similarly, showing an uncaptioned film in a dark room makes the interpreter useless. To further complicate an already difficult situation, the teacher may interject a comment here and there to emphasize the highlights of the film. The student is 'left in the dark', not only with respect to the contents of the film but also the cues given by the teacher about important aspects of the film which might eventually be covered on the examination.

> **SF:** *I used several strategies regarding the use of media. First, I handed out copies of material which I intended to put on the overhead. This enabled students to spend more time concentrating on what I was saying, and less time trying to copy the overhead. Second, I waited a few minutes after putting up an overhead to give students time to read it before beginning my elaboration. Third, I paused between comments in order to give students time to write notes; sometimes this required vigilance on my part, watching students to see if they were*

finished and had looked up before I continued. I planned to use a videotape, film and slide show for the class. While the film was available in captioned format, the other materials were not. For those not captioned, I took advantage of the partial lighting feature of this room, which permitted the dimming of lights at the back of the room while leaving enough light at the front for Mr Holcomb to see the interpreter. Additionally, I made the videotape and slide show available to Mr Holcomb and the interpreter outside of class so they could review them at their leisure.

TH: *The groundrules which Professor Foster and I established enabled me to actively participate in discussions about the information presented. This is in contrast to experiences in other classes where I was limited to trying to unscramble all the data that were being projected on the overhead, with no opportunity to internalize the information and share my thoughts with the class. Also, I asked Professor Foster to share with me ahead of time the list of media she planned to use for the class. I did some checking, and found that one of the films was available in a captioned version. Professor Foster then arranged to use this version so that I could enjoy and benefit from this programme as much as did my classmates. For those media without captions, I had to settle for the nearly impossible task of watching the screen and following the blur of the interpreter's hands as he attempted to keep up with the rapid dialogue of the film.*

Barriers Associated with the Use of Interpreters

The skills of the interpreter can contribute significantly to the level of participation by the hearing-impaired student. If the interpreter is skilled in translating both sign language into spoken English and spoken English into sign language, the student is more likely to actively participate in the classroom. Unfortunately, it takes many years to develop the skills necessary to interpret well enough to allow students to participate freely. This problem of weak interpreting skills has created a feeling of inhibition among many hearing-impaired students, since they do not wish to be poorly represented to their teacher and classmates and are understandably reluctant to rely on interpreted information which may be incorrect.

TH: *In order for me to appear intelligent and present myself as a capable student, the interpreter must articulate my comments accurately, that is, use appropriate vocabulary along with inflections that match the intent of my message. Otherwise, my comments might appear choppy, unintelligent, or downright inappropriate. Furthermore, it can be awkward and discomforting to have an interpreter who does not possess adequate skill to comprehend my signing; for example, there had been*

> *times in past classes when I had to repeat myself several times before the interpreter could understand me, leaving my classmates and teacher hanging and all eyes on me as I struggled to make myself understood. One solution is to make sure that the interpreter is competent and qualified for the job. The interpreter for the course I took with Professor Foster was reputed to be one of the best in the area. In fact, I requested him because both I and Professor Foster were familiar with his skill and comfortable with his style. Because of his high level of competence, he was able to interpret my signs into spoken English accurately, giving me an equal opportunity to demonstrate to my classmates my understanding of the material and enabling me to make appropriate and interesting contributions to class discussions.*

SF: *Even though I had used interpreters before, I regretted the loss of direct communication with Mr Holcomb. I learned from Mr Holcomb that in conversations with a hearing-impaired person who is using an interpreter to voice comments, one should look at the hearing-impaired person. This can be difficult for hearing people who are used to attending to whoever they hear speaking. Even though I knew what I **should** do, I still found myself wanting to turn and look at the interpreter when he was voicing for Mr Holcomb rather than maintaining eye contact with Mr Holcomb. I remember wondering if the hearing students had the same sense of distance from their hearing-impaired classmate, and whether this influenced their interactions with him.*

The interpreter and hearing-impaired student must become a close team if the student is to actively participate in classroom activities. For example, during discussions, hearing-impaired students can be at a disadvantage because the information is being passed through a third party (interpreter) and the process of delivering the message through the medium of sign language usually takes a few seconds (interpreter lag). It can be a challenge for these students to process the information and find the right place to interject their comments. In order to be better able to participate, the student and interpreter need to be in synch, that is, they need to develop a system that allows the interpreter to give the cue for the student to begin speaking or signing at the right moment.

TH: *A system was devised by the interpreter and me where he would acknowledge my intent to make a comment (I would sign a lead-in word such as 'but' or 'I think') and begin to speak at an appropriate time during the discussion. This was especially helpful when the discussion became heated and students did not want to wait until recognized to speak. This experience stands in contrast to previous situations in which the interpreter was 'too busy' interpreting the comments of others to facilitate interjection of my thoughts.*

Barriers Associated with Teaching Style

Teaching style can range from didactic to participatory. If active dialogue between students is emphasized and grades based heavily on this interaction, it can place incredible stress on hearing-impaired students, since interpreter lag makes it difficult for them to participate in discussions that are characterized as heated or rapid fire. Typical attempts to participate in a discussion would be for hearing-impaired students to raise their hand and wait to be recognized by the teacher; if the teacher prefers to keep his or her involvement in the classroom discussion minimal, the hearing-impaired student may have to wait practically forever to be called on. Furthermore, it can be impossible for the interpreter to interpret a situation where several dialogues are taking place simultaneously, compounding an already difficult situation.

SF: *This was perhaps the most challenging part of my experience. My plan for the course was based on an intensive seminar format in which students were required to read materials and discuss them in class. More importantly, my past experience in seminar classes had led me to the belief that the best discussions are those which could be characterized as 'rapid fire', in which students were so excited that they forgot to raise their hands and frequently jumped into the conversation. In other words, I was expecting, even hoping for unrestrained dialogue among the students and between the students and me. My conversations with Mr Holcomb brought me to the quick conclusion that a discussion rated successful by these standards would be a disaster for him. I had to readjust my expectations and set ground rules for group discussions which precluded rapid fire or overlapping discussion. Moreover, I had to be prepared to enforce these rules, frequently reminding students to wait or pause in their conversation. Interestingly, I found that by asking students to take turns to speak, and by pausing between comments, more students were drawn into the discussion and their comments were often more thoughtful and well phrased.*

TH: *When I learned that Professor Foster's class was a seminar in which the emphasis is on dialogue among students, I decided that I must take a firm stand and make very clear the need for turn taking and waiting for the interpreter to catch up. As a result, Professor Foster agreed to play an expanded role as moderator and make sure people spoke only when recognized. Even so, I found it necessary to be assertive and remind my classmates to wait a minute or give me a chance to join the discussion. Our combined efforts paid off, and I felt really equal to my classmates. I knew that I had the same opportunity as my classmates to participate and share my thoughts; the degree of my participation was based solely on my motivation and command of the material.*

Barriers Associated with the Attitudes and Behaviours of Hearing Classmates

Hearing classmates must be willing to work with the hearing-impaired student and teacher to follow the established procedures and make them work. While the teacher has a responsibility to set the tone and demonstrate appropriate behaviours, the students must be willing to follow this lead and learn from the experience. As noted earlier, the creation of a positive learning environment for the hearing-impaired student often results in increased access to learning for all students. As a result, it has been our experience that hearing students who work to develop and maintain such a class setting will find it rewarding.

TH: *As mentioned before, teachers sometimes make a conscious effort not to treat hearing-impaired students any differently. I have found this approach to be detrimental to the overall classroom climate; often in these situations, the students and teacher feel uncomfortable and awkward for the entire semester about deafness in general and about communicating with a hearing-impaired student. From the beginning of the semester, Professor Foster was clear about the fact that the class would be unique simply because there was a hearing-impaired student in the class. The 'Communication Courtesy' handout was reviewed in order to help students better communicate with each other in the classroom. Hearing students were encouraged to ask any questions they might have about this special situation; as a result, they were more relaxed about having a hearing-impaired student in the class and made an extra effort to include me in their interactions. Another important factor that made the classroom climate positive and comfortable was the fact that Professor Foster knew some sign language and expressed an interest in learning more. This demonstration of interest paved the way for the hearing students to become even more motivated to communicate directly with me. In all, I found this class to be the most enjoyable and enriching in terms of my relationship with classmates because of the way Professor Foster and I approached this situation.*

SF: *The hearing students in this class expressed a genuine willingness to modify their behaviour in order to assure equal involvement of every student in class activities. This was probably due in part to the fact that they were all enrolled in programmes related to education and human development. At the suggestion of Mr Holcomb and the interpreter, I allotted part of the first class to review the 'Communication Courtesy' handout with the class and gave students an opportunity to ask questions. As we note at the end of this handout, it is very important that people feel comfortable and learn from their mistakes. Although there were a few awkward moments, I felt that the group was quite successful in including everyone during class discussions. I noticed that Mr Holcomb was less successful in accessing informal conversations in* *which students engaged before class and during breaks; this left me frustrated and wondering what more I could do. Should I request that students refrain from casual conversation unless the interpreter is present? Should I suggest that such conversations be conducted only in writing? These alternatives, while insuring that nobody would have access to informal information unless it was also available to Mr Holcomb, seemed radical and likely to make everyone uncomfortable and self-conscious. I must admit sometimes feeling defeated in this area of integration, and wonder if it would be more successful in classrooms where people spend considerably more time together.*

Barriers Associated with Unspoken Rules and Expectations

The inability to participate in casual conversations with classmates can have far-reaching implications. Without access to these conversations, hearing-impaired students are unable to participate in the exchange of information regarding the art of surviving in and passing the course. The informal exchange of information within the classroom often refers to the teacher's reputation; for example, the grading system (how to get an A with the least amount of work), pet peeves (spelling errors, sloppy penmanship, missed deadlines), horror stories from previous classes (including how these problems were handled) and other seemingly trivial but critical pieces of information. Similarly, throughout the course students often discuss issues such as frustrations in dealing with difficult materials and the amount of work required to complete assignments; at the end of the course tips are exchanged on completing the term project, such as helpful resources, acceptable length of paper, and so forth. All this information is often lost to hearing-impaired students; instead, they must rely on their keen sense of survival and ability to decipher unspoken rules and expectations and hope for the best.

> **TH:** *I find it interesting that Professor Foster was especially frustrated about the inequity in terms of informal communication and information exchange. This did not frustrate me as much, perhaps because as a hearing-impaired person this kind of segregation is a way of life. However, this inequity occasionally caused problems for me as a student at the university. Because I cannot always play the 'university game' right, I have found myself subject to scorn or missing an opportunity. For example, there were times when I needed information or assistance with paperwork (registration, parking stickers, receipts, and so forth). It took me longer than most to discover that some secretaries are more helpful than others; apparently, the university game includes access to information about which secretaries are the most cheerful, understanding and resourceful. Another example is related to financial aid. One of the most widely held beliefs among the students is that applications for financial scholarships are routinely rejected initially, but that those who write a letter of appeal are*

considered. As a hearing-impaired student, I did not have ready access to this information. Fortunately, a hearing friend who knows sign language told me at the last minute and I sent in my appeal; other hearing-impaired students may not be so lucky. Similarly, in past courses I often did not have the slightest clue of what the teacher's expectations really were other than what was documented in the handouts or articulated in the class. In a few classes where I was fortunate enough to have a hearing classmate who could communicate in sign language (such as Professor Foster's class), I was frequently amazed at the amount of knowledge students share with each other about teachers. Additionally, students reinforce and support each other in times of frustration and despair regarding coursework; for example, in Professor Foster's class the major complaint among the students was the amount of work required of us. If I had not had my hearing friend to 'clue me in', I would have thought I was the only one struggling with the course load, since I would see only the students' smiling faces and completed assignments during the formal part of the class.

SF: *In an effort to put all the students on equal footing regarding class assignments and expectations, I provided the class with extensive written documentation about the class schedule, assigned readings and requirements for term projects. Additionally, I took a substantial amount of time at the beginning of the course to review these materials and answer questions. Lastly, I encouraged students to see me individually. However, I realized that these steps could not fully compensate for the informal exchange of information which occurs among students. Since I am naturally excluded from these discussions, I cannot provide hearing-impaired students with this information.*

Concluding Comments

As we noted earlier, it was not easy for either of us to approach the other, accept new roles and openly discuss our mistakes as well as our successes. If it was difficult for us, it may be even more difficult for those who are in similar situations but lack the underlying friendship which motivated and sustained us. Still, we would encourage others to establish working partnerships with their students, teachers and classmates. As we learned, the results can be very rewarding for everyone.

At the same time, we acknowledge that we were not successful in making the classroom completely accessible. Hearing students continued to discuss readings and other assignments informally before class and during breaks; Mr Holcomb was largely excluded from these conversations. Sometimes students had to be reminded to wait until the interpreter finished before injecting their comment into the discussion, even towards the end of the semester. Several hearing students never completely mastered the idea that they should look at Mr Holcomb when he was making a comment; instead, they watched the interpreter who was voicing the signed comments. Sometimes Professor Foster called on students without giving Mr Holcomb sufficient time to catch up and join in the discussion. Mr Holcomb did not always interrupt to ask others to slow down or wait their turn. Perhaps more time is required to completely modify these persistent behaviours; perhaps they cannot be overcome within the classroom until they have been addressed on a larger societal level, that is, until human diversity is not only tolerated, but welcomed.

In closing we would like to make several points. First, each educational environment is in some ways unique; teachers and students in different settings may find that the strategies we used are not appropriate or sufficient. For example, teachers in high school classes may need to take a larger role in initiating contact with the hearing-impaired student. In other cases, the student may not feel that changes are necessary. Sometimes neither the student nor teacher knows what to do in order to make a classroom fully accessible; in these situations outside help in the form of consultants may be required. What *is* important is that teachers are willing to consider making changes and recognize that for some hearing-impaired students, integration without such accommodations is meaningless.

Second, our experience may have implications which go beyond meeting the needs of hearing-impaired students. The importance of initiating and maintaining dialogue with students who may have special needs within an integrated class, the idea that non-disabled classmates must be motivated and involved, and the notion of collaborative effort are all generalizable to people with other kinds of disabilities. In particular, the concepts of accessibility and accommodation can be applied in situations involving students with disabilities other than hearing impairment; the notion of full access remains the greatest challenge.

Lastly, we learned that the concept of three levels of integration (institutional, personal and group) may be more useful as a vehicle for organizing ideas than it is for day to day practice. In fact, these three levels are so interdependent that to pry them apart distorts the description of life in a complex system such as a school. Mr Holcomb's experience regarding academic scholarships at the university involves both institutional and personal barriers to integration. Moreover, his lack of access to the implicit rules surrounding the awarding of academic scholarships might have directly affected his ability to enroll in courses at the university and therefore his ability to participate in an integrated group setting. Similarly, there is considerable overlap between personal integration and the informal interactions of students within the classroom. Studies of integrated schools must take into account both the differences between levels of integration and the ways in which these levels overlap or impact on each other to produce a complex and dynamic system.

In summary, we feel that by talking with each other openly about our concerns and feelings regarding accessibility and accommodation within the integrated classroom, we were able to create a setting in which all students experienced enhanced opportunities for participation. We acknowledge that in some ways our experience fell short of our goal of total accessibility. However, we choose to think of our experience as a beginning rather than an end, and look forward to our next opportunity to work together within an integrated class.

Appendix

Communication Courtesy

In this class, we will be using an interpreter to facilitate communication between hearing and hearing-impaired participants. The following are general guidelines for communication in class:

Visual line of communication

Hearing-impaired class participants need to maintain a clear line of visual contact between themselves and the interpreter (or, if they are lip-reading, the teacher). It is therefore important to be aware of this need and take care not to block the line of vision.

Waiting for the interpreter to catch up

Due to the nature of his/her task, the interpreter will finish the communication in sign language a few seconds after the speaker has completed his/her comment. Hearing-impaired class participants who are using the interpreter for communication will not be in a position to respond or join the discussion until the interpreter has finished. It is therefore important to allow for this 'lag time' in class discussion in order to insure an opportunity for full participation by everyone.

Recognizing speakers

The interpreter will indicate who is speaking before beginning to interpret the speaker's comment. In order to insure that all class participants are able to follow the discussion clearly, individuals are asked to wait for recognition by the teacher or discussion leader before beginning their comment.

Asking questions

The interpreter will explain his/her role at the first class. However, if something comes up over the next few weeks, don't hesitate to approach the teacher, interpreter, or a hearing-impaired class participant for more information or clarification.

Relaxing with each other

Perhaps most important, we must all make an effort to relax and feel comfortable with each other. It's OK to forget to wait before jumping in the conversation — try to remember next time. It's OK to feel shy about tapping someone on the shoulder and asking them to slow down their speech or move back in their seat — but they probably won't mind at all. If we can help each other to communicate, we will have not only a good working relationship, but some terrific discussions and a great class!

References

ANTIA, S. D. (1982) 'Social interaction of partially mainstreamed hearing-impaired children', *American Annals of the Deaf*, 127, 1, pp. 18–25.

ENGLISH, R. W. (1971) 'Correlates of stigma toward physically disabled persons', *Rehabilitation Research and Practice Review*, 2, pp. 1–17.

FICHTEN, C. S., AMSEL, R., BOURDON, C. V. and CRETI, L. (1988) 'Interaction between college students with physical disabilities and their professors', *Journal of Applied Rehabilitation Counseling*, 19, 1, pp. 13–20.

FOSTER, S. (1988) 'Life in the mainstream: Reflections of deaf college freshmen on their experiences in the mainstreamed high school', *Journal of the American Deafness and Rehabilitation Association*, 22, 2, pp. 27–35.

FOSTER, S. (1989) 'Reflections of a group of deaf adults on their experiences in mainstream and residential school programs in the United States', *Disability, Handicap and Society*, 4, 1, pp. 37–56.

FOSTER, S. and BROWN, P. (1989) 'Factors influencing the academic and social integration of hearing impaired college students', *Journal of Postsecondary Education and Disability*, 7, pp. 78–96.

GARRESTON, M. (1977) 'The residential school', *The Deaf American*, 29, pp. 19–22.

GRESHAM, F. (1982) 'Misguided mainstreaming: The case for social skill training with handicapped children', *Exceptional Children*, 48, pp. 422–33.

GRESHAM, F. (1986) 'Strategies for enhancing the social outcomes of mainstreaming: A necessary ingredient for success', in MEISEL, C. J. (Ed.) *Mainstreaming Handicapped Children: Outcomes, Controversies and New Directions*, Hillsdale, NJ, Lawrence Erlbaum Associates, pp. 193–218.

HIRSHOREN, A. and BURTON, T. (1979) 'Willingness of regular teachers to participate in mainstreaming handicapped children', *Journal of Research and Development in Education*, 12, pp. 93–100.

LARRIVEE, B. (1985) *Effective Teaching for Successful Mainstreaming*, New York, Longman Inc.

MACDOUGALL, J. C., MUNHALL, K. G. and DESTOUNIS, B. V. (1981) 'Reverse mainstreaming of the physically handicapped', *Physiotherapy Canada*, 33, pp. 2–4.

MERTENS, D. and KLUWIN, T. (1986) Academic and social interaction for hearing-impaired high school students. Paper presented at the 1986 meeting of the American Educational Research Association, San Francisco, CA.

RAUTH, M. (1980) *Mainstreaming: A River to Nowhere or a Promising Current?* Washington, DC, American Federation of Teachers.

RAWLINGS, B., KARCHMER, M. A. and DECARO, J. (1988) *Guide to Post-Secondary Programs for the Hearing Impaired*, Gallaudet College, Washington, DC and National Technical Institute for the Deaf at Rochester Institute of Technology, Rochester, NY.

REYNOLDS, M. C. (1980) 'Public Law 94–142: The challenge of the integration movement to teachers and teacher–educators', *Prevention and Integration: Priorities for the 80s — Education Seminar Proceedings*. Vancouver, Canada, World Congress of Rehabilitation International.

SAUR, R., LAYNE, C., HURLEY, E. and OPTON, K. (1986) 'Dimensions of mainstreaming', *American Annals of the Deaf*, December, pp. 325–9.

WRIGHT, B. A. (1980) 'Developing constructive views of life with a disability', *Rehabilitation Literature*, 41, pp. 274–9.

11
Integration of Special Needs in Further Education

Mary Hutchinson

General Background

The aim of integration should be to develop each student individually thus enabling them to achieve their full potential. Integration should be seen as a process of increasing participation in the educational and social life of further education and students/pupils with special educational needs should be as fully integrated, as possible, within the College.

The North Lincolnshire College is a large further education establishment situated on three separate centres at Lincoln, Gainsborough and Louth. Whilst relatively small, the Gainsborough Centre is well equipped and offers a wide range of full and part time courses to students from a wide area. The emphasis at the Centre is on integration for all students wherever possible with the additional help of a support tutor where necessary.

The work with 'special needs' students originally started with 14–16-year-old pupils from the local secondary and special schools. This is now progressing through the Centre with students post-16 on full and part-time courses. This continuum of education is being further developed for some special needs students who, after taking part in a school link course, are now enrolled on full-time courses with additional support. Other handicapped youngsters are integrating into various modules of existing full-time courses as 'tasters' with a view to participating more fully next academic year. The importance of social integration is emphasized for these pupils within College where they are able to make use of all the facilities.

The Gainsborough Centre started a TVEI pilot scheme and in 1984, under this scheme, they ran City and Guilds courses 685 and 693 in conjunction with the three secondary schools. In 1986 pupils from the local special school for moderate learning difficulties participated in the Foundation courses. These pupils were able to choose from four vocational areas: Commercial Studies, Community Care, Construction and Engineering.

As well as the mainstream pupils there were nine statemented pupils, seven of whom finished the course and six who obtained City and Guilds Foundation Course Certificates. The pupils attended College on three half days a week. The syllabus was divided into four main components, each of which were interrelated and overlapped providing a fully integrated programme of study. The pupils also studied the two vocationally biased components in their own school using the expertise from both centres.

The main aims of the special school pupils participating on this course were:

1 integration with their peers from the mainstream schools;
2 the curriculum was educationally and vocationally relevant to their needs;
3 the possibility of accreditation by an external examining body.

The HMI report stated that 'the quality of the pupils' thinking and their motivation was good'. It also commented that the 'behaviour and motivation of the special educational needs pupils was markedly better than that displayed by the mainstream pupils'. Many showed a particular aptitude to practical work and where the written work showed a weakness various forms of information technology were used. Although not previously identified as having special needs, some of the mainstream pupils had specific learning difficulties and at times needed varying degrees of additional support.

During the course it became evident for many that their exam results would not do them justice — in the main they had completed and understood the course work but found it difficult to put this on paper especially under exam conditions. An approach was made to City and Guilds requesting extra time for these pupils, however this could only be granted for statemented children and was of no help to mainstream pupils who had learning difficulties. The alternative was to register the pupils on a College-based assessment taken entirely on their course work. Examples of work convinced City and Guilds assessors that the College — School links should be validated.

The pupils attended College at the same timetabled period on three half days each week regardless of the subject taken. Sympathetic members of staff with special needs training were available during that time to provide extra support to all pupils. Extra help could be negotiated in advance between subject tutor and support tutor or the subject tutor could call for assistance during the lesson via a radio pager. The support team further enhanced the programme with extra help in basic numeracy and literacy skills. This support was funded by TVEI.

It was felt by all staff concerned that the School-College link was a valuable experience for the special needs pupils and that it was important to continue with this integration at College. However, because of the end of the TVEI pilot scheme the secondary pupils no longer attended College. During this time the College was in the process of submitting a request for TVEI extension to commence in September 1990. The special school pupils continued in 1988/89 and the Foundation Course was replaced by the joint BTEC/City and Guilds Foundation Programme of Pre-Vocational Studies.

In order to continue links with the special school the College developed a modular curriculum package based on the City and Guilds Programme. April 1989 saw the second group of special school pupils start on the course. It has to be recognized that, because of lack of numbers and lack of mainstream links, these pupils worked together as a group. However the importance of social integration within College has been a valuable experience and should not be undervalued. Many of the pupils have benefited from using facilities such as the refectory alongside full time students, being responsbile for their own spending money and fitting into College life in general.

September 1989 saw the courses change yet again. Under TVEI the secondary pupils in their fifth year were able to join the special school pupils on the joint BTEC/City and Guilds Foundation Programme for Pre-Vocational Studies. These pupils are fully integrated into four groups and study four different case studies on a seven week carousel. The aim is to provide areas of study which are not available in the schools — Electricity in the Home, Motor Vehicle Maintenance, Brickwork and Home Maintenance. Working with the subject tutors are two support tutors, one offering technical and practical support in the workshops and the other offering support for learning difficulties. In addition another group from a secondary school in a nearby town attend College to study a similar group of case studies. Although from a mainstream school, ability and behaviour are mixed. This time the support tutor is provided by the school, who also travels to the College with the pupils and a behavioural support tutor is available through county to help with individual pupils with specific behavioural problems.

The City and Guilds Foundation Course

The Foundation Course was divided into four main areas with the pupils choosing their subjects in consultation with staff concerned.

Community Care

The Community Care Programme was intended to introduce pupils to a career in the Community Service field and to provide experience in a range of occupational activities so that pupils can explore their own range of interests and abilities. Pupils gained an insight into the structure of the community services and an understanding of the needs of all client groups within the community. Through this they would be able to develop practical skills required for work in this area and extend their interpersonal and communication skills. The course would also enable the pupils to undertake simple projects and provide an appreciation of the environment in which we live. It would also help pupils recognise good design in manufactured goods and assess the quality of services.

Construction

This course aimed to provide pupils with an insight and experience of the construction industry and a knowledge of processes, procedures and materials used. It also aimed to develop the mathematical skills and scientific principles necessary for a full understanding of the vocational and environmental aspects of the course. The pupils had an opportunity to undertake simple projects and to develop an ability to recognize quality, reliability and good design. The course also offered an appreciation of the environment and an insight into the functions of local and national government and the services they provide.

Commercial Studies

This course covered a wide variety of basic skills. The pupils had the opportunity to use modern equipment in a model office. The course also provided an insight into banking and business organisation. Throughout the course the pupils were expected to research information and record this using various forms of modern information technology. Use of the telephone gave pupils a chance to improve personal communication skills required for this type of work experience.

Engineering

This course was intended to give an insight into the structure, processes, procedures and materials used in the engineering industry. It also provided the pupils with the mathematical skills and scientific knowledge necessary for a fuller understanding of the vocational and environmental aspects of the course. Through this the pupils could develop their interpersonal and communication skills required in situations in everyday life. It also helped them to recognize quality, reliability and good design. It also provided an insight into the functions of local and national government and the services they provide relevant to the engineering industry.

As some pupils had problems with written communication it was felt that sitting an examination would jeopardize their chances of receiving a City and Guilds Certificate despite having successfully completed the course work.

The Locally Devised Scheme

The course coordinator discussed the fact that some pupils would not gain accreditation for the successfully completed coursework. The board granted the College's request to submit locally devised schemes in three main areas: the main subject area, communication skills and social and environmental studies. Through the course work and these locally devised schemes the pupils could be assessed in the following areas:

the industrial, social and environmental factors relevant to the subject;
the relevant industrial skills and practices;
the relevant technological and scientific skills;
the level of communication and interpersonal skills.

These assignments were designed to cover a wide range of knowledge and skills acquired during the course. The pupils were encouraged to use word-processors and the Kroy printing machine in order to present their work attractively. The support tutor was on hand to help with this whilst the subject tutor could continue with revision work for those taking the examination. On the whole the locally devised scheme was well accepted by the pupils and most were delighted to receive City and Guilds accreditation. However one or two of the pupils who had a good grasp of the subject felt they should have been allowed to take the examination. The choice of locally devised scheme or examination had been discussed with pupils but the ultimate decision had been with the schools who paid the examination fee. Again the support tutor was able to help with counselling and support for individual pupils. They were also able to form a liaison between school and college and between individual and establishment.

The communication assignment involved a survey of the facilities at the local leisure centre. The first task was to phone the leisure centre to make an appointment to visit the manager and discuss what was available. In order to cause as little disruption as possible one of the pupils' calls was actually directed through to the leisure centre whilst the others were set up on the internal phone system within the College. Unknown to the pupils the tutor was able to listen in and assess their ability. The community care assignment involved the pupils in investigating provision in the town for the elderly. They visited various establishments, asked questions and then wrote up their findings. For engineering the pupils acquired an old reaper, stripped it down and then renovated it. This also involved them in finding out about modern machinery, visiting a local museum and talking to local farmers about their farm implements. Much of this work was photographed throughout the course so that pupils had a visual record of their work.

The Combined Curriculum Package

The Foundation Course proved a valuable experience for the special school pupils and staff at both establishments felt it important to retain this link. The College was asked to participate in the development of a modular curriculum package for 14–16-year-old pupils with moderate learning difficulties. This package was based on the joint BTEC/City and Guilds Foundation Programme for Pre-Vocational Studies (FPPS). The pupils participated in six vocationally based modules each of which were twenty to thirty hours duration.

The modules were designed to develop the skills and experience which would assist the pupils in transition from school to adult life. The functional, locational and social integration was aimed at building further their personal competencies. The modules also provide opportunities for progression to continuing education, training and/or employment. As with the Foundation Programme additional members of staff were available as support tutors.

Staff meet both within the College and between institutions on a regular basis to discuss pupils progress and problems and to develop future patterns of learning.

From September 1989 the local special school became an approved centre for the BTEC/City and Guilds 14–16 FPPS and established links and developments with the College should continue.

The six modules studied were Catering Operations, Community Care, Office Procedures/Starting a Youth Club, Introduction to Electronics, Moped Maintenance and Construction.

Catering Operations

The aim of this module is to investigate and carry out basic catering operations and to undertake a 'function' as an end result of the course. During the course it is hoped pupils will acquire knowledge and understanding of hygiene, health and safety as applied to the catering industry. They should produce a variety of dishes according to the individuals practical ability. They should also acquire basic knowledge and skills applied to restaurant operations. At the end of the course the pupils prepared, cooked and served a lunch for school and College staff and the pupil's guests. This enabled them to experience working as a team in the planning and organizing of a social function. A video of this was made so that the pupils had a good record of this major project.

Community Care

The aim of this module is to provide the pupils with the background knowledge of care of the different client groups within the community. It is intended to introduce them to a wide range of skills and practices in community care. The course also aims to develop interpersonal and communication skills required in the main occupations in the community services. It will also contribute to the pupils development of social and leisure skills and personal qualities. An overall view of the services available locally is to be provided by several visits to residential establishments.

Office Procedures/Starting a Youth Club

The aim of this module is to provide the pupil with an insight into the organizational and clerical aspects of starting an organization. It is hoped the pupils will work as a team, delegating tasks as necessary and making critical evaluations from the information obtained. This module also gives them an opportunity to develop written and oral skills. It also provides an opportunity to work in and use the up to date equipment in a model office.

Electronics

The aim of this module is to make the pupil aware of modern electronics and construction methods as well as acquiring confidence in a new role. It is hoped that dexterity, neatness and the need to plan logically would be mastered through developing the pupils soldering and construction ability, starting with basic soldering exercises and leading to the construction of the 'heads and tails' game. This module also involves the use of measuring instruments and should develop the pupils competence in practical communication and use of mathematics. An overall view of the electrical industry and domestic electricity supply was provided by a visit to a local electricity generating station.

Construction

The aim of this module is to involve the pupils in the various processes required to build a brick wall, construct a window casement and fit this into the wall. The pupils would use a wide range of skills used in the construction industry as well as developing their interpersonal and communication skills. They would also need to recognize danger points and show responsibility for their own and their colleagues safety whilst in the workshop. The module would also help to improve their dexterity with the use of various tools in the industry. The pupils would also be responsible for handling information, identifying stages for decision making and participating in group work.

Moped Maintenenance

This module aims to make the pupil aware of the different types of mopeds and motorcycles and identify the different parts of the bike. Again the pupils would need to recognize the importance of safety in the workshop and be able to participate in group activities as well as working as a team. They will undertake a number of simple repair and cleaning tasks in the workshop and be able to recognize the need to observe safety when using the bikes on the roads.

Support System

The main purpose of the support system is to offer help in a variety of ways wherever and whenever the need arises. To implement the policy of integration support was offered to all pupils so that those with special needs were not specifically singled out amongst their peers.

The support tutor was able to help with the following:

preparation of teaching material suitable to the varying needs of the individual;

reproduction and presentation of individuals work where written skills show a limitation — the maximum use of computers and word processor being employed;

arranging and accompanying staff/pupils on visits

an extra pair of hands in the workshop working alongside the subject tutor;

liaising with individual and subject tutor;

liaising between school and college;

being responsible for the keeping of detailed and confidential records and schemes of work.

The support tutor arranges in advance with the subject tutor when the additional help could be used most effectively. However the support tutor could be contacted at any time during the session via a radio pager and the subject tutor could receive immediate help should the need arise. At regular intervals the support team and subject tutors met together to hold regular reviews of pupils progress and all pupils could be monitored and their work assessed. All members of the support team were issued with safety shoes and overalls to encourage safe practice within the workshops. All pupils were also issued with overalls when working in the workshops.

The support team leader acted as a liaison between staff at school and College so that problems could be identified and dealt with effectively. It was felt that the pupils at College should have someone at College whom they could identify and relate to whilst on the premises, especially in the settling in period when problems were most likely to arise. Such problems as late transport, meal arrangements, finding workshops inevitably cropped up and pupils could find the support tutor thus coping with problems immediately rather than taking them back to school. The support tutor checked on pupils who were absent and these names were phoned through to the school after the lesson started so that anyone wishing to play truant could be traced immediately and the pupils knew someone was checking on their attendance. The subject tutor could discuss appropriate learning techniques and assessment procedures with the support tutor so that each individual pupil could be helped. The effective use of computers, word-processors and printing techniques enabled some pupils to improve the presentation of their work and also develop limited keyboard skills. Although the support tutor usually worked with the slow learners sometimes subject tutor and support tutors' roles were reversed as this was felt to be important for interrelationships.

Effective Development for Students 16+

A mainstream pupil on the Foundation course had been identified at school as being dyslexic but was offered no additional support. Whilst attending College she received support and gained a City and Guilds accreditation for her work. She was subsequently accepted for a two year course in catering and the College has been able to fund additional support for basic literacy. This year after completing her first year on the catering course and being successful in all her exams she has started on her final year. As course tutors became aware of this extra help several students were identified as having learning difficulties and they are able to receive individual help on a regular basis. One of the special school pupils on the combined curriculum course was accepted on the two year full-time City and Guilds 331 Residential Care Course. One of the secretarial students who was not ready for work experience out of College was able to assist the support tutor producing work on the typewriter or word-processor for use with the students with learning difficulties.

The special needs coordinator now has time available to identify special needs students enrolling for full or part time courses at college and is able to offer either appropriate help to the student or help and advice to the tutor. For most of these pupils it is a case of inobtrusively monitoring their progress and then offering help if or when it is needed. In a few cases help will be on a more regular basis.

Assessment

This is an integral part of the pupils' programme. In 1988/89 pupils received assessment profiles for all the modules they successfully completed together with a college certificate acknowledging the modules completed. In each module the tasks clearly stated what was required of the pupils in order for him/her to acquire the desired learning and demonstrate the identified skills. The differentiated statements for the skills were used to generate the outcome statement for each task. These statements then provided the basis for the reports to appear on the final documentation. The areas of assessment were clearly marked at the end of each module and the pupils were aware of these areas of assessment as they worked through the modules. The final assessment sheets and profiling were worked out with discussion between tutor and pupil.

The Future

It is difficult to predict what future developments will be. However September 1989 brought its usual changes. Pupils from the secondary schools have been able to join the special school pupils on a fully integrated BTEC/City and Guilds Foundation programme. These pupils attend College for one half day each week. They are divided into four groups and study four case studies on a seven week carousel basis. The case studies, Home Maintenance, Brickwork Project, Electricity in the Home and Motor Vehicle Maintenance were designed to provide extension and enhancement to the pupils school curriculum. Workshop facilities in College provide the pupils with actual 'hands-on' experience in all four areas of study. Two support tutors are available to provide help and back up during these sessions. One support is a technician and able to provide expertise in the workshop. The other tutor is able to provide help for pupils with learning difficulties or behavioural problems and help with the filling in of students own assessment/profile sheets.

The success of this integration and support system has encouraged the College to adopt this policy for other students at the Gainsborough Centre. Several students with special needs are already integrated into full-time courses with the back up of a support tutor. Adults from employment training agencies are now being allowed to integrate into individual modules of a variety of courses. In particular adults with learning difficulties are able to take advantage of the practical modules in some areas and also basic literacy classes. Several physically handicapped adults are able to study areas like computing, GCSE and 'A' Level subjects and take advantage of modified workshop facilities.

Progress in this area has been slow and at times frustrating when the demands of individuals have been difficult to meet or finance. The model of 'integration with support' is not a panacea for all students with learning difficulties. It is more likely to be one small point on a continuum of tapering support and provision.

What this programme does demonstrate is that given the cooperation of vocational tutors, special school teachers and national validating bodies it is possible to provide, within the existing physical constraints of FE, a programme that caters for the aspirations and needs of at least some of those with special educational needs and open up the full range of NVQ potential.

Part Four:
Integration and Pupil Skills

12
Language Skills: The Child with Down's Syndrome in Ordinary Classes

Pat Le Prevost

Introduction

Every child entering a class for the first time is a stranger to the teacher and the other children. The teacher, however, with her knowledge, skill and experience can soon assess that child, pick out his strengths and weaknesses and very quickly help to settle him into the group. The children will also accept him particularly if he is able to join in their games and activities as an equal. The unknown factors about his abilities, behaviour, personality etc. are soon recognized and from the teacher's knowledge of children, the stranger becomes 'Mark', 'Peter', 'Sue' or 'Anne' with similar problems and characteristics to the 'Mark', 'Peter', 'Sue', and 'Anne' who moved into the next class at the end of last term. No child is alike but there are enough similarities for us to feel comfortable with their individual personalities to be confident that we can do the best for each one.

The difficulty arises when the child entering the class already has a new, different and forbidding label attached to it. This child is not just 'Mark' but 'Mark with Down's Syndrome', or 'Anne' but 'Anne with Special Educational Needs' and immediately there are questions to be asked and answered before that child's abilities, behaviour and personality can be recognized and he or she can become a true member of the class.

The label 'Down's Syndrome' on a new born baby has, in the past been the end of any attempt at formal education, and an automatic closing of doors to opportunities granted to everyone else. In addition, the problems were self-perpetuating for without help and training the children did often become aggressive, non or poorly communicating, unattractive adults whose behaviour, manner and speech set them aside from the general population and made them stand out as 'different'.

The turning point for many of these children came in 1970 with the Education Act (Handicapped Children) when it was recognized that every child had a right to education. It was from that time that people really started to look at the problems involved and how to overcome some of the difficulties that the children face in dealing with the everyday world.

I would like to share with you some of the work we have carried out over the last ten years, and perhaps the explanations and discoveries that we have made — particularly in how children with Down's Syndrome learn language — so that we may help to make that new entrant into your class less of an unknown factor.

In the mid 1970s, following the Education Act, the development of services to special schools and children with special needs meant that we really began to look closely at ways of teaching and learning, and to ask questions about what was really being achieved. It was during this time also that the use of signs in the form of structured vocabularies and language programmes began to be introduced to the mentally handicapped population. This was to see if this means of communication was easier for them particularly if they had failed to learn speech. From the good results obtained with adults these programmes were then introduced into special schools where equally rewarding results were gained with the younger children. However, there was still a lot of opposition to the use of signs, particularly with children with Down's Syndrome as it was felt that this would lead them to become lazy in their attempts at speech and that they would not try to talk at all. Their ability to mime had long been recognized as a 'party trick' and not felt to be of any use to learning. It was often actively discouraged as being detrimental, and some children were forbidden to gesture their needs at all in case it hindered their speech development. Thus, when signing systems were introduced into special schools in this county in 1976 the children chosen to be taught were often not those with Down's Syndrome. However, it soon proved to be an impossible task not to teach them, as they picked the signs up from other children using them, and it was also found that whereas it had been thought to be detrimental to the child's learning speech — the opposite was often the case. Children with Down's Syndrome entering school at three to four years with no speech picked up a few signs and suddenly started to produce words as well. Children who had been total non-communicators began to try, and often speech began to appear. The criteria for the use of signs, however, was always — try only after normal speech has failed to come at the expected age.

By this time the Education Service had realized the importance of early stimulation and the parents' need for help in the very early years of a handicapped child's life. The pre-school Teacher Counsellor Service had been set up to help parents to teach their children with their early milestones. Schemes like 'Portage' began to be explored and structured training and help was found to be very beneficial in all areas of development bar one — and that was language and communication and particularly where the child had Down's Syndrome.

Would the introduction of signs early help or hinder the development of language in these children? We did not know — and there was no means of testing the teaching or not teaching of signs to the same child, it was just not possible. In 1979 one very brave set of parents decided to risk the experiment and, under guidance, introduced a limited number of signs to their 10-month-old child with Down's Syndrome. The results were then monitored over the following five years. This study answered so many questions, and led to so many new areas of progress, that many children all over the world have now benefited from that initial case.

Problems of Mental Handicap

Before talking about the results that came from all this however, it is probably useful to look at exactly what was wrong with the speech and language of the children that we were struggling with in the special schools, and just what we were trying to change.

Firstly, what does having mental handicap mean in relationship to your ability to learn? First of all it means that your ability to hold, remember, process and alter information in your head is not as great as the 'normal' person. The more handicapped you are the less information you can store, remember or use. Using words which have to be learned, understood and remembered is one of the hardest skills to achieve. Your use and also the number of words you are able to use will also depend on how handicapped you are. Another skill that is difficult is that of concentrating; if you are not able to concentrate for even a short time then you only look or listen to things superficially and do not really learn them. It was realized very early on that merely exposing handicapped people to lots of different experiences did not mean that they learned anything from any of them. Their inability to concentrate meant that they merely flitted from one thing to another without taking in any of them.

Another skill that we take for granted is that of being able to generalize information. If a young child learning language learns to say 'dog' he will initially call all four legged creatures 'dogs'. He is already beginning to try to sort out the information he is gathering in into categories and establish patterns and order in his thinking. He very quickly learns that all four legged creatures are not dogs and also that dogs come in all shapes and sizes, but are still dogs — in other words he has learned a concept. This is a necessary part of processing inner language if we are going to be able to switch, change and modify ideas in our heads when we want to use them as speech. This ability to generalize categories and modify ideas is also one of the brain functions that is impaired to a greater or lesser degree with mental handicap. Names of objects get stuck to the original object on which they were used and it takes time and help to move them to their wider aspects.

In the normal pattern of child development a lot of major changes take place in the first four years. From being a small fairly helpless infant, unable to sit up unsupported, unable even to hold a fairly small object, we become a walking, talking, running, jumping, highly skilled achiever, able to use our hands independently, pick up tiny objects, place things inside one another, use tools such as spoons and pencils and have experienced many, many activities in such a short space of time. If your brain development is such that these motor skills are taking much longer to mature, for example if you are unable to hold your head up and sit up unsupported for the first 12 months of your life instead of the usual 3 to 6 months, then the amount of actual variety of experiences that you can achieve is going to be much less and therefore you learn slower. If your hands will not grasp and hold an object until 12 months, when the normal baby is already bashing the daylights out of its rattle at 6 months, your learning experience is also reduced so that, even if your brain is capable of doing it, because your body is taking longer to achieve good muscle tone you are already falling behind in the learning stakes.

These are just some of the difficulties that someone with mental handicap has in-built before he starts. Any help which is going to be successful will not only have to accept these difficulties, but plan ways to alleviate and therefore minimize the problems involved. For example, to experiment with both hands may need special seating so that a baby whose back cannot support him, can be safely propped up and can learn to play like his normal counterpart. A child who has difficulty in generalizing needs experience of lots of different objects of the same category for direct comparison. To learn what 'big' means, means lots of different 'bigs' — moving into all areas of experience. These are some of the basic underlying problems of mental handicap, which although cause many difficulties — having been recognized — can at least be taken into consideration when programme planning.

Language Difficulties in Down's Syndrome

Now let's look at Down's Syndrome in particular and see just what some of the problems were that were causing so much difficulty when the children or even adults tried to talk.

Firstly, their onset of language or rather the beginning of speech was never regarded as usual until about the fifth year of life — in other words nobody expected the children to talk until they were 5 and the majority didn't. Secondly, when they did start to talk, a lot of the children had difficulty in making up their own sentences. Instead of the usual curious questions and everlasting exploration of words, the children were often very good at babbling nonsense, but clear words were only obtained if the object was produced, in other words there was no development of concepts of words and no extension of inner language; asked to name an object, no problem, but take the object away and ask what it was and the child couldn't do it. This went right on into adulthood. Ask the child what he wanted, how he felt, what was wrong, etc. and again he was totally unable to find the right words for the occasion. But popping in and out of this mess of language were 'little phrases' that had been learned previously and were then used again and again merely to make conversation. The 'Hello, how are you?' types of phrase which we all recognize as a greeting, were used time after time just to try and keep conversation going without any reference or understanding of their meaning. They had been learned as being useful to keep people's attention and were therefore a means of doing just that. Finally, with large floppy tongues and poor tongue movement, the way the children even said the words they did know, was often so distorted, that nobody understood them anyway. Speech and language for many people with Down's Syndrome was no mean feat!

These were all the problems that we were trying to alleviate when we started the initial experiment in 1979. One reason we wanted to try new methods of procedure was because despite all the difficulties lots of children seemed to be making such good strides in other areas of development provided the learning processes were broken down into small enough steps. Was it perhaps our methods of teaching that were producing the poor results?

Results from the Initial Study

The very first thing our baby with Down's Syndrome taught us was that she needed help with looking at the important things going on around her. In other words she needed help to develop her concentration. As her mother used nice normal gestures and a few structured signs she very soon learned to look for them and they would help her understand. Her mother worked hard in the early months making sure that her daughter turned to watch the important things in her life and also listened to their names. The signs were never used without good clear speech and babbling was encouraged as much as possible.

The second thing she taught us was that despite all her difficulties she could understand very well what words meant and could respond to them well at the age of 18 months. At this age she had no hope of saying anything close to the word itself, she could nevertheless recognize words when we said them and by using a simple sign indicate that she had done so. By this age too, she was identifying most of the pictures in her baby books and differentiating between cows and cats, dogs and horses.

However, two major stumbling blocks also came to light which answered some of the questions we had been asking. Firstly, she found it very difficult to distinguish between similar sounding words. Particularly words with the same vowel sound in the middle and with quite similar sounding consonants at the beginning and end, so words like 'see', 'tree', 'she', 'knee', would be interpreted as the same, thus leading to a great deal of confusion. This has since been confirmed as a common problem in all the children. In fact it is recognized as a short stage in normal language development, but it is usually passed through and corrected so quickly that many parents may only notice the odd error as an amusing episode which is immediately put right. With children with Down's Syndrome however, this stage goes on for quite a long time, and if left, merely piles confusion upon confusion. With the use of the visual symbol by the child, not only is the error recognized, but immediately corrected.

Secondly, the children's ability to recognize symbolic or even photographic pictures is not always accurate, therefore a round, red object can be either a ball, a balloon or even an apple. We recognize the extra little additions like stripes, a string or a leaf that change pictures into different things, the children don't. Therefore, they misread pictures and again confusion sets in. By adding the visual medium or an extra dimention to their language experience we were able to help the children understand language much earlier and help them through the many hazards of distinguishing one picture from another. In other words, the children were using their eyes to help their ears.

Moving from their development of understanding language to their ability to express themselves, this then became the next area of interest. The children were telling us that they wanted to communicate long before 5 years, in fact much closer to the normal age of language and speech development in young children. They just couldn't do it with speech however. Firstly their floppy tongues just would not produce the sounds needed. If you pick out the vowel sounds in a sentence — 'oo a a ee', that means very little to anyone especially if it is out of context. Often the children could not even produce the correct vowel, so the speech would be 'u u u ee' — even more difficult to interpret. Is it — 'Who had a sweet?', 'Look at that tree', 'You can have these'? Without some other clues it is impossible to tell. It is no wonder the children were reputed to be good at mime.

Many words we use are not simple two or three sound words either, words like 'm̲ e̲', 's̲ e̲e̲' only contain two sounds, but presented with a word like 't̲ e̲ l̲ e̲ v̲ i̲ si̲ on̲' or a phrase like 'b̲ r̲ ea̲ d̲ a̲ nd̲ b̲ u̲ tt̲ er̲' you can have up to eleven different sounds, not only to say correctly and accurately but also to get in the right order. This skill of listening and repeating sounds in the correct order is something the children find very difficult indeed. Word *patterns* however, are much easier — 'he̲l̲/l̲o̲' for example — has two syllables, starts high in pitch and goes downwards, this is no problem; 'b̲re̲a̲d̲ / a̲n̲d̲ / b̲u̲t̲/t̲e̲r̲' and 't̲e̲l̲/e̲/v̲i̲/s̲i̲o̲n̲' both have four syllables, word patterns and pitch change are not so hard to copy, but getting the right sounds in the right place as well really is very hard indeed.

Earlier in this chapter I spoke of the use of 'nonsense babbling', here patterns of speech and words have been picked up but there is no idea as to the correct sounds needed to turn those patterns into words. Again this is a stage of normal speech development that all little children go through, again often without the parent noticing what is going on, but they very quickly realize the importance of the 'consonant' sounds and practise them by the hour — just to amuse themselves. This is fine if your muscles will actually do it, but if your tongue is so sluggish it won't produce the sounds you are back to plain vowel sounds again and 'oo a a ee' which tell nobody anything. This is what had happened to many of the children.

As we watched our first little girl developing her speech between the ages of 18 months and 3 years, she showed us very clearly that she had the normal desire of any child to explore language, play with speech and use it with us, but she needed to rely very heavily — particularly in the early stages — on the signs. She would look at pictures and sign them to herself, she would use signs to hold conversation with her mother and always they were accompanied by some sound, but as far as we could tell the sounds were nowhere near the correct patterns for the words she wanted. Often they were just sounds going up and down with the correct rhythm of the sentence but nothing else. Very gradually over the months these patterns became more accurate and her need for signs dropped away. She still used them as a quick memory aid but often they were so slight as to be hardly noticeable. For example, when she was about 3½-years-old she was doing a puzzle with me and pointed out a piece in the shape of a tree. The correct sign for tree is to make the shape of a tree by extending the fingers of one hand and raising your arm so that it becomes the trunk and the fingers the branches. Instead of moving her arm up and extending her fingers as she used to do, she merely extended her fingers on the table and turned her wrist, she was now able to say the word accurately enough for me to understand what she said, but still needed a back-up. She was still using the sign — linked to the word — but now it was fading and the word was taking precedence, because she was able to make it clearly enough.

All the way through her first years she used signs first with odd sounds, then gradually the words took shape and then took over. Watching her, and other children since, it became clear that their listening skills were their main weakness while their visual skills were their strength. Unfortunately this can sometimes lead the children into trouble, and cause more difficulties than intended if language and the understanding of it are developing slowly.

Children in the Classroom

The child in your class may not have reached the skill of understanding the words you use to such a high degree as the other members in his class. All children learn the names of things around them first, then they learn simple action words, then they learn the meaning of words such as — big, new, little, in, on and under. They soon start joining these ideas together, for example: big book, dolly sleep, in box, new shoes, etc. While they are at this ability level, the rest of the words in sentences we use are in the background as it were, waiting until their meaning can be absorbed as well. This is fine most of the time, particularly if it is a small child of 2-plus years that we are dealing with. We adjust our language and help the child through the situation, taking them and showing them what the words mean.

When a child reaches 5 however, we are beginning to expect them to have passed this stage and to understand the whole of what we say. Problems arise then in this sort of situation, for example you may say: 'Go and get your outdoor shoes they are by your coat'. Most children of 5 will understand the words underlined. But the child with less understanding ability may only understand: 'Go and get — shoes — coat'. Which is what he will do. He is wrong. He has done the wrong thing. So the next time when instructions are given, because he does not trust his own ability, he does precisely what we all do in these circumstances. He waits until someone else does it and then copies — in which case he gets it right and is credited with full understanding, or he just waits until someone takes him and helps him through it. In which case it is assumed he understands nothing, or is being stubborn because he understood before! But to him, each time, it is reinforced in his mind 'Don't trust what you hear!'

One of the ways we make life easy for ourselves is to develop patterns, routines and short-cuts. We always put things in certain places so that we know where to find them: we always do one task followed by another. It saves time, effort and thought. However, we can easily break that pattern when circumstances change, for example: Thursday is the day we go into the hall for PE, but the hall is being used for a display so we have to go outside instead. A quick word with the class and most of them will have listened to the message, understood it and prepared for the change. No-one gets upset, it doesn't matter, they may even quite like the idea of doing something different. Not so the child with language difficulties who has misheard or even stopped listening. PE time — clothes are changed ready to go into the hall — suddenly confusion! He may get angry, upset or just refuse to move. He likes patterns and routines, they make him feel safe and he doesn't have to worry about the future. Change that and he is lost until he can get adjusted again. A simple hand held and reassurance, plus another child to help may be all that is needed to avoid some of these problems. A new experience can be safely added, which will help next time, this one will have lost its fears.

Another difficulty with still having simpler language structures is that the ability to think in sequence is also more limited — playground / gate / road / danger / hurt — for instance is a sequence of five connected links. Break that down to two links, the — danger / hurt — bit may well be taught, but if you only think as far as — playground / gate — you may not always stop to think of the trouble ahead. Having got to the gate you may link it with — gate / home — or even — gate / shops — so off you go again; trouble. Even if someone explains that you don't go out until home-time. Home-time is not here and now and therefore not established until routines are well established and we have already explained the problems with those!

This may sound all very depressing and you may be saying 'this child' has too many problems, but if you are aware that:

The children learn by what they see;
They like routine because it doesn't need explaining; — but
They can accept change and should learn to trust what they hear;
The more they do and take part in the class, the more they learn;
The more they learn, the less these problems occur and the more secure they feel;
The more secure they feel, the more they learn; — and then
The more they can link what they *see* to what they *hear*.

Another point to remember is that the child with Down's Syndrome is still a child first and foremost, and as such is the same or different as any other child. He can be as good, kind, happy and willing to learn as any other child, he can also be as cheeky, lazy, wilful and just plain naughty as any other child. You will have your own ways of dealing with good and bad behaviour and he needs to be treated the same way. Any child who throws his pencils on the floor is made to pick them up. He is a child with learning difficulties, but he is a child first and foremost.

Watching our experimental children grow up we have realized many things. Firstly, that they are capable of learning language, but they need to see what is happening then they can understand and apply the language.

Some of them have been very lucky and been able to produce words clearly enough for us to understand very early on, this has meant they could practise speech and by the time they reach you they are already quite capable of putting their own sentences together, thinking in sequence and learning the more detailed aspects of our own grammar system. Our grammar system that can change — time / dinner — to 'It isn't time for dinner yet', so that they don't have to watch your facial expression, the other children and anything else that will make sense of it for them.

Some of the children will be halfway there and need a little help from you — a frown, a shake of the head — will soon tell the child that difficult words like: isn't, can't, won't and haven't, mean NO.

Some of the children will have been able to listen to words, practise them and are able to say them so that they can be understood without any help at all. Others will have been struggling with large, flaccid tongue muscles, and continuous hearing problems from blocked-up ears and noses, so that they haven't been able to hear properly let alone learn to listen. These children may be still at the stage where they need to listen to words carefully, and continue to practise them before they are able to really say them clearly.

It must always be remembered that producing words clearly is a learned skill and all skills need good tools and lots of practice before they can be achieved. No one would be expected to knit a patterned Fairisle jumper until they had learned and practised the basic stitches in knitting, and no child can produce a complicated pattern of sounds without having had plenty of practice at them first. Expect a jumper from a novice and you get a crumpled mess of wool and dropped stitches, expect long clear sentences from a child who needs basic practice and you could stop him trying or make him try so hard he stammers over it. Lots of listening and looking and building up carefully, a step at a time, and success can be the answer.

Some of the best teachers of children who need help with their speech are other children. If they really play together — they *don't* talk down to one another but *with* one another at a level each one can understand. They must regard one another as equal partners in the game however, and not treat the child with Down's Syndrome as a toy or plaything. The teachers' attitude to the handicapped child can help so very much in this, if she regards the child as just another member of the class, so will they. If she separates him out as something different, then he becomes different in the eyes of the other children. Realizing that his needs are different from the others and catering for them is not the same as regarding his Down's Syndrome first and the fact he is a child second.

As I mentioned earlier, one of the hardest things the children have to live down is the label 'Down's Syndrome', it is hung around their necks at birth and has built up so many prejudices against them that no one wanted to really look at the actual child. They were left without help, without understanding and without hope. Place any child in a cot for the first three years of its life and it will be very far behind its peers. Place a child, who has difficulty learning anyway, in a cot for three years and it is lost for the rest of its life. Yet, that is exactly what was not only done, but advised, by many 'experts'. 'You will have a good baby', they said, 'and we will look at him when he is 3 to see if there is anything we can do.'

Understanding the way he can learn by giving him good, clear speech with lots of visual clues, and helping him over the time when he has begun to understand language but cannot yet say anything clearly by using signs, has helped us to realize that many of these children can learn to express themselves to say what they want when they want it. They can ask questions and they can learn. By using their strengths to help their weaknesses, they have learned to master the skills of communication to the best of their ability. Some of the children may have as much ability as a normal child. Some may have very little ability to learn more than a few basics of life, but at least they are now having the right to try and by accepting them into your class you are converting the letter of the 1970 Education Act into fact.

13
Art Therapy and Special Education

Jenni Wallace and Diane Waller

Art therapy is a form of psychotherapy in which the client or patient is encouraged to use a variety of basic art materials — paint, clay, collage, etc — to help to get in touch with unconscious feelings. The image-making process takes place within the boundaries of a secure space, in the presence of a qualified art therapist. Art therapists work with both individuals and groups in a wide range of institutions concerned with the care, treatment and education of children and adults.

Art therapy is a recognized profession within the NHS and has its own career and salary structure. In order to train as an art therapist, it is first necessary to have a degree (usually in Art or Design) followed by at least one year's working experience in the health or social services or related area. These qualifications are necessary to apply for entry to the Postgraduate Diploma in Art Therapy, currently offered by the University of London Goldsmith's College, Hertfordshire College of Art and Design and the University of Sheffield. The Diploma lasts for one year full-time or two years part-time and is a highly intensive course of training, combining theoretical studies with practice in hospitals, schools, day centres, etc. The Goldsmiths' course has an Educational Mode, open only to qualified teachers who wish to work subsequently within special educational needs services, or as therapists within mainstream education.

The British Association of Art Therapists (BAAT)

The BAAT is the professional association for art therapists in Britain. It was formed in 1963 from a group of artists and psychotherapists who had been working in hospitals throughout Britain and meeting occasionally at exhibitions or at working parties concerned with the promotion of art therapy. Although the term was first coined around 1940 by the artist Adrian Hill and a number of people had been trying to develop the notion of art (or creative activity) being valuable in rehabilitation, it was not until 1963 that a coherent attempt was made to define what was really meant by the term, in order to go ahead with such major decisions as: who would be suitable to train; what the training should consist of; what kind of standards of practice should be required. Even then, it was obvious from the numerous ways that would-be members of BAAT described their work, that there was only the vaguest general agreement about the scope of art therapy among those that wished to promote it.

The brief which was given to the first Council and Officers of BAAT by its membership (in 1964 about 30) was threefold:

1   To investigate ways in which it would be possible for the art therapists currently employed on a range of diverse salary scales to be given salaries and conditions of service appropriate to their age and experience: which was, normally, an art diploma and teaching qualifications.
2   To devise suitable training and encourage well qualified entrants to train.
3   To set standards for practising art therapy.

This was a very ambitious task for a small group of people and in 1967 BAAT became a Central Association of NUT in the hope of gaining help in fulfilling the brief. The aim then was to have all art therapists employed under the adult education umbrella and seconded to hospitals and other centres. Some members were employed in this way, and enjoyed salaries and conditions far superior to their colleagues who were employed on 'ad hoc' rates in the NHS, roughly equivalent to those of an occupational therapy helper.

BAAT continued to be a Central Association of NUT until 1977, when it was clear that there was a much better chance of achieving a reasonable career structure for art therapists within the Whitley Council structure of the NHS, and that the union ASTMS was in a better position to help BAAT achieve its aims. The period of the mid-1970s to 1982 was characterized by intense campaigning for training at postgraduate level and for acceptance of art therapy as a graduate profession by the DHSS. To some extent the aims were achieved through the help of ASTMS, the input from existing training centres at Herts College of Art, Goldsmith's and Birmingham Polytechnic, and parliamentary lobbying by art therapists in cooperation with bodies such as the Royal College of Psychiatrists. In 1982, the DHSS issued a Personnel Memorandum which confirmed the view of BAAT that, in order to practise as an art therapist in the NHS, it was necessary to possess a degree plus a Postgraduate Diploma in Art Therapy from a recognized institution of further or higher education. The memorandum also specified the career and salary structure which was equivalent to that of the professions allied to medicine.

Although this was not considered ideal, it was certainly a big step forward and enabled BAAT to devote time to internal organization and to the next stages of development, i.e., to create a similar structure within the Social Services and education.

As well as negotiating for members on questions of salary and conditions of service, determining criteria for training courses and standards of professional practice, BAAT also sees itself as having an educational and public relations function. It holds regular conferences as part of its Annual General Meeting, and encourages its regional groups to mount study days and workshops for both members and the general public.

In 1985, BAAT joined with Goldsmith's College and the International Society for Art and Psychopathology in hosting a Triennial Congress which was attended by delegates from as far afield as Chile, the USA, Hungary and Bulgaria.

The journal INSCAPE is published twice a year and consists of articles on and around art therapy. There is also a bibliography, a book service for members and, one of the most time-consuming services, answering enquiries from the general public.

All the above functions are carried out by a Council, assisted by the membership who are divided into regional groups and cover England, Wales, Scotland and N.Ireland. There are four officers of Council, elected every two years, and eight members. Most of the day-to-day work is carried out by sub-committees, including membership, registration, training and education, member's work problems, INSCAPE, and more recently, the Social Services and Education sub-committees. The work is all done voluntarily, with the exception of routine enquiry services, liaison and mailing, for which a small amount of paid secretarial assistance is available. There are now over 700 members, registered, associate and trainee. One of the interesting features of BAAT is its close link — right from its beginnings — with the Trade Union Movement. So strong is this link that in 1976 the AGM voted that 'all full members of BAAT must be members of a recognized trade union'. Another feature is that BAAT has never received funding other than its member's subscriptions and a small amount of finance from sales of publications which cover their cost. It could be said, then to be truly a 'grass roots' organization.

Registered Art Therapists

The first Register of British Art Therapists was published in March 1986. It is printed annually and amended periodically throughout the year, and is intended mainly for employing bodies seeking professional staff. The initials used by Registered Art Therapists are RATh, and they have:

1 reached academic standards approved by BAAT. These standards are endorsed by the DHSS and serve as qualifications for work anywhere in the NHS;
2 agreed to work according to the objects and constitution of BAAT and within its guidelines 'The Principles of Professional Practice';
3 satisfied the BAAT as to their legal indemnity cover, either through Trades Union membership alone, or with additional insurance cover for those who are self-employed.

BAAT and Special Needs Provision

Art therapists have always worked with children as well as with adults. Many are employed in Child and Family Units attached to hospitals (e.g., Guys, St. Thomas', Bethlem and Maudsley in London). Others are employed as 'art teachers' in mainstream or special education even though they may be trained as art therapists and performing that function for much of the working week. Recently, BAAT set up a sub-committee to investigate the position of art therapists in schools. Experience gained from the three training centres shows that many schools actively seek student art therapy placements to help cope with some of the emotional and behavioural difficulties of children which cannot be contained within the classroom. Several headteachers have tried to get funding to employ a sessional art therapist, and one or two have succeeded. However, the position is at the 'ad hoc' stage similar to the NHS in the 1970s and before. Research is currently taking place at Goldsmith's Art Psychotherapy Unit into Art Therapy in Mainstream Education, where the process of integrating children with special educational needs will be examined in the context of a videotape consisting of interviews with headteachers, with art therapists in schools and case studies demonstrating the effectiveness of art therapy with particular children. This follows an earlier video entitled: 'Art Therapy with Children: Special Needs', which discussed art therapy in a school for learning disordered children and a psychiatric adolescent unit.

It is, of course, important to stress that art therapy should be carried out by qualified therapists, even though they may be officially designated as 'teachers'. There is a considerable difference between the two roles. Cooperation between teacher and therapist is essential, but blurring the role can lead to confusion and ineffective practice.

We are though beginning to see more and more art therapists working within special education and employed by education, but the question to ask is — How are they employed? and — Where are they employed? Certainly not as art therapists, as such a post does not exist within the structure. There are headteachers, advisors and inspectors who realize the worth of art therapists and find ways of employing them through various routes. But how did they know about their work in the first place? Well, perhaps one of the training colleges sought a placement for one of their students so, the awareness raising process began, and the benefits of having an art therapist on the team were fully realized. This model is certainly worth supporting as it keeps the higher education college in touch with developing practice in schools.

This role confusion is certainly handicapping the potential of some very exciting innovational work. We know where the good practice is taking place, but it very much comes under the umbrella of special educational needs, and the art therapist is loath to come forward in fear of upsetting the system — (i.e., not being allowed to practice art therapy). The teacher/art therapist could be a supply teacher, support teacher or employed by the home tuition service — no matter how they are employed, they are recognized by their art therapy role second and as a teacher first. The person who was trained as a teacher first and as an art therapist second has to make a decision about where they choose to work on completion of their training. Whereas the salary structures for teachers and art therapists are roughly the same, possibilities for career development and promotion are not as favourable.

It is here where we need to examine how they received their training. It is now very unlikely that an educational authority would pay or release anyone for this training. It is usually done in one's own time and often at the students own expense. Though there are examples where the authority has been quite supportive. So what we see are that the terms of release for training have a bearing on the role the person may take up on their return.

Take a case example

A teacher worked in a school for children with physical disabilities and had a part-time art post. The headteacher supported an application for an art therapy training, clearly seeing the benefit to the school. The teacher elected to do a part-time course and attended in her own time. Taking 2 years to complete the course was both important for the teacher and to the school, as both needed time to look at how this work could be integrated. It became clear that if the teacher was to initiate the ground rules within the school early on, people were more likely to cooperate; the boundaries were made clear, and it ruled out the possibility of confusion.

The role was now explored with the headteacher and this was the outcome.

She remained in the role as art teacher;
A third of her week was given over to art therapy;
She would run a staff day on art therapy, to explain the role to colleagues, allowing time for people to explore some of their fears and have access to further information;
That the class teachers made referrals in writing to the art therapist, with reasons why they thought art therapy would be a useful medium;
That the sessions were called 'Special Art', the notion being that children had individual attention in the art room;
That parent's permission was sought before sessions were able to start;
That the child referred also agreed. All the parties gave support, as each saw the benefit of the child having an opportunity for a one to one relationship.

The sessions were time-based, initially half an hour to an hour depending on the nature of the disability. Some children with poor motor control needed more time and physical support to make a visual art object. It was also agreed at each half-term that the situation would be reviewed, so all concerned could be consulted as to whether the sessions would continue.

Progress was slow, though there were always rewarding signs of increased self-confidence and the raising of some self-esteem, but the larger concern of 'Coming to terms with one's disability' was a much longer process. This was the basis of all the work she was involved in, and it was clear that the parents and the teachers needed to explore their feelings of the children's disability as much, if not more than the child. What became clear was that we can often be 'the handicapping adults', expecting youngsters to be making changes in an environment that shows little understanding of the real problems. It was important at this stage that the art therapist work at a level where she did not raise anxiety, to work at a pace which the child and the teachers felt comfortable with and above all to build in her own support.

Figure 1:   The advantages and disadvantages of working in a special school as an art therapist may see it

Advantages	Disadvantages
1 Being able to work in a school setting	1 No clearly defined role
2 Making a contribution to the whole school, rather than withdrawing child to child guidance setting.	2 Little contact with other therapists working in a similar situation.
3 Being able to work in a one-to-one situation.	3 Teachers may not know what you are there for, they may not have been consulted.
4 Being able to work with a whole group.	4 Unsatisfactory work conditions. Lack of designated room, poor resources.
5 Being able to contribute to the staff development in the school.	5 Lack of support from teachers
	6 Recommendations may not be implemented.

To paint a rosy picture with this case example would be untrue. The teachers at times were quite critical, and some of their observations were very pertinent.

The second case illustrates an example of good practice with a mainstream comprehensive school which supported integration.

Debbie, a 15–year-old girl with 'spina bifida' had been integrated from a special school into the comprehensive at 12–years-old. She was one of several children with a physical disability integrated that year, and the school was thought to be one of the leading comprehensives in this field of integration. Their policy was one of treating all children the same, no special allowances being made for them except for attendence to physiotherapy. There was good access into the building

Figure 2:   As the teacher may view the art therapy situation within school

Advantages	Disadvantages (to the therapist)
1 I like James being withdrawn for therapy – it gives him some individual attention and it gives the class and myself a break away from him.	a You only come in once a week.
	b You can teach in a one-to-one situation.
	c We have twenty other children's needs to consider.
2 I like the idea of a partnership as we both have different skills to offer the child.	
3 I believe in a team approach to support individual children.	d You are very expensive resource
4 I like working alongside the therapist in the classroom	e You are not here when the therapy finishes, we are left with the resulting behaviour.

and there was some welfare support. One of the deputy heads had overall responsibility for their well-being; and a good pastoral support system was in operation.

At fifteen, four years after her entry into the school, Debbie was being discussed in a case review. Her textile teacher observed that she had difficulty with spatial concepts during some design exercises, other members of the staff acknowledged that she was 'hard to communicate with'. One of the teachers present at the review was the link teacher from the special school where an art therapist practised. They made a referral. At first, the therapist felt that the referral may not be appropriate, as the reasons given were not really connected with the role of an art therapist. However, it was agreed that the art therapist meet with Debbie to talk to her about some of the difficulties she was having in some art activities. The therapist explained the sort of work that she did with children, and said that there could be an opportunity to work in a one-to-one situation with Debbie if she was to agree. The art department was fully supportive, and they managed to find an hour spare in one of the studios each week. It was clear to the therapist that Debbie just needed private time. There was so much that she had bottled up during her struggle for survival within this large school that it was causing her to become blocked in more and more areas of her life. It was agreed with Debbie and the school that the therapist seek permission from the parents to attend an hourly session of art therapy within the school week.

The parents' attitude was very positive towards the extra time Debbie would be having in the form of therapy. Though there was a concern that hopes and expectations could be raised in an unrealistic way. In the end, like any parents, all they wanted was for their daughter to gain independence and to achieve a 'full-time job'. They understood that she needed to build up confidence and self-esteem first, before the latter could be realized.

The first session was about getting to know each other, with the therapist instigating most of the conversation in the form of questions about school and how she spent her leisure time. It was clear that Debbie had few friends out of school, and she started to tell the therapist about one girl, who was much younger and lived in some flats nearby.

The therapist asked if she could draw a picture of herself and her friend, which she agreed to do. She drew herself as able-bodied but larger than her friend. Debbie was in fact confined to a wheelchair. The drawing was small and faint, and she seemed saddened by the result. She said she found it hard to explain how she felt, but it was *in the picture*. This insight that Debbie discovered revealed both to herself and the therapist that there was a place for the drawing in the meetings.

Over the next few sessions Debbie explained to the therapist how it felt to be in a wheelchair in this particular school. She felt that the children didn't care, as they would let doors swing shut on her and push past her in a hurry. Once some boys had swung her around in her chair, and she said that she regarded her chair now as a weapon and didn't care if she ran into other children. She explained that her chair was part of her and people should understand that by touching her chair they were touching her. The therapist asked if she would like to get out of her chair to do her next painting, and that they would together find a way of supporting her. She agreed, and said that painting a big picture could be fun.

After explaining that she had permission to paint what she wanted, that the finished product would not be judged and whatever was painted would be acceptable, Debbie was eager to start. The therapist took a large piece of paper and stuck it to a table top that was the right height for Debbie to stand at. She stood, with the aid of calipers and a helping hand from the therapist and began to experiment with large brushes, and a full range of polymer paints. She started by making blobs of colours that began to merge and became darker and darker.

The sessions continued like this over a number of weeks until she felt able to talk about them. She enjoyed having a large collection of paintings which were kept safely in the artroom. She would always look over what she had done the previous week and request to paint a new one. She indicated she wanted to talk about them when she realized they were all looking alike. The therapist asked her what she thought they may be about, 'Anger' she said, 'I feel angry'. With time, a breakthrough was made. Debbie in later weeks was able to say she was angry at being disabled, and had never been able to say this before. She came to believe in the right to feel angry and tested this feeling out in her paintings. It was at this point that she did more talking than painting. She had experimented with her subconcious feelings and by using an art medium, she was able to produce an art object that enabled communication between Debbie and the painting and Debbie and the therapist.

This next stage she was involved in was to practise with her verbal skills to improve her communication, to speak aloud about how she was feeling, and to test out the experience of it being listened to and accepted. When Debbie had brought out her anger into the open, she was able to discuss her disability in a more realistic way. She wanted to explore more about spina bifida, she wanted to ask how and why, all sorts of questions that she felt no-one would want to discuss with her for fear of upsetting her.

Debbie agreed that the next stage she wanted to work on was a strategy of putting her anger on one side so that she could look at possibilities for her future. The therapist suggested that she return to her drawings to help with this exploration. She did this by drawing an outline of her head with little boxes inside. One box had anger in, another had a friend and the other boxes were 'don't knows'. Her strategy for coping was to acknowledge that she was made up of all sorts of feelings, fears and aspirations. Her drawing helped her to see that she could pull down any of the boxes one at a time when she needed them, or tuck them away when she felt that they were stopping her getting what she wanted.

This case example illustrates a part of a change process that a 15-year-old girl was going through. Appropriate referral, consultation and team work gave the right sort of support. It would be true to say, that any of the other therapies may have been just as successful here, but on this occasion, art therapy worked.

I think the school was wrong to treat all children the same. It would be better if they took the position that all the children were individuals but that they had rights of equality.

What we have described is a lesson in partnership. There was good communication between the therapist, the teacher and the school, and because of this, neither one was threatened by the other's role. It could be useful for the art therapist to be involved in staff development within the school so that roles could be explored and clarified, and both sides could learn how to access each other's expertise.

For effective integration to take place, we must be prepared to examine and challenge our own assumptions, otherwise boundaries are fudged, roles are confused and the child ultimately loses out.

References

DALLEY, T., WALLER, D.E., BEACHAM, J. Art Therapy and Children: Special Needs. Videotape. Tavistock 1987. (Series — Tavistock Educational Videos. Now Routledge)

WALLER, D.E. (1984) in Dalley, T. 'Similarities and differences between art teaching and art therapy', *Art as Therapy*, Tavistock.

WALLER, D.E. (1990) Becoming a Profession: A History of Art Therapy 1940–1982. Routledge.

Training Courses

Goldsmith's College, University of London. Art Psychotherapy Unit, 27 Albury Street, London SE8 3PT.

Hertfordshire College of Art and Design, 7 Hatfield Road, St. Albans, Herts.

University of Sheffield, Art Therapy Training Programme, 85 Wilkinson Street, Sheffield S10 2GJ.

Further Information on BAAT

Available from: 11A Richmond Road, Brighton, East Sussex BN2 3RL. Comprehensive Brochure — £5, made payable to BAAT Ltd.

14
Reading Skills and Special Needs: Survey of Recent Research

Sylvia Baldwin

This review will reflect the current interest in the early stages of reading and writing and will try to look at some of the implications for practice. Studies of young children learning to read, especially young fluent readers (Francis, 1982), longitudinal studies of large groups of children from birth onwards, work on patients with acquired dyslexia (Coltheart and Harris, 1986) and models of the reading process (Ellis, 1984) are some of the different aspects drawn together by cognitive psychologists interested in reading. Whether explanations at this level have any use for the teaching and instuctional level is discussed by Reason (1988) and her colleagues: they try to find ways of reconciling the views of the language experience approach (omnipotent in colleges of education for so long) and those of cognitive psychologists. Pinsent (1988) feels that the two approaches are not necessarily antagonistic and can be seen as complementary.

Importance of Early Reading Skills

There are a number of studies showing the best single predictor of reading ability at age 11 is word recognition scores at age 7. Share and Silva (1986), in a New Zealand longitudinal study, identified a group of children with reading difficulties at 7 whose problems persisted throughout their time at primary school. The National Child Development Study, (Hutchison, 1979), found 7-year-old attainment scores the best predictor of literacy levels at 16. Disadvantaged children show a cumulative deficit throughout their years at school (Cox, 1983). There appear to be good educational reasons for concentrating on the early years of learning to read, apart from the intrinsic interest of the research.

Some may object that word recognition scores at 7 are nothing to do with 'reading' and bear no relationship to the skilled reading of text for meaning. There are several ways of answering these objections: Perfetti and Lesgold (1979) and Oakhill and Garnham (1988) argue strongly that automatic efficient word recognition skills are necessary, although not sufficient, for the development of higher order comprehension skills.

Stanovich (1986) draws attention to Matthew effects in reading. 'For unto everyone that hath shall be given, and he shall have in abundance: but from him that hath not shall be taken away even that which he hath' (Matthew, Chapter 25: 29). The relationship of early cognitive advantages and learning to read is a two-way reciprocal process. Children with better language skills on entry to school read early: consequently they develop better vocabularies, make better use of their educational experiences and shape and influence their environment, especially parents and teachers, in ways which reward and increase their reading skills and so on ... Negative Matthew effects show how 'the poor get poorer': disadvantaged on entry, they are further behind the others after the first term in school; they have less successful exposure to print and increasingly avoid reading, becoming increasingly unmotivated and unrewarding to their teachers. Learning to read has important cognitive and social consequences.

Failure to take children's learning history into account has been responsible for preoccupation with two long running controversies which are to some extent interdependent: the existence of specific reading and spelling retardation and the current status of deficit theories.

Specific Reading Difficulties

Definitions of dyslexia by exclusion have long been out of favour, but there is now doubt about using IQ methods to identify a group of children as specifically reading retarded on the basis of discrepancy between their levels of reading and the levels predicted on statistical grounds on the basis of age and ability.

Rutter and Yule (1975) use the most statistically valid way of measuring the discrepancy in actual and predicted reading age through the use of a regression equation. Because of the excess number of under-achievers in reading (the hump in the distribution) they divided children with reading difficulties into two groups: the specifically reading retarded and the generally backward. They thought that these two groups differed qualitatively, because, although both groups had speech and language difficulties, they varied in other respects: sex difference, prevalence of motor difficulties, level of intelligence and educational outcome. It was thought that the differences might be of educational significance, and the two groups of children might need different kinds of educational treatment. The existence of this 'hump' in the distribution was accepted for several years, but has now been challenged. Rodgers (1983), in a national sample which was part of the Child Health and Education Study, did not confirm the over-representation of children with severe under-achievement. Van Der Wissel and Zegers (1985) thought that the hump was an effect of the artificial ceiling of the reading tests. They also thought that the difference between the two groups was due to the IQ-based selection and did not indicate qualitative differences. Share *et al* (1987) did not find any difference between the observed and expected frequencies of severe under-achievement, using the two standard error cut off point, either in individual or group data. Humps could be achieved through creating false ceilings in the reading scores, and the effects were not specific to one reading measure. Share argues strongly for treating under-achievement on a continuum.

Pennington (1986) points out that the regression approach, using a large normal sample similar in age, education, sex and S.E.S. as the children to be identified, with the same IQ and reading tests, ensures that the discrepancy will be equivalent statistically across all children. However, the choice of what constitutes a significant discrepancy will still be arbitrary. Does this mean that if there is no distinct cut-off point, the concept of specific reading retardation or if you like, dyslexia, has no value? Ellis (1984) uses the analogy of obesity. Unlike measles, obesity has no definite diagnosis and only an arbitrary cut-off point: however, this does not prevent useful work being done on understanding its causes and ways of preventing it. Bryant and Bradley (1985) also argue strongly for a continuum of children with reading difficulties; they compare Scott Fitzgerald's remark 'the rich are different from us' with Hemingway's comment 'yes, they have more money'. Part of the confusion has been caused by the traditional use of IQ as the most useful predictor of reading attainment. There is now evidence that there may, at least for the early stages of reading, be much better predictors (Stanovich, 1985). Intelligence correlates only weakly with reading ability in 5–7-year-olds, more strongly in later childhood, and more strongly still in adults.

Difficulties with Deficit Theories

The view that a group of children could be clearly identified as having 'specific reading retardation' has been closely connected with the search for deficits in the children as the cause of their reading failure. Looking back it is easy to see why belief in unitary deficit explanations (in terms of perceptual, sensory or cognitive deficit) of reading failure was so attractive: hunt the deficit and cure the child. Reaction against this in the 1970s was very strong for a number of reasons. Firstly, there was a strong dislike of labelling children, and the feeling that the deficit theory ignored what is known about learning being an interactive process between the child and his environment.

However, it is difficult to get away entirely from some form of deficit theory, even if it is a very general one (e.g., poor verbal skills), or a mismatch theory (e.g., between the children's stage of reading development and the type of teaching). Deficits may be dangerously shifted to another area, perhaps to sociological explanations of why children fail to read, without the grounds for this being made explicit (Tomlinson, 1988). A stronger form of this kind of objection to deficit theory were the very strongly held views about the psycholinguistic nature of the reading process. What has been called the 'new orthodoxy' (Pinsent, 1988) sometimes prevents teachers from being able to consider new research. It was probably very useful in the 1970s that Smith (1978 and 1982) and Goodman (1967) stressed the importance of 'learning to read through reading' in the prevailing educational atmosphere of practice in useless sub-skills and reading-readiness tests. However, these views about the nature of skilled reading are now being challenged as they seem to be based on very poor experimental evidence (Mitchell, 1982). They often used reading procedures remote from normal reading or looked at reading where the stimulus quality was poor. There is now increasing evidence against skilled readers using top down processing of print: they use orthographic skills to analyze words rapidly into morphemes. They do not use orthographic redundancy and the effects of context to predict meaning. It is in fact poor and beginner readers who rely most on context (Perfetti and Roth, 1981), and they do so inefficiently. Smith's rejection of deficit theory was based on misconceptions about the importance of context as facilitating word recognition. Context facilitates the recognition of words in *speech* by reducing the number of possible words to be identified, and can be important if the perception of speech is slow or inefficient. However in *reading*, context appears to influence word identification through the process of checking back after the word has been read (Coltheart and Harris, 1986; Oakhill and Garnham, 1988). Moreover, as Oakhill and Garnham point out, Smith is extremely vague about suggesting ways of teaching children, apart from insisting that they should be immersed in interesting and meaningful reading material.

A second source of objections to deficit theories was their poor methodology. When researchers began to compare good and poor readers, even if they tried to control for IQ, they found so many differences between them that the notion of a specific deficit began to be undermined, suggesting rather that there were many and rather general cognitive differences. It was also equally likely that any identified deficit could be the cause or the effect of the child's poor reading. However recent research (e.g., Bryant and Bradley, 1985) has used reading age matched controls, comparing poor readers with younger children who are reading at the same level. They have combined these with longitudinal studies complemented by small training groups. These are more likely to show that any identified deficit is causally tied to the child's reading development and not a third factor correlated with both. It is also possible that cognitive processes may be interlocked with reading in relationships of reciprocal causation; Ehri (1979 and 1984) shows that in the early stages of learning to read this is what happens between phonological awareness and reading.

Revised Deficit Theory and Different Kinds of Language Processing

There is a current focus on different kinds of language processing deficits which may contribute to reading failure. The four that seem to be of most interest are phoneme discrimination, phonological awareness, verbal short term memory and word naming. These may occur singly, or in combination or be linked to some more general deficit (what Ellis, 1984, calls general left hemisphere inefficiency.) There is most interest, at the moment, in phonological awareness, usually described as understanding that there are segments of sound in speech and of knowing that you have this understanding. Interest in this is parallel to interest in other metacognitive processes in young children and their ability to reflect on what they know. Phonological awareness helps children to see how print maps on to speech;

some children discover this for themselves and it seems to be closely tied to early progress in reading. In others, the lack of this awareness seems to cause great confusion. 'If the light were not so gradual in dawning, the relationship between speech and print might count as one of the most remarkable discoveries of childhood' (Perfetti, 1985).

Stanovich (1986) thinks that this awareness has particular importance as a developmentally limited relationship: it is necessary and very important at early stages of reading, but does not determine reading progress at all levels. When it occurs early enough in a child's education it acts as a second order facilitator by a kind of 'boot strapping' mechanism. Developmentally limited specific relationships are one of the ways in which Stanovich tries to bring some order into the confusing multiplicity of differences between good and poor readers.

Phonological awareness still shows a significant relationship with reading achievement in studies which control for IQ (Rosner and Simon 1971), and there are now a number of training studies (e.g., Bryant and Bradley, 1985). Singleton (1987) suggests that tests of phonemic processing would probably be just as powerful predictively as the Aston Index or the Bangor Dyslexia Test. It also seems to have a strong association with socio-economic status: Warren-Leubecke and Warren Carter (1988) found that by the age of 7 disadvantaged children differed from others in phonemic awareness rather than in their attainment in basic skills. It seems to fit well with emphasis in Marie Clay's (1985) approach on encouraging children to use verbal discussion of different strategies, and would explain the very variable success of different phonic approaches. Chall (1967) long ago emphasized the importance of making phonic teaching explicit. Lack of phonological awareness also seems to be acceptable to deficit theories which look at mismatch: 'what a child needs that he doesn't have when he comes to school' (Gibb and Randall, 1988).

Children's phonological awareness has been measured in a number of ways: identifying the odd man out in a string of three words by the initial medial or final sound, or detecting which word in a string does not rhyme (Bryant and Bradley 1985), and by phoneme and syllable counting (Leibermann, Shankweiler, Fischer and Carter, 1974). Looking at these tasks it is not absolutely clear how much they depend on good working memory. Bradley and Bryant have tackled this by partialling out short term memory in some of their studies but did not say how much of the variance reading and spelling at 7+ it accounted for.

Verbal short term memory is another area of current research interest. Baddeley (1978) thought that a deficit in 'working memory' interfered with phonological coding and the later development of comprehension. The relevance of short term memory here seems to be in processing, and it seems to be specific to tasks which involve verbal coding and/or rapid sequential processing. One of the main components of this is the articulatory loop which stores a small amount of verbal material and preserves order in it. This is interrelated with 'lexical retrieval' or word naming. In both phonological processing and naming activities a visual stimulus word or a picture invokes a phonological name code from long term memory. Difficulty in producing these names could also make it harder to encode material into working memory and make it harder for children to become aware of phonemes. Naming deficit studies have used reading age matches and have been shown to be predictive of early reading skills in two longitudinal studies (Jansky and de Hirsch, 1972; Wolf, 1984).

It seems to be worthwhile to revive a modified version of deficit theory when it pinpoints areas like phonological awareness where the research has been methodologically sound, and where the findings seem to be of practical use for the teacher in the classroom. There are important implications for earlier intervention and for the type of assessment, with more emphasis on observation of the child's abilities and more time spent on better methods of recording and monitoring progress. Reason and colleagues (1988) emphasize the importance in obtaining a child's full reading history before deciding on whether to offer more of the same or an alternative teaching approach.

Cognitive-developmental Theories about the Acquisition of Literacy

Research into phonemic awareness is closely linked to theories about stages in the acquisition of literacy, based partly on observation of young children learning to read (Francis, 1982) and current understanding of the reading process in skilled readers.

Marsh, Friedman, Welch and Desberg (1981) describe five stages in learning to read. Stage 1 (linguistic guessing) describes how young children, often pre-school, can recognize a small set of words by sight. The children have no strategies for dealing with unknown words except guessing, and this will only be on the basis of fitting the context. There is no attempt to use initial letters. Interestingly, the child's parents do not see this as 'reading'. The children's writing skills at this stage are very limited, although they may write initial letters representing whole words.

At stage 2 (discrimination net learning) the child is still identifying words by sight but is more willing to guess at unknown words, sometimes using a degree of initial letter similarity. His guesses will usually be drawn from the set of words he knows he has met in his reading before. The child's knowledge of which words he has met is remarkably accurate. He does not use letter order cue or phonological cues.

Stage 3 (sequential decoding) describes the child's discovery of phoneme/grapheme correspondence. New and unfamiliar words can sometimes be decoded. At this stage he will sometimes produce non-words in his attempts (which children at the first 2 stages will not). His use of phonics is not yet context sensitive, (e.g., long vowel before final 'e'). He may not have to decode all words completely before he recognizes them and so he can use an incomplete decoding approach to some irregular words.

At Stage 4 (hierarchical decoding) he begins to use context sensitive rules and can cope with homophones. This merges into Stage 5 (Morphophonemic analogy) where words are processed in terms of their constituent morphemes and new words are decoded through analogy. This represents the beginning of the final mature stage of reading.

Uta Frith (1985) thinks that in order to explain how the strategies of skilled readers develop over time we need a developmental model of reading. Reading acquisition does not fit a simple model of developmental change by steady improvement, but more a pattern of stops and starts. She describes three phases, logographic, alphabetic and orthographic. New steps in development come from the merging of old and new strategies which allow transition from one phase to another. She identifies the transition from the logographic phase, which combines Marsh's first and second stages, to the alphabetic phase as the point where many children fail. She describes this as 'classic phonological dyslexia'. Frith feels that one reason for the transition to the next phase lies in the development of phonemic awareness and the child's increasing ability to write.

Alphabetic strategies are first adopted for writing, perhaps because in writing, inaccuracies in using this new strategy are less likely to be detected. At this stage there is dissociation between the child's reading and writing skills and he continues to use logographic strategies for reading. (This fits with Bradley and Bryant's earlier findings that children at early stages of development write words which they cannot read.) In the alphabetic phase the child begins to use grapheme/phoneme correspondence in both reading and writing. Letter order and phonological cues are crucial at this stage. The child begins to be able to read unfamiliar and nonsense words, and this phase corresponds to Marsh's Stages 3 and 4. Towards the end of the alphabetic phase reading again becomes the pacemaker, and the child first acquires orthographic skills in reading. In this phase a knowledge of language structure is important, and he can analyse words directly into morphemes (the minimum unit of meaning). This allows infinite recombinations, and the number of words he can read increases tremendously. It is not like the early logographic phase because it is analytic, and it is not like the alphabetic stage because it is not phonological. Strategies from earlier phases continue to be used.

When a child fails to make a transition from the logographic to the alphabetic stage his unsuccessful attempts at writing and reading unfamiliar words will be obvious. He may still make some improvement in his reading through logographic strategies, but his development of literacy from this point on will be abnormal, even if his overall reading age goes up. Frith, followed by Snowling (1987) feels that the basic cognitive deficit is a dysfunction in phonological skills but it is not yet clear in what ways this affects the acquisition of the alphabetic strategy, whether through phoneme segmentation, phonological assembly or articulation. Children with speech and hearing problems are particularly vulnerable to failure at this point.

Frith also looks at failure to advance from the alphabetic phase to the orthographic one: this transition may not be made completely for those children who have become good readers but are still poor spellers. It is usually the case that the child acquires orthographic competence in reading first, because precise orthographic representation is not necessary for reading although it is for spelling. Good readers who are poor spellers may fail to pay full attention to all the letters in words, and this may be partly a consequence of teaching which reflects the view that reading is a psycholinguistic guessing game.

Implications for Practice

Frith's idea of developmental phases in reading is productive of new ways of observing children's reading and spelling progress. Her work raises questions about heterogeneity: are all poor readers different and therefore need individualized programmes and one-to-one teaching? This has been the traditional approach. But, if as she believes, many children fail to make progress at the transition between the logographic and alphabetical phases, and develop different compensatory strategies to cope with this, either as a reaction to teaching methods (Barr, 1975) or because of different temperaments (Roberts, 1988), why don't we teach these children in groups which might enable us to offer them more intensive help, perhaps on a daily basis?

There are other questions which cannot yet be answered; do all children need to pass through all stages of reading development? Or should some children whose phonological difficulties are extremely severe be helped to bypass the alphabetic stage and go straight on to using orthographic strategies? In practice this approach would be taken by a multi-sensory approach to teaching with a heavy emphasis on spelling patterns. However, there is increasing evidence about the importance of the alphabetic stage as providing children with dual route to word recognition. Having this alternative route seems to be important in comprehension, providing the articulatory loop which allows even skilled readers another run through of a phrase that is hard to understand or has several interpretations.

The link between cognitive developmental theories of reading acquisition and models of the reading process (Coltheart and Harris, 1986; Ellis, 1984) are at present part of a research project being undertaken by John Morton, funded through the Medical Research Council.

The degree to which these cognitive psychologists' theories about reading are accepted will determine how we view the provision of remedial help. Reason and her colleagues (1988) want to preserve the balance of approaches. They feel that it is possible that severe reading difficulties can be overcome through enhanced opportunites for natural language based reading experience, with the addition of techniques like paired reading which have important behavioural effects. They feel that intervention should be based on knowledge of the child's educational history: we no longer need to worry about the definition of specific learning difficulties if the severity of reading problems is seen as a function of the amount and the quality of the previous teaching. A decision to try complementary approaches, probably using a multi-sensory approach, would be made after considering the amount of progress that has been made through more traditional approaches. On balance, this group feel that even if cognitive developmental theory has identified the difficulties of some children being associated with phonological awareness, the research is not sufficiently advanced to know what intervention will help to deal with this deficit.

Stanovich (1986) feels that negative Matthew effects are so powerful that educational interventions which provide more of the same will not be successful, and that the only way to halt the cycle of escalating under-achievement is by more targeted help. He accepts the danger inherent in returning to some form of process training of an identified deficit, but feels that the earlier process training acquired a bad name by training irrelevant processes and training them too late, after the developmentally limited specific factors had ceased to be powerful and more general cognitive difficulties were appearing. He feels that attempts to prevent negative Matthew effects should ideally be preventive, and quotes the training studies of Lynette Bradley because he feels that even small gains early in development can engender large differences later. If a preventive approach is not possible, he suggests that later intervention strategies should be targeted to diminish one of the most powerful causes of negative Matthew effects: differential amounts of reading practice.

With the arrival of local financial management, early assessment and the National Curriculum, schools may decide on a systematic reappraisal of how they are matching the level of the children's skills and abilities in their schools from within school resources, and what extra sources of help might be available or bought in. Schools could consider a whole range of different approaches which could be used at different developmental points in a child's reading history. For example, at nursery or reception class level there are already many activities which help children to acquire phonological awareness. These include practising listening skills, participating in rhymes and songs, memory games, perhaps even Letterland, and these could be given more emphasis without the need for much change. However, this is unlikely to be powerful enough to help children with severe delays in phonological awareness, especially those with speech and language difficulties.

Lynette Bradley's work gives many details of her assessment and training procedures (Bradley, 1984). It is important to notice that in some of the training studies children were not only taught to categorize sounds through pictures, but some of her experimental groups were given additional training in using plastic letters to make the words they had been listening to. Bradley thinks that this kind of 'making connections' is very important in helping children to realize the connection between speech and print, and later to generalize and to use analogy.

After one or two terms in school it will be clear that some children are going to have great difficulty in making the transition from logographic to alphabetic strategies. Teachers need to be alert to signs that they are perhaps ready to use these strategies in their writing and need to give them encouragement to make this step forward. It is perhaps at this point that teachers would become interested in Marie Clay's (1985) Reading Recovery procedures. She identifies the end of the first year of school as a time when some children become confused about the whole process of learning to read, and develop bad learning strategies. Her programme provides intensive time-limited help on an individual basis for the poorest readers, (the bottom 10–15 per cent), selected by their teachers purely on the basis of their poor reading. Her aim is to enable these children to catch up with the average band in their class; her methods encourage independent learning strategies so that the children can continue to cope when help ceases. If this help is given at an early point in the child's educational career he does not have such a long way to go to close the gap with his peers. The cost of this in teaching time is half an hour per day per child each week day, for twelve to twenty weeks. Her results, from follow-up over time, indicate that these children continue to make average progress. I have found that it is very easy to get teachers interested and enthusiastic about this approach which is so close to their own philosophy, and needs no special material apart from a large supply of varied reading books. The methods of recording progress are extremely thorough, and show the teacher even small signs of improvement.

Other schools may have more children with severe reading difficulties who are generally immature. They might wish to offer these children intensive intervention a little later, perhaps in the top infants or first year juniors, by offering a precision teaching approach individually, or a group programme like Reading Mastery. This has been extremely carefully designed to increase time spent in successful reading activities and provides help on a daily basis. It teaches for independent learning skills and recognizes the importance of ensuring this through helping the child to develop meta-linguistic skills. It avoids dependence on one to one help and makes use of group effects. It too has inbuilt ways of recording progress. Long-term follow up of children who have used it seems to show continued progress. Its aim is to help children to achieve automatic word recognition skills at the end of a year's programme, but it also improves comprehension and spelling skills. Its cost in terms of teaching time will be twenty to thirty minutes each week day for a group of seven to nine children over a year. Teachers dislike it at first sight, and to get started, need support from other teachers who have used it successfully. Children enjoy it very much.

In most schools there will also be a large number of children in the second and third junior years who have made a start with reading, but who have not acquired sound reading habits and reading practice, despite the use of real books and a language experience approach. This is where programmes which encourage the differential practice mentioned by Stanovich, through using parents, volunteers and peer tutors, seem most appropriate. From the research literature, it seems as though this sort of approach is most effective when used for a time-limited project, and employing methods like Paired Reading or Pause Prompt and Praise. It also needs to be remembered that even a parental involvement project will consume teacher time, as it will be important to set up the project carefully and to maintain the enthusiasm of parent-child pairs through encouragement and discussion.

For children who have reached the orthographic stage but are still poor spellers, the use of micro-computers and word-processing programmes in particular has great potential, and is increasingly being used.

Psychologists and teachers need to read some of the research themselves before deciding whether they will follow Reason's modified acceptance of its importance, or Stanovich's more challenging approach. What seem to be points of agreement among those writers who are attempting to apply research to teaching is that we should in the future be far less involved in traditional forms of assessment and selection of a few children to be given intensive help. Our time would be more effectively spent on helping teachers to develop new strategies which lock on to children's clearly observed difficulties, and to find better ways of observing and recording progress. We may need to act as advocates of earlier intervention, on the grounds that in the long run it will be shown to be more cost effective, and we may need to remind teachers of earlier studies which helped them to plan for the most effective use of their time (Southgate, 1986).

References

BADDELEY, A. D. (1978) 'The trouble with levels: A re-examination of Craik and Lockhart's framework for memory research', *Psychological Review*, 85, pp. 139–52

BRADLEY, L. (1984) *Assessing Reading Difficulties: A Diagnostic and Remedial Approach*, (Second edition), London, Macmillan Education.

BRYANT, P. and BRADLEY, L. (1985) *Children's Reading Problems*, Oxford. Blackwell.

CHALL, J. (1967) *Learning to read: The Great Debate*, New York, McGraw Hill.

CLAY, M. (1985) *The Early Detection of Reading Difficulties* (Third edition), London, Heinemann.

COLTHEART, M. and HARRIS, M. (1986) *Language Processing in Children and Adults*, London, Routledge and Kegan Paul.

COX, T. (1983) 'Cumulative deficit in culturally disadvantaged children', *British Journal of Educational Psychology*, 53.

EHRI, L. (1979) 'Linguistic insight: Threshold of reading acquisition', in WALLER, T. & MACKINNON (Eds) *Reading Research: Advances in practice and theory*, New York, Academic Press.

EHRI, L. (1984) 'How orthography alters spoken language; competencies in children learning to read and spell', in DOWNING and VALTIN (Eds) *Language Awareness and Learning to Read*, New York, Springer-Verlag.

ELLIS, A. W. (1984) *Reading, Writing and Dyslexia: A Cognitive Analysis*, New York, Lawrence Erlbaum.

FRANCIS, H. (1982) *Learning to Read: Literate Behaviour and Orthographic Knowledge* London, George Allen and Unwin.

FRITH, U. (1985) 'Beneath the surface of developmental dyslexia' in PATTERSON, K.E., MARSHALL, J. and COLTHEART, M. (Eds) *Surface Dyslexia*, London, Routledge and Kegan Paul.

GIBB, C. and RANDALL, P. E. (1988) 'Meta-linguistic abilities and learning to read', *Educational Research*, 30, 2.

GOODMAN, K. S. (1967) 'Reading: A psycho-linguistic guessing game', *Journal of the Reading Specialist*, 6, pp. 126–35.

HUTCHISON, D., PROSSER, H. and WEDGE, P. (1979) 'The prediction of educational failure', *Educational Studies*, 5 pp. 73–82.

JANSKY, J. and DE HIRSCH, K. (1972) *Preventing Reading Failure*, New York, Harper and Row.

LIEBERMANN, I. Y., SHANKWEILER, D., FISCHER, F. W. and CARTER, B. (1974) 'Explicit syllable and phoneme segmentation in the young child', *Journal of Experimental Child Psychology*, 18, pp. 201–12.

MARSH, G., FRIEDMAN, M., WELCH, V. and DESBERG, P. (1981) 'A cognitive-developmental theory of reading acquisition', in MACKINNON, G. E., and WALLER, T. G. (Eds) *Reading Research: Advances in Theory and Practice*, New York, Academic Press.

MITCHELL, D. C. (1982) *The Process of Reading: A Cognitive Analysis of Fluent Reading and Learning to Read*, Chichester, John Wiley.

OAKHILL, J. and GARNHAM, A. (1988) *Becoming a Skilled Reader*, Oxford, Blackwell.

PENNINGTON, B. F. (1986) 'Issues in the diagnosis and phenotype analysis of dyslexia: Implications for family studies', in SMITH, S. (Ed.) *Genetics and Learning Disabilities*, San Diego, College Hill Press.

PERFETTI, C. A. (1985) *Reading Ability*, Milton Keynes, Open University Press.

PERFETTI, C. A. and LESGOLD, A. M. (1979) 'Coding and comprehension in skilled reading and implications for reading instruction', in RESNICK and WEAVER (Eds) *Theory and Practice of Early Reading*, vol.1, New York, Lawrence Erlbaum.

PERFETTI, C. A. and ROTH, S. (1

role in reading skill' in LESGOLD A. M. and PERFETTI, C. A. (Eds) *Interactive Processes in Reading*, New York, Lawrence Erlbaum.

PINSENT, P. (1988) 'The implications of recent research into early reading', *Journal of Child Development and Care*, 36.

REASON, R., BROWN, B., COLE, M. and GREGORY, M. (1988) 'Does the "specific" in specific learning difficulties make a difference to the way we teach?', *Support for Learning*, 3, 4.

ROBERTS, T. (1988) 'Reflection — impulsivity and lack of success in reading', *Support for Learning*, 1, 2.

RODGERS, B. (1983) 'The identification and prevalence of specific reading retardation', *British Journal of Educational Psychology*, 53.

ROSNER, J. and SIMON, D. P. (1971) 'The Auditory Analysis Test: An initial report', *Journal of Learning Disabilities*, 4, pp. 384–92.

RUTTER, M. and YULE, W. (1975) 'The concept of specific reading retardation', *Journal of Child Psychology and Psychiatry*.

SHARE, D. L. and SILVA, P. A. (1986) 'The stability and classification of specific reading retardation: A longitudinal study from age 7 to 11', *British Journal of Educational Psychology*, 56, 1.

SHARE, D. *et al.* (1987) 'Further evidence relating to the distinction between specific reading retardation and general backwardness', *British Journal of Developmental Psychology*, 5.

SINGLETON, C. H. (1987) 'Dyslexia and cognitive models of reading', *Support for Learning*, 2, 2.

SMITH, F. (1978) *Reading*, Second edition, Cambridge University Press.

SMITH, F. (1982) *Understanding Reading*, New York, Holt Rinehart and Winston.

SNOWLING, M. (1987) *Dyslexia: A Cognitive Developmental Perspective*, Oxford, Blackwell.

SOUTHGATE, V. (1986) 'Teachers of reading: Planning for the most effective use of their time', in ROOT, B. (Ed.) *Resources for Reading: Does Quality Count?*, UKRA.

STANOVICH, K. E. (1980) 'Towards an interactive compensatory model of individual differences in the development of reading fluency', *Reading Research Quarterly*, 16, pp. 32–71.

STANOVICH, K. E. (1982), 'Individual differences in the cognitive processes of reading', *Journal of Learning Disabilities*, 15, pp. 549–54.

STANOVICH, K. E. (1985) 'Cognitive processes and the reading problems of learning disabled children: Evaluating the assumption of specificity', in TORGESEN, J. and WONG, B. (Eds) *Psychological and Educational Perspectives on Learning Disabilities*, New York, Academic Press.

STANOVICH, K. E. (1986) 'Matthew effects in reading: Some consequences of individual differences in the acquisition of literacy', *Reading Research Quarterly*, 21, 4, pp. 360–407

TOMLINSON, S. (1988) 'Why Johnny can't read', *European Journal of Special Needs in Education*, 3.

VAN DER WISSEL, A. and ZEGERS, F. C. (1985) 'Reading retardation revisited', *British Journal of Developmental Psychology*, 3.

WARREN-LEUBECKE, A. and WARREN CARTER, R. (1988) 'Reading and growth in metalinguistic awareness in relation to socioeconomic status and reading readiness skills', *Child Development*, 59, pp. 728–42.

WOLF, M. (1984) 'Naming, reading and the dyslexias: A longitudinal overview', *Annals of Dyslexia*, 34, pp. 87–116.

15
Language Skills and Pupil Needs: Oracy in the Classroom

Sarah Tann

The term 'oracy' has been with us now for over twenty-five years. Despite this it is the area of the language curriculum which is often the one with which teachers are least confident and in which they often feel least competent. Yet, every day each teacher's classroom reverberates with talk. It is important to look more closely at the talk that takes place in our classrooms so that we can understand the nature of the talk — the quantity and quality, the purposes and audiences, the language and social skills that are required and the demands that 'oracy' makes of both the listeners and the talkers.

It has been estimated that for two-thirds of any class session there is talk and that two-thirds of that talk is from the teacher (Flanders, (1970). This finding — which has been confirmed by other studies (Galton, Simon and Croll, 1980; Bennett and Desforges, 1984; Rutter *et al.*, 1979) — has important consequences. Because it is the teacher who dominates the talk it means that the children are predominantly listeners. Because the major proportion of teacher talk is for the purpose of directions, explanations, information or control, this forces the children into a relatively passive reactive role of absorbing and acting upon teacher talk, rather than entering into an interactive discussion mode.

If we are now, within the framework of the National Curriculum, to promote children's abilities in both speaking and listening then we need to review our own classroom practice and identify more precisely what kinds of speaking and listening opportunities children actually experience, how we can manage a classroom where there may need to be a wider range of opportunities and, very importantly, how do we monitor the speaking and listening which we may thereby generate.

Management Issues

The Physical Environment

In an integrated primary classroom there will always be a significant proportion of children with hearing difficulties. This is clearly of particular concern if we are considering 'oracy'. These hearing difficulties will probably affect all of the children for some of the time. Many diseases, as ordinary as the common cold, affect hearing. Work at the Audiology Unit of the Royal Berkshire Hospital suggests that on any one day up to 20 per cent of children in a primary classroom may be suffering from temporary loss of hearing in a mild form. This clearly will add to the strain of trying to concentrate throughout the day, in what is often a noisy environment. In addition, children suffering from middle ear or conductive fluctuating hearing loss experience considerable distortion and hence disorientation.

Apart from loss of hearing, there are also cases where hearing can be 'too good', as when children suffer from not being able to 'filter out' extraneous noise to which they do not wish to attend. Such children are also under extra strain and are frequently highly distractable because they are overly aware of everything that is going on around them.

In either situation, the classroom environment is of crucial significance if, as teachers, we are trying to promote good listening and speaking habits. Background noise can be reduced by a number of relatively simple measures. These include reducing the chance of reverberation from high ceilings and hard reflective surfaces such as lino, concrete, paint and plaster. Such environments are poor in terms of acoustics, apart from also looking bare and hostile. Hence, primary classrooms which are at least partially carpeted or have cork-type tiles, classrooms which have drapes as background to displays, which have soft board on the walls or which break up the spaces into smaller bays by using dividers made of sound absorbent materials, not only look more friendly and inviting but they are also better acoustical environments.

Whilst hearing is certainly an important factor in oral communication, there is also a great deal of the 'message' which is conveyed by para-verbal and non-verbal means. Hence, being able to see the speaker so that their face and body can be 'read', and being able to see the listener for the same reason is an important adjunct to oral communication. The physical positioning of all those involved in the oral communicative process, therefore, is an important aspect to consider. Participants need to see and be seen. Those with hearing difficulties need to have a full front view and need to be at an appropriate distance to the speakers and away from sources of distraction and surfaces with reflection.

Further, seating can be linked (intentionally or otherwise) to status. The 'round table' approach is important physically and psychologically! If there is to be a 'leader', their location can be crucial in facilitating a 'chairing' status. By the same token if no 'chair' is required it is important that no individual locates themselves in such a way that they appear to be playing that role.

The Language Context

Within the primary school there will be many different contexts in which children are asked to listen or to speak. These need to be analyzed in terms of the particular demands they make of children and how this could relate to helping or hindering the development of oracy. Such an analysis might include the following variables:

(a) audience size — one-to-one: child to teacher, or known adult
child to unknown adult
child to child
small group: children with adult
children playing/working unsupervised
large group: whole class, whole school

(b) purpose — presentation e.g., report back on process or product
(formal) or 'giving news' . . .
transmission e.g., offer/receive instructions,
information, feedback
exploration e.g., exchanging ideas, opinions,
(informal) (creative/problem-solving)

(c) source — person-to-person (non-verbal clues also available)
telephone ⎫ no non-verbal clues and possible
tape-recorder ⎭ sound distortions

Many additional variables may also be pertinent, including familiarity or unfamiliarity with the audience, with the content, with the location in which the speaking and listening is taking place, with the purpose and style of language which should be appropriate to both the purpose and the audience.

Listening can also be greatly affected by aspects of language itself. For example, although there are only about forty sounds in any spoken language, some sounds are much harder to hear than others — particularly those with a high frequency or pitch and which have little intensity (e.g., s, t, p, sh). Such sounds do not easily carry across distances. Particular sounds are also more likely to cause difficulties in speech production (e.g., th, sh, s, f and r) not only in terms of pronunciation but in articulation especially for those with lisps or stammers. Children from different linguistic backgrounds, with different community language experiences and different regional influences may also demonstrate differential speaking and listening behaviours with relation to some consonant clusters (where additional 'vowels' may be inserted between the consonants to make them more 'pronounceable'), and with certain vowel sounds.

The Affective Environment

Because speaking and listening usually occur in a social context, the social relationship of the participants is of utmost importance. Attitudes amongst the participants to each other, to the particular task or purpose of the oral context and the attitudes to the value of oracy itself as a means of learning is crucial. In the primary classroom, therefore, where, in general, the younger the children the more rapidly fluctuating are their friendships, this can pose quite a challenge in terms of handling group dynamics.

Further, there are many parents (and 'therefore' also children) for whom 'talking' is seen as contrary to 'learning'. It is clearly very important for colleagues, parents and children to understand the nature of what is being learnt through oral means. The increase in the status of talk will come about by a mixture of factors: the National Curriculum itself which demands that children should develop specific speaking and listening skills, by the research which is emerging to show how this can more easily be successfully achieved, by the careful monitoring of children's progress and by their increasing understanding of their progress and their own individual objectives through their growing awareness of the strategies and skills they could develop in order to become more competent in a wider range of contexts and purposes. Hence it is important to encourage a valuing of the children, a valuing of what they say and a valuing of oracy itself.

Managing the Teacher's Talking and Listening

If we start from the assumption that it is the teacher who is the predominant talker in the classroom it follows that the children are predominantly the listeners. We frequently hear teachers (and parents) complain that children never listen. We need to examine more closely what might be meant by such an assertion, and what teachers can do to help children in their role as listeners.

'Listening' can refer to many different components. The instruction to listen can mean general aspects such as 'pay attention', 'understand/follow', 'remember', 'respond', or more specifically it may direct a child's attention to focus on fine aural distinctions to increase phonic awareness or to check a teacher's pronunciation of an unusual name. These differences relate to different levels of aural precision, as well as a range of cognitive and social demands. Such a request to 'listen' therefore requires different roles and types of response. Hence, it is important for children to be clear as to why they are listening, what precisely they are listening to and what their role is in the listening activity. For example, are they to listen 'appreciatively' to music or poetry? Are they expected to listen very precisely in order to 'discriminate' between (phonic or environmental) sounds? Are they to listen to instructions in order to then 'react' in a particular way (immediately by going to line up, or in the future by bringing their library book back tomorrow)? Are they to listen in order to 'respond' and make a comment or answer a question? Or, are the children being asked to listen in the constructive and critical 'interactive' context of a group discussion where their role of listener will rapidly alternate with being a speaker as well?

Such alternative role expectations frequently change as a learning session develops. Is it clear to the children when they are expected to shift from one role to another and how the rules might change? For instance, during an initial 'elicitation' session some calling out may be welcomed as an indication of enthusiastic participation, but would be rejected in a 'checking' situation. Naming a child is sometimes a reward for not calling out, but sometimes a control strategy for misbehaviour. Further, the listener's role may change frequently, for example whilst acting as a response partner listening appreciatively to someone's story draft, and then moving to comment constructively, ask questions, make critical suggestions possibly in a group situation where it is important to listen to others' views as well.

The National Curriculum requires children to participate in discussions (i.e., interactively). It also requires children to listen and respond to stories (responsive), and to listen and follow instructions (reactive). This is to take place in a one-to-one teacher–child context, small-group and whole-class contexts, and with known and unknown adults, in person and on the telephone. Most of these situations already occur in many classrooms and should not create too much difficulty.

There is no direct mention of 'discriminative' listening, yet this is the area which is most frequently resourced in any classroom and the area on which children are most often offered special help. Perhaps it is the easiest to isolate from the 'seamless web'. Perhaps it is easiest to teach and to measure the results. Perhaps it is the aspect of oracy which is assumed to be most obviously linked to the dominant goal of literacy.

However, for children who find any of these listening situations difficult, how can they be helped? First, it is necessary to conjecture as to why listening poses a problem. Is it the passivity with which it is often associated? Is it because the purpose of listening is not immediately obvious — as so much of the information may seem to be directed at others? How can we tackle either of these?

When children first come to school, one of the key features of their classroom to which they have to adapt is that they are a member of a large group (Willes, 1983). To manage such a group the teacher needs to organize and plan and therefore give instructions relating to daily activities (who should do which activity), and classroom procedures (where things are kept and how to behave). Many of these soon become fairly routine as classroom patterns are established. The more routine they are, the more passively the children listen and the more likely they are to follow what other children do rather than listen to the instructions.

A key strategy for any teacher must be to try to make listening as active an activity as possible. For example, with regard to routines, this activity can be changed from being predominantly reactive to increasingly interactive. The children can be asked to remind each other of what the procedure is. Alternatively children can be invited to suggest a procedure to deal with a certain situation so that they are actively involved in devising routines and can therefore see the purpose of it. If they are actively engaged in determining their own environment then they have a very real interest in the discussion and are more likely to be active listeners. This shift from reactive to interactive has the added bonus of shifting the teacher's role from being predominantly a talker to being a listener. Thus the teacher can demonstrate that she values what a child says, that talking is worthwhile and also she can demonstrate how to listen interactively and follow up with questions, comments, clarifications, modifications, explanations. Hence the teacher gets a chance to model the strategies which children need to adopt themselves in a discussion situation.

Apart from trying constructively to reduce the amount of teacher talk, it is also necessary to examine how to improve teacher talk, so that it can provide positive models of talk. Teachers do need to give instructions and expositions/information which may be of a prolonged nature. These need to be carefully structured so as to assist the listener and at the same time that structure made evident so as to model how to structure 'talk' so that children can learn to do this themselves (for example for 'report back' sessions or perhaps 'news').

Conventional wisdom varies between alerting the listeners to the fact that you will say this 'only once', to suggesting that you should 'tell them what you are going to say, say it and then summarize what you have just said'! Brown and Edmundson (1988) offer some clear guidelines for positively modelling an 'exposition':

— give a clear and consistent signal to gain attention;
— wait till attention has been gained;
— delivery should be interesting and varied in voice tones;
— state what the children are to listen to and why (purpose);
— state how they are to respond/react (to reduce passivity);
— 'chunk' the information so that children don't have to listen for too long before having a chance to interact;
— by identifying what they already know and what they need to know;
    — selecting main points (keys)
    — sequencing these logically, using simple sentence structures, introducing new vocabulary with explanation in parenthesis
    — providing practical examples to elaborate
    — reinforcing with visual reminders
    — summarizing each phase before proceeding to the next one
    — encouraging children to give feedback to check understanding
— conclude by reiterating purpose/end result;
    — information keys/procedural steps
    — outcomes/children's follow up.

Regular modelling of such expositions is important in helping children to internalize the particular structures of 'information text'. In addition, teachers who provide opportunities for children to listen to models of expositions read aloud from non-fiction text (or to read for themselves) could help in this area, particularly if the structures unique to such expositions are then discussed with the same rigour with which fictional text is often discussed. Within the National Curriculum guidelines, children need to be familiar with both kinds of structure so that children can describe an event, give a talk (English AT 1), explain an investigation (maths AT 1,9; science AT 1), or to check and review (English AT 3; maths AT 1,9; science AT 1).

Apart from helping children to develop their listening skills by clarifying the purpose and making the process more active, and by both helping children to listen and at the same time modelling expositions, teachers can also model how to value and encourage others' talk, how to listen to others and how to respond in an interactive situation. The most limited interactive situation often found in the primary classroom is the question-and-answer sessions that can occur when a teacher is trying to check understanding (and attentiveness). If, however, questioning is to be used to stimulate thinking and to explore ideas, then the differences between these functions of questioning must be made clear. This can also be indicated by para-verbal features such as a more tentative tone of voice, and also non-verbal features such as a more relaxed body position.

In encouraging children's responses, a key factor is how long we pause for a response. Generally, this is only two seconds before we either repeat the question, re-phrase it, re-direct it to another child, or answer it ourselves! If we are to encourage responses and allow time for children to think (particularly the less impulsive ones) we must both present the question less threateningly and give longer response time. We need also to vary our range of questioning strategies to include inviting other ideas, information or experiences, to compare these and identify similarities and differences, to comment upon/extend/add, to modify/limit/focus, to query and clarify, to seek evidence and explanation, as well as to challenge and reject (Brown and Edmundson, 1988). Again the more these kinds of strategies are articulated and made explicit the more chance there is of children being able to be aware of them, understand and use them (Tann and Armitage, 1986). Hence teachers need to be alert to their own talking and listening in the classroom and ask themselves:-

1 How does it help children to listen — by clarifying the purpose and making the listening less passive;
2 How does it help to provide a positive model of talk — through their own expositions and by making such phases evident to children when they are trying to structure any such presentations or reportback sessions themselves; and
3 How do their own listening-and-responding techniques help to model good practice amongst their children.

Monitoring Listening and Speaking in the Primary Classroom

There are two major aspects of monitoring within the National Curriculum that need to be clarified. First, we are asked to monitor teacher provision, in terms of the skills, concepts, knowledge and attitudes identified in the attainment targets and levels of achievement which are likely to be needed in pursuing each activity — so that we can check what opportunities exist for children to develop a particular range of skills. Secondly, we need to monitor the progress made by each individual child in terms of their skills as well as concepts, knowledge and attitudes.

In trying to determine which activities to plan, or to encourage, we need to be sure in our own minds about the role that such an activity might make in furthering skill development. Given the background of many attempts to 'meet special needs' in the primary classroom, it is frequently the case that 'special' and separate activities are planned, often supported by special and separate teachers often in a special and separate room or corner, away from the mainstream life of the class. We have to consider what such practice can offer children. Does it focus the mind of the teacher on a specific aspect of the child's learning so that it can more easily be assessed and the difficulties be diagnosed so that the problem can be more precisely addressed? Does it allow the child to focus on a specific skill and feel more successful in tackling it so that confidence grows? If the skill is practised in such isolation, how does the child perform when the skill is submerged in a broader task? Is the child able to transfer the skill from the isolated context to a situation of more general application? What help might they need to make this kind of transfer? Finally, in focusing on a specific aspect of talking or listening are we really trying to develop that isolated aspect or is it instrumental to some other goal? If so, which?

There are a number of classroom materials which have been produced with the claim that they serve to develop listening skills. The majority of these, in fact, focus on children making fine aural distinctions in discriminatory listening. For example there are a considerable number of lotto-type 'phonic' games, and games which demand the identification of environmental sounds. There is no evidence that identifying environmental sounds helps in identifying phonic sounds. Or, that identifying phonic sounds encourages a child to learn to read for meaning rather than merely decode — though of course initial phonic recognition is one of many useful strategies, so long as a child does not become overly dependent upon it so that it distracts from their search for meaning. However, such matching games may serve an important subsidiary purpose in helping to encourage the child to concentrate and pay acute attention for a growing time span. In so far as concentration and attention are preliminary factors in learning to listen then such materials may facilitate listening.

A second type of classroom material is the type of game which includes turn-taking, and even missing a turn! The contents of such games vary considerably though many are associated with reading (or number work). Again there is little evidence that such games help reading, or the phonic listening components of some aspects of reading. But, such games could contribute to developing children's social skills, their willingness to participate, their need to listen to each other, to wait for each other, and could contribute to increasing their confidence in a group situation — where luck as well as skill play a part, and where 'gaming' and losing appears less threatening to the individual than 'working' and failing.

Other activities involving listening can also be instrumental in developing further skills. For example, imaginative play, role play, drama and read-aloud-plays all require listening in a social context. We know that pre-school aged children are quite capable of 'taking the role of the other', of understanding others' perspectives, of empathizing with another's situation (Dickson, 1982) despite the dominance of the rhetoric of 'ego-centric' behaviour at this age. Any such dramatic encounters are very valuable opportunities for developing children's oracy skills, because of the children's involvement and intense need to both listen and learn in order to participate. Listening to story tapes can also provide opportunities for children to enjoy stories in a shared context. It also provides access to a wider vocabulary and occasions for children to grow to appreciate 'how stories work' and be able to predict story structure which can help in their own developing reading skills.

Hence, in a classroom situation where there are so many materials on offer and so many activities to choose from, it becomes essential for the teacher to analyze the tasks and resources so that the learning opportunities are monitored — not just in terms of what the activity is claimed, or may be intended, to achieve but what the individual children actually get out of it.

The second aspect of monitoring makes different demands on the teacher. Monitoring the children is more usefully done in the ongoing situation of the classroom. This may be useful in diagnosing how a child responds and what a child may be learning, but it is also more difficult to do given the busy context of the primary classroom with so many other children also demanding attention.

The National Curriculum requires teachers to monitor children closely and to be able to identify individual needs and then provide individual plans of work. So far, the main guidance in this area has been the recommendation to use the ILEA Language Record which suggests employing a mixture of observation, interview, diagnostic marking of written work and use of miscue analysis as tools for assessing children in the real context of their classroom learning rather than assessing their tests or tasks. Comprehensive monitoring of all children in the class, all the time, on all the statements of attainment listed, at each level, for every Attainment Target is clearly impossible. Rigorous selection is needed to choose which children to observe, when, doing what, on which attainment items to focus and to choose how to record the information and what then will be done with it.

Alternative formats can be used for varying purposes. This might include a 'diary' approach to record close observations of everyday behaviours. A 'conference' report, focusing on feelings and expectations, can be made of discussions held with the child, their parents and other adults with whom the child comes into contact. In addition some 'systematic observations' can be conducted. This could quantify the amount of specific actions and interactions in particular learning contexts on which a teacher wants more information can be collected on tally sheets.

Each of these techniques can give different kinds of information, each of which could add an important dimension to a teacher's understanding of a child in the mainstream classroom. Clearly, such detailed monitoring can only be done very selectively. To be effective, and to be efficient in terms of time spent, it must always be done in a very purposeful fashion with particular information goals precisely defined.

There remains the close monitoring which many teachers instinctively do whilst hearing a child read, or when talking to a child about a story they are reading or a book they are using to pursue a line of enquiry. Again, these occasions can be used for focusing on specific issues to help to fill gaps in our understanding of a child. Finally, there is a great deal of information to be gained from both watching a child engaged on a written task, from discussing the work in progress with the child and later from analyzing its contents and structure for miscues and achievements.

Monitoring can easily become chronically overburdensome. Time, or lack of, will establish its own limitations. However, it is important to make time for observation so that the information we collect is less partial, less subjective and less random. The higher the quality of our information the better we can support each child's special needs.

Developing Listening and Speaking Skills

Because oracy is by its nature an activity which takes place with others, it is important to remember that in aiming to develop oracy, we are developing social skills, language skills and cognitive skills simultaneously. This is clearly a demanding goal. It is unique in that it can provide collaborative support (and thereby be less threatening), and can offer a rare opportunity for the child who has literacy difficulties to be able to demonstrate skills in these other areas (as it can release a child from the additional demands of either reading or writing).

Research always shows girls to be superior to boys in literacy skills throughout the primary ages. However, in oracy the boys can begin to hold their own (APU, 1988), even though, currently, they are now blamed for being too domineering so that we hear frequent exhortations to encourage girls to be less submissive.

An enormous range exists of classroom activities for developing oracy, which are based on the principle of maximizing active participation in both listening and talking. The following suggestions are just a few in the wide repertoire of most primary teachers.

Discriminative Listening

(a) Musical register-time: the teacher sings 'Good morning' to each child in a different way (altering pitch, timing, rhythm etc.), to which the child has to listen very carefully and then imitate — or vice versa — while the rest of the class listens to judge accuracy.

(b) Rhyme time: every nursery and infant teacher has a stock of finger rhymes and action songs to which the class has to listen so they can join in appropriately.

(c) Story time participation: this is particularly suitable in traditional tales where the reader can encourage the class in choral speaking of the repeated refrain, spell, admonition (Fee Fi Fo Fums, etc.) or where the children can participate in choral sound effects (for the giant's footsteps for example).

(d) Sounds recognition: having listened to identify/match such sounds (whether natural, domestic or urban) to encourage a more demanding and active task, the children could then be asked to decide how they might classify their sounds (thus turning a relatively passive listening activity into an interactive discussion).

(e) Focused listening: some stories or poems lend themselves to this kind of activity (for example, Rosen's Hairy Tales and Nursery Crimes or Dahl's BFG) when children can be encouraged to listen to spot the deliberate 'mistake', or, a reader could deliberately insert such 'mistakes' . . .

(f) Spelling strategies: simultaneous oral spelling can help those who find their visual memories an inadequate aid — adding steps (Look Trace Say Cover Write Check) can help to focus aural memories; children can also be encouraged to 'have a go' in trying a word, then when it is corrected the child can 'photograph' it and vocalize it before attempting to reproduce it themselves.

Reactive Listening

(a) Listening to instructions: as already mentioned children can be helped a great deal to listen actively if they are told specifically why they are listening, for what, and what they will do with the information afterwards; children can be encouraged to pass on instructions to each other so that their experience of both roles helps to direct their attention on the demands and need of each party and to consider how to construct 'good instructions'.

(b) Listening to extract information: again the purpose of collecting the information must be clear, the nature of information needed should be focused and the means of recording the information varied and as visual as possible (e.g., using D.A.R.T.s techniques and procedures developed by the Nottingham team with Lunzer and Gardner, 1985; key word or picture symbol). Note-taking in pairs can be encouraged so that partners can support each other in recalling and recording information; motivation is increased if the need is perceived as 'real'. For example, if only part of the class have been undertaking an investigation (of listening to a programme or conducting an interview) which is integral to the class activities it would be necessary for others in the class to listen carefully so that they can extract the information they need for the follow up activity.

(c) Listening to extract information in interviews: this requires an ability to extract and process information very quickly so that a subsequent question can be posed if necessary. (Very often if interview questions have been prepared a speaker's answer can easily include the answer to a later question, yet the question is still posed because of the difficulty of asking, listening, extracting and reformulating questions almost simultaneously! — practice in this in 'mock interview' and simulation activities can help to develop this kind of listening for information.)

Critical/Responsive Listening

(a) Listening to books: listening to a story-teller or to a story being read aloud can make considerable demands in terms of concentration — this can be facilitated by the reader maintaining a high level of eye-contact and aided by dramatic performance with variation of voice and expression. Encouragement to listen can be enhanced if listeners are then invited to discuss the characters and events, to predict the next episode, to note/draw their predictions and then test them against the next reading session, or, if listeners are encouraged to listen so that they can then devise questions for another group to answer when they listen to the story/tape.

(b) Listening to others' stories: as a response partner to another child the listener has a very definite responsibility to listen purposefully knowing that what they say can be acted upon and therefore be consequential. (Children can be encouraged to listen for two things they liked before asking for clarification and then making suggestions.)

(c) Listening to own story: this may be a story which the child has taped in draft form to which they want to listen in order to be their own response partner, or, it could be a tape of their own reading performance which they can then check against the text to spot discrepancies. (Such self-correction can then be remedied by re-making the tape and can be less threatening than have someone else to do the correcting.)

Interactive Discussion

(a) Brainstorming: this encourages participants to offer any idea they can think of, hopefully, in an unthreatening context where everything must be accepted before ideas are sorted and evaluated.

(b) Problem-solving/action-planning as an extension of brainstorming: this requires additional skills of initiation, asking for clarification/details/examples/reasons, acceptance, modification, extension, hypothesis, rejection, evaluating, testing, reviewing, deciding, concluding as well as the social skills of turn-taking, supporting, inviting, soothing, compromising, directing, etc. . . .

(c) Open-ended opinions-based discussions: these require all of the above skills and sensitivities, but can be preferred by some children, for, if the task is an imaginative or fantasy one then nothing is 'wrong' and it could be less threatening — though the openness of the task may itself be threatening to those that prefer tight parameters.

Speaking

(a) Recitation: children from a very young age can enjoy reciting favourite rhymes, poems and jokes . . . (Recitation is now required by the National Curriculum in Key Stage One).

(b) Choral speaking: the security and support from a group performance can be useful for shy children and can begin with refrains in ballad poems, chorus work in plays and musicals.

(c) Dramatic dialogue: even if the performance aspect is an individual one, the fact of being 'in role' can provide security or opportunity to be 'bigger' and different to usual.

(d) Process report: children working in groups, or alone, can be asked to report back on work so far, thus highlighting the strategies they are using to tackle the task (locating/extracting information, designing tests, sorting and handling data) and outlining any problems or gaps they have got (thus inviting others to make suggestions and participate interactively), rather than reporting on findings.

(e) Presentational report: this is an opportunity to formally present findings and requires the same kind of careful planning, ordering and structuring of information as was suggested for structuring of teacher expositions.

Conclusion

Oracy in the integrated classroom of the primary school is going to become an increasingly important feature of classroom life. It always has been important, for it has long been recognized that young children, in particular, have done so much of their learning through oracy if only because they are at a pre-literacy stage. But oracy has for too many years suffered from this lower status of being a preliminary stage before children progress to the 'proper stuff' of literacy. However, now that the National Curriculum has given equal weight to oracy, reading and writing, throughout the primary years, the 'Cinderella' of language may well be growing up into the Princess.

For many teachers this will allow them to continue the excellent work in which they have already been engaged, but without having to bend over backwards to justify and protect the time which they invest in oracy as a means of developing children's listening and talking and above all their learning. For many other teachers it will mean that greater attention must now be paid to the listening and talking opportunities in their classrooms. This will mean increased monitoring and analysis of provision and of individual children's progress. Learning to undertake these tasks may well require special support to meet these new special needs which teachers will experience.

The higher status of oracy may well mean that children with special literacy needs may be able to join in more tasks without feeling disadvantaged. However, it may also highlight different children who though competent and confident in literacy tasks, may lack the social skills needed in many oral situations. Equally the new status of oracy may highlight children who are of a reflective nature (whether intellectually 'able' or 'less able') and who don't find it easy to operate in the 'cut and thrust' of debate, or those who are retiring who may find real difficulties in being in the 'spotlight' of more open and public oral contexts.

All of this adds up to the necessity to reassess children's difficulties and to redefine our notions of needs in the new ERA. It may need greater attention to the ways in which children are grouped for different activities and to a more detailed analysis of the demands and nature of the different kinds of tasks which are undertaken in the classroom (Tann, 1988).

However, in legitimating a wider range of competencies in the primary classroom, the National Curriculum may well change the way we teach and the way children learn. It could provide a broader stage on which more children have a chance to find areas in which they can succeed — which must surely help to provide a better experience for all our children and meet the most basic need of all, that of positive self-esteem.

Author's Note

This contribution owes much to information and ideas offered by the team of Oxford City Special Needs Advisory Support Teachers.

References

A.P.U. (1988) *Language Performance in Schools*, London, HMSO.

BENNETT, N. and DESFORGES, C. (1984) *The Quality of Pupil Learning*, London, Lawrence Erlbaum.

BROWN, G. and EDMUNDSON, R. (1988) 'Asking questions', in WRAGG, E. C. (Ed.) *Classroom Teaching Skills*, London, Croom Helm.

DICKSON, W. P. (Ed.) (1982) *Oral Communication in Children*, New York, Academic Press.

FLANDERS, N. (1970) *Analysing Teacher Behavior*, Reading, MA, Addison–Wesley.

GALTON, M., SIMON, S. and CROLL, P. (1980) *Inside the Primary Classroom*, London, Routledge Kegan and Paul.

LUNZER, E. and GARDNER, K. (1985) *Learning from the Written Word*, Edinburgh, Oliver and Boyd.

RUTTER, M. *et al.* (1979) *Fifteen Thousand Hours*, London, Open Books.

TANN, S. and ARMITAGE, M. (1986) 'Time for talk', *Reading*, **20**, 3, pp. 184–9.

TANN, S. (1988) 'Grouping in the integrated classroom', in THOMAS, G. and FEILER, A. (Eds) *Planning for Special Needs*, Oxford, Basil Blackwell.

WILLES, M. (1983) *Children into Pupils*, London, Routledge and Kegan Paul.

Notes on Contributors

Sylvia Baldwin is an Area Educational Psychologist with Berkshire County Council. She read Classics at Oxford University and then went on to teach at St. George's School in Switzerland. She read Psychology at Goldsmith's College, London, and then took her training as an Educational Psychologist at University College, London. She has practised as an Educational Psychologist working in Oxfordshire and then in Berkshire from 1983. She is particularly interested in the education of children aged 5 to 8 years, in the way young children learn to read and the difficulties that arise.

Barry Carpenter is currently Inspector of Schools for Solihull Education Authority with particular responsibility for Special Educational Needs. He has taught in the spheres of both moderate and severe learning difficulties, specialising in curriculum development and augmentative communication. He has been course tutor to the B.Phil (Ed) course in special needs at the University of Warwick. In addition, he was a tutor for the British Institute of Mental Handicap, and a teacher-supervisor for schools experience from Westhill College, Birmingham. He contributes extensively to in-service training of teachers throughout the UK, particularly regarding the education of children with profound and multiple learning difficulties. He has published on such issues as curriculum development and integration, and is currently editing a book on the National Curriculum and its impact on children with special educational needs. He has been appointed to the DSS National Development Team to monitor child initiatives.

Rosalia Chow is a Research Fellow at the Department of Applied Social Studies, Hong Kong Polytechnic. She has a special interest and expertise in mental handicap as this relates to integration, community living skills and vocational skills training. She qualified in Psychology at Oxford University before taking her Masters Degree in Counselling and Consulting Psychology at the Graduate School of Education, Harvard University. She followed her research interests at both Oxford University and at the Massachusetts Mental Health Centre in America before taking up her present work, formulating programmes of management for behaviour problems, and counselling clients and their parents. She is part-time tutor for the Open College, the University of East Asia, Macau.

Mary Cobb is the Integration Support Teacher at Blythe Special School, Warwickshire. She has taught in both mainstream and special schools and has an expertise in the implementation of partial integration projects linking pupils with severe learning disabilities with their mainstream peers. She is currently studying special education on an MEd course at Warwick University.

Mary Field was until recently Deputy Head of William de Ferrers School, Essex, England, where she took a special interest in the integration of physically disabled pupils, in multicultural education and education/industry collaboration. She read Geography at Girton College, Cambridge, and has worked in grammar and comprehensive schools, and as Head of Geography at the Further Education Centre in Cambridge. In 1987 she was seconded for a period to the Training Agency.

Susan Foster is Research Associate and Assistant Professor at Rochester Institute of Technology's National Technical Institute for the Deaf in Rochester, New York. She received her BA degree in English and American literature from Northwestern University and her MEd in Special Education from Bridgewater State College. She completed her PhD in 1983 at Syracuse University studying Special Education. She has worked as a Program Coordinator at a residential school for children with multiple disabilities, an English teacher, and as a Qualitative Research Consultant before taking up her current post at Rochester Institute of Technology. She has written in the professional journals on issues relating to the education and employment of people who are deaf and is the author of *The Politics of Caring* (1987).

Gillian Fulcher is Lecturer in Sociology in the Department of Anthropology and Sociology, Monash University, Australia. She specializes in education policy, disability and social policy in the welfare state. She has written *Disabling Policies? A Comparative Approach to Education Policy and Disability*, (1989) and is an overseas Editor for the journal *Disability, Handicap and Society*. She has produced the following government reports: *Finding the Handicapped Migrant: Conceptual and Policy Issues* (1984) (For the Department of Immigration and Ethnic Affairs, Canberra); *Integration in the Victorian Education*, (1984) (Report of the Ministerial Review of Educational Services for the Disabled); and *Towards a Policy Direction on Integration* (1986) (with Lyn Gow) (Report to the Commonwealth Schools Commission on Integration in Australia). She is currently Director of Research, Association for the Blind, Victoria.

Lyn Gow is Reader in Rehabilitation Sciences and Applied Social Studies at Hong Kong Polytechnic. She has a special interest and expertise in the field of mental handicap and the integration of the disabled. She first qualified as a primary school teacher, worked in colleges of teacher education, and then took up a staff post in ordinary and special education at the University of Wollongong from 1980. She has published over 180 articles in scientific and professional journals, and written chapters in five books on matters of integration, de-institutionalization, leisure programmes with people with disabilities and staff training. She conducted the Australian Review of Integration for the OECD and has written 4 reports for the Australian Government. She has been a member of many professional and voluntary societies and since 1987 has been a special member of the Integration Task Force of the International League of Societies for the Disabled.

Thomas Holcomb is Assistant Professor at the Rochester Institute of Technology's National Technical Institute for the Deaf in Rochester, New York. He read Psychology at Gallaudet University, studied for his Master's degree at Rochester Institute of Technology, and completed his PhD in Education at the University of Rochester in 1990. He was employed as Admissions Counsellor at Gallaudet University prior to taking up his present post at the Rochester Institute of Technology. He has written extensively on matters relating to the education of deaf students and is regularly involved as a speaker to conferences and conventions on matters relating to deaf students.

Mary Hutchinson is Tutor in Special Needs and Course Tutor on the National Association of Maternal and Child Welfare Course at North Lincolnshire College (Gainsborough Centre). She trained in teaching at Ilkley College (Leeds University) and studied for her degree in education at the Open University. She has also followed the Open University studies in special needs leading to the Advanced Diploma in Education. For three years she taught in a comprehensive school in Brigg before joining the staff at Gainsborough College of Further Education.

Pat Le Prevost is Speech Therapy Manager and Clinical Specialist in Severe Learning Difficulties at the Slade Hospital in Oxford. Over the past ten years she has been actively engaged in work as part of an Early Intervention Service in the region. From 1958–61 she was speech therapist in charge for the Wiltshire County Council Education Authority; she then worked at Leavesden Hospital at Watford before joining the Oxford Health Authority in 1974. She is a Fellow of the College of Speech Therapists.

Wen Lin is an Educational Counsellor and works as a researcher and consultant for the Secretary of Education of Minas Gerais State in Brazil. She can be contacted at Rua Agenor Goulart Filho, 207, Bairro Ouro Preto, 31. 310 — Belo Horizonte — MG, Brazil. She specialized in the integration of pupils with special educational needs and presented a paper on these issues to the International Conference on Disability, Handicap and Policy in Bristol, July 1988. She studied integration policy and practice at Lancaster University where she obtained both a Masters Degree and Doctorate. She has written 'The Development of Special Education in Brazil' in the *Journal of Disability, Handicap and Society*, 2, 3, 1987.

Mollie McPherson is Head of House at Dartmouth High School, Sandwell. She trained for teaching at Goldsmiths College, London (in physics and chemistry), later studying for a degree in Psychology through the Open University and a Master in Education at Birmingham University. She has also trained in computer assisted learning, active learning techniques, pastoral care management, youth counselling and thinking skills. She has taught at Buckpool and Longlands comprehensive schools in Dudley, at Harry Cheshire School in Kidderminster, and Four Dwellings School, Birmingham.

Harry Silverman is Associate Professor in the Department of Special Education at the Ontario Institute for Studies in Education. He trained as an Educational Psychologist and practised in Ontario school boards before taking a faculty position. His research has included applications of Feuerstein's Instrumental Enrichment with mentally handicapped people and penitentiary inmates. He is currently consultant to the Ministry of Education in the North-West territories of Canada on a training project to increase the in-school resource support available in schools in isolated communities.

Sarah Tann is Reader in Education at the School of Education Oxford Polytechnic. She has a special interest and expertise in primary language development — especially oracy and topic work. She has co-authored *The Reflective Teacher in the Primary School* (with Andrew Pollard) 1987; and edited *Developing Topic Work in the Classroom*, 1988. She is a Member of the United Kingdom Reading Association Teacher Education Committee.

Jenni Wallace is tutor for Staff Development and Further Education at London University Institute of Education. Her areas of interest and expertise are those of art therapy and group work. She has jointly authored *An Opportunity for Change* (with Deborah Cooper and Joanna Richards) 1988, which is a practical guide to in-service training for special needs staff in further education and training establishments, for the National Bureau for Students with Disabilities (SKILL). She is a member of the Governing Council for SKILL.

Diane Waller is Head of the Art Psychotherapy Unit and Senior Lecturer at Goldsmiths College, University of London. She has a special interest and expertise in art therapy and group therapy, in the history and development of art therapy as a profession, and in training in art therapy. She has co-edited *Images of Art Therapy* (with T. Dalley), 1988, and co-authored two videos (with T. Dalley and T. Beachan) called *Art Therapy in Children*, 1987. Her current research interest is in developing a short term intensive treatment programme for recovering alcoholics, based on group interactive art therapy. This has grown out of ongoing work at the Centro Italiano di Solidarieta in Rome, a coordinating centre for treatment of substance abuse. She is Life President of the British Association of Art Therapists and adviser in art therapy to the Department of Health. She is a member of the Health and Medical Studies panel for the Council for National Academic Awards.

She has been Consultant to the World Health Organization for a funded project to establish an art therapy service within the Bulgarian National Health Service through the University of Sofia.

Paul Williams is Director of the Community and Mental Handicap Educational and Research Association. His main areas of interest and expertise are in normalization, service evaluation and self-advocacy by people with learning difficulties. He has jointly published *We Can Speak for Ourselves: Self-Advocacy By Mentally Handicapped People* (with B. Shoultz), 1982. He has also written many chapters on issues such as normalization, evaluation, self-advocacy and values-led approaches to service development. He was a founder member of the Campaign for People with Mental Handicaps (CMH) and the Community and Mental Handicap Educational and Research Association (CMHERA). He has been a member of the Health Care Evaluation Research team in the Wessex region with Dr Albert Kushlick, evaluating new forms of residential care for people with severe handicaps. For ten years he was a Tutor at Castle Priory College, the Spastics Society's Staff Training Centre at Wallingford.

Anne Jordan is Associate Professor of Education at the Ontario Institute for Studies in Education in Canada. She trained as a teacher and worked in primary education in Sheffield. She then worked as Research Assistant and Assistant Professor at the Universities of York and Queen's in Ontario. From 1980–81 she was seconded to the Ontario Ministry of Education to consult with school boards on the implementation of special educational legislation and policy. Since 1988 she has been Chairperson in the Department of Special Education at the Ontario Institute, Toronto. She is a member of the editorial board of the *Canadian Journal of Special Education* and a field reviewer for the *Journal of Exceptional Children*. She is a member of the board of trustees for Hugh McMillan Centre School. She has published *Consumers Guide to Bill 82: Special Education in Ontario* and has in preparation a volume on the role of the resource teacher and the development of skills in classroom consultation.

Pamela Wotton is a special educational needs teacher with the Oxfordshire County Council. For over twenty years she has taught pupils with special needs and qualified in this area through the Open University. She is currently Teacher in Charge of an Assessment Unit for pupils with behaviour problems, based in a First School.

Index

PASSING
see Programme Analysis of Service
Systems' Implementation of
Normalization Goals
pastoral role of teacher, 149
PE
see physical education
pedagogical issues, 12, 16
pedagogic supervisor (PS), 31, 34–6, 38n4
peers, 134, 147, 191
teaching through, 73, 143, 144, 148,
211
Perfetti, C. A. (1985), 206
and Lesgold, A. M. (1979), 202
and Roth, S. (1981), 205
Perrin, B. and Nirje, B. (1985), 61
personal
hygiene, 131
skills, 132, 144–5
phenomenology: MEIIP, 27–8, 36
phonic approaches to reading, 205, 206,
207
physical education (PE) lessons/teachers,
128, 134
physically handicapped: integration of
secondary pupils, 123–37
physical needs of SEN child in
mainstream, 129–31
physiotherapist, coordination with, 133
physiotherapy, lack of, 127
Pickering, D.
and Gow, L. (1987), 62
et al (1988), 62
Pinsett, P. (1988), 202, 204
playgroups, 86–90
policy, integration, vii, 3–22
politics/political factors of integration
policy, 3–22, 30, 37, 63
Polloway, E. A. (1984), 60
Portage Project, 86–7, 88, 184
potential, achieving individual, ix
power, 5, 8, 29, 37
prejudice, vii
preventative framework: teachers' beliefs,
69, 70, 71, 72, 78, 80
primary assessment unit, 101–22
primary schools/classroom, ix, 221–4
principals and exceptional children, 69–81
problem-solving: group work, 149
professionalism/professional control, 7, 8,
11, 14, 16
profiles/records, xi, 94, 95–7
programmes/programming, 70, 72, 74,
184

Programme Analysis of Service Systems
(PASS), 44–5
Programme Analysis of Service Systems'
Implementation of Normalization
Goals (PASSING), 44–7
PS
see pedagogic supervisor
psychological dimension, 28, 30, 36, 72
pupil
skills and integration, 181–228
see also records; students

Quicke, J. (1986), 16

Rauth, M. (1980), 157
Rawlings, B. et al (1988), 153
reading
approaches, 209–12
development, 207, 208, 209
difficulties, 203–4, 205–7, 210
and intelligence, 203–4
and meaning, 202, 205
programmes, 210–11
skills and special needs research, 202–14
testing, 203–4
research, xi, 17–18, 42, 57, 69–80, 86,
202–14
need for, 63, 64
Reason, R., 211
et al (1988), 202, 207, 209
records/record-keeping, xi, 35, 95–7, 211,
223–4
referral of exceptional children, 72
regular schooling/classes
see mainstream
remedial interventions, 209–12
remedial teacher, x
see also support
reports, 133, 227
Reschly, D. J. (1980), 79
Resource Room, x
resources, 51, 56–7, 58, 59, 62, 64, 80
adapting, 98
financial constraints, 25, 56
lack of, 25, 107
sharing, whole school, ix, 92, 97
staff, 72
Victoria, 11, 12, 13, 16, 17
see also playgroup; preventative
framework; support
respect, teacher-pupil, 146, 149
responsibility, pupil-, 140, 144, 145, 147,
157